Reformation Readings of Paul

Explorations *in* History *and* Exegesis

EDITED BY MICHAEL ALLEN
and JONATHAN A. LINEBAUGH

An imprint of InterVarsity Press
Downers Grove, Illinois

InterVarsity Press
P.O. Box 1400, Downers Grove, IL 60515-1426
ivpress.com
email@ivpress.com

©2015 by Michael Allen and Jonathan A. Linebaugh

All rights reserved. No part of this book may be reproduced in any form without written permission from InterVarsity Press.

InterVarsity Press® is the book-publishing division of InterVarsity Christian Fellowship/USA®, a movement of students and faculty active on campus at hundreds of universities, colleges and schools of nursing in the United States of America, and a member movement of the International Fellowship of Evangelical Students. For information about local and regional activities, visit intervarsity.org.

While any stories in this book are true, some names and identifying information may have been changed to protect the privacy of individuals.

Cover design: Cindy Kiple
Interior design: Beth McGill

Images: Martin Luther in the Circle of Reformers / Deutsches Historisches Museum, Berlin, Germany / © DHM / Bridgeman Images

ISBN 978-0-8308-4091-5 (print)
ISBN 978-0-8308-9909-8 (digital)

 As a member of the Green Press Initiative, InterVarsity Press is committed to protecting the environment and to the responsible use of natural resources. To learn more, visit greenpressinitiative.org.

Library of Congress Cataloging-in-Publication Data
Reformation readings of Paul : explorations in history and exegesis / edited by Michael Allen and Jonathan A. Linebaugh.
  pages cm
  Includes bibliographical references and index.
  ISBN 978-0-8308-4091-5 (pbk. : alk. paper)
  1. Bible. Epistles of Paul—Criticism, interpretation, etc.—History—Modern period, 1500-   I. Allen, R. Michael, editor.
  BS2650.52.R43 2015
  227'.0609—dc23
                                                                                         2015027322

P	24	23	22	21	20	19	18	17	16	15	14	13	12	11	10	9	8	7	6	5	4	3	2	1
Y	35	34	33	32	31	30	29	28	27	26	25	24	23	22	21	20	19	18	17	16	15			

For our siblings,

Jennifer, Jonathan and Josh

Contents

Abbreviations	9
Introduction	11
Jonathan A. Linebaugh	
Galatians and Martin Luther	
1 Martin Luther's Reading of Galatians	23
David C. Fink	
2 The Text of Galatians and the Theology of Luther	49
John M. G. Barclay	
Romans and Philipp Melanchthon	
3 Philipp Melanchthon's Reading of Romans	73
Robert Kolb	
4 The Text of Romans and the Theology of Melanchthon	97
Mark Seifrid	
Ephesians and Martin Bucer	
5 Martin Bucer's Reading of Ephesians	123
Brian Lugioyo	
6 The Text of Ephesians and the Theology of Bucer	143
Wesley Hill	
1 & 2 Corinthians and John Calvin	
7 John Calvin's Reading of the Corinthian Epistles	165
Michael Allen	
8 The Text of 1 & 2 Corinthians and the Theology of Calvin	187
Dane C. Ortlund	
The Letters of Paul and Thomas Cranmer	
9 Thomas Cranmer's Reading of Paul's Letters	211
Ashley Null	

10 The Texts of Paul and the Theology of Cranmer *Jonathan A. Linebaugh*	235
In Conclusion: The Story of Reformation Readings *Gerald Bray*	255
Contributors	275
Scripture Index	277

Abbreviations

ASD   Desiderius Erasmus. *Opera Omnia Des. Erasmi Roterodami.* Edited by Jan Hedrink Waszink, Union Académique Internationale, Koninklijke Nederlandse Akademie Van Wetenschappen. Amsterdam: North Holland, 1969–.

CCSL   Corpus Christianorum. Series Latina. Turnhout: Brepols, 1953–.

CD   Karl Barth. *Church Dogmatics.* Vols. I-IV. Edited and translated by G. W. Bromiley and T. F. Torrance. Edinburgh: T&T Clark, 1973, 2007.

CGC   "Cranmer's Great Commonplaces"

CO   John Calvin. *Ioannis Calvin Opera quae supersunt omnia.* 59 vols. Corpus Reformatum 29-88. Edited by G. Baum, E. Cunitz and E. Reuss. Brunswick and Berlin: C. A. Schwetschke, 1863–1900.

CP   Martin Bucer. *Common Places of Martin Bucer.* Translated and edited by David F. Wright. Appleford, UK: The Sutton Courtenay Press, 1972.

CSEL   Corpus scriptorum historiae byzantinae

CWE   Desiderius Erasmus. *Collected Works of Erasmus.* 86 vols. planned. Toronto: University of Toronto Press, 1969–.

ET   English translation

FC   Fathers of the Church. Washington, D.C., 1947–.

fol.   folio

LW   Martin Luther. *Luther's Works [American edition].* 82 vols. planned. St. Louis: Concordia; Philadelphia: Fortress, 1955–1986; 2009–.

MBW   Philipp Melanchthon. *Melanchthons Briefwechsel.* Edited by Heinz Scheible. Stuttgart-Bad Cannstatt: fromann-holzbog, 1977–.

MO   Philipp Melanchthon. *Philippi Melanthonis Opera quae supersunt omnia.* Edited by C. G. Bretschneider and H. E. Bindweil. Corpus Reformatorum 1-28. Halle and Braunschweig: Schwetschke, 1834–1860.

MT	Masoretic Text
MWA	*Melanchthons Werke in Auswahl [Studienausgabe]*. Edited by Robert Stupperich. 7 vols. Gütersloh: C. Bertelsmann, 1951–1975.
NovTSup	Novum Testamentum Supplements
NPNF	A Select Library of the Nicene and Post-Nicene Fathers of the Christian Church. 28 vols. in two series. Edited by Philip Schaff et al. Buffalo, NY: Christian Literature, 1887–1894.
PG	*Patrologia cursus completus*. Series Graeca. 161 vols. Edited by J.-P. Migne. Paris: Migne, 1857–1866.
PL	*Patrologia cursus completus*. Series Latina. 221 vols. Edited by J.-P. Migne. Paris: Migne, 1844–1864.
r, v	Some early books are numbered not by page but by folio (leaf). Front and back sides (pages) of a numbered folio are indicated by *recto* (r) and *verso* (v), respectively.
SJT	*Scottish Journal of Theology*
WA	*D. Martin Luthers Werke, Kritische Gesamtausgabe: [Schriften]*. 73 vols. Weimar: Hermann Böhlaus Nachfolger, 1883–2009.
WABr	*D. Martin Luthers Werke, Kritische Gesamtausgabe: Briefweschel*. 18 vols. Weimar: Hermann Böhlaus Nachfolger, 1930–1983.
WADB	*D. Martin Luthers Werke, Kritische Gesamtausgabe: Deutsche Bibel*. 12 vols. Weimar: Hermann Böhlaus Nachfolger, 1906–1961.
WATR	*D. Martin Luthers Werke, Kritische Gesamtausgabe: Tischreden*. 6 vols. Weimar: Hermann Böhlaus Nachfolger, 1912–1921.
WTJ	*Westminster Theological Journal*
WUNT	Wissenschaftliche Untersuchungen zum Neuen Testament

Introduction

Jonathan A. Linebaugh

THE REFORMATION FOUGHT and conquered in the name of Paul. . . . Reformation exegesis reads its own ideas into Paul, in order to receive them back again clothed with Apostolic authority."[1] So opens Albert Schweitzer's *Paul and His Interpreters*, and much Pauline scholarship, especially since the Second World War and the American civil rights movement, has echoed his diagnosis. Writing in 1911, Schweitzer could complain that "the study [of Paul] continues to be embarrassed by a considerable remnant of the prepossessions with which the interpretation of Paul's doctrine was approached in the days of the Reformation," that it was then "assumed *a priori* that Pauline theology can be divided into practically the same individual doctrines as that of Luther, Zwingli, and Calvin."[2] The only way behind this apostle of Reformation faith and back to the Paul of history, as Schweitzer saw it, was for "the spell which dogma had laid upon exegesis . . . to be broken."[3] One way to characterize a major trend in Pauline research since at least Krister Stendahl's essay "The Apostle Paul and the Introspective Conscience of the West" (1963) is to see it as a carrying out of Schweitzer's call to dis-spell the theological assumptions of the Reformation—Pauline

---

[1] Albert Schweitzer, *Paul and His Interpreters: A Critical History*, trans. W. Montgomery (New York: Schocken Books, 1964), p. 2.
[2] Ibid., p. 33.
[3] Ibid., p. 2.

scholarship as a kind of defense against the dark arts of Reformation dogma.[4]

Take, for example, the "drastic difference between Luther and Paul, between the 16th and the 1st century" that Stendahl attempts to expose by contrasting the "robust conscience" of the apostle to the Gentiles and the "introspective conscience" of Martin Luther.[5] In Stendahl's account, Luther is a "pioneer" in the religious and social climate shaped by the "Black Death" and "late medieval piety and theology" with its "system of Penance" because he asked that world's question ("How can I find a gracious God?") and dared to answer it with "Paul's words about a justification in Christ by faith, without works of the Law."[6] For the student of Paul, however, this calls for research:

> The first issue at hand is whether Paul intended his argument about justification to answer the question: How am I, Paul, to understand the place in the plan of God of my mission to the Gentiles, and how am I to defend the rights of the Gentiles to participate in God's promises? or, if he intended it to answer the question, which I consider later and western: "How am I to find a gracious God?"[7]

Stendahl's answer is evident in his opinion that the second question is "later and western," but it is given representative expression by James D. G. Dunn: "'Justification by faith' was Paul's answer to the question: How is it that Gentiles can be equally acceptable to God as Jews?"[8] On this reading, the reformers were right to "see justification by faith as a polemical doctrine," but, as N. T. Wright suggests, the "target is not the usual Lutheran one of 'nomism' or '*Menschenwerke*,' but the Pauline one of Jewish national pride."[9] The reason for this change of target is that, according to Wright, "justification means that those who believe in Jesus Christ are declared to be members of the true covenant family" and so the Pauline polemic against "'justification by works' has nothing to do with individual Jews attempting a

---

[4] N. T. Wright speaks less of defense than contrition: Pauline scholarship is "trying to repent of projecting late-medieval or Reformational soteriological categories back onto [Paul]" (*Paul and the Faithfulness of God* [London: SPCK, 2013], p. 43).
[5] Krister Stendahl, *Paul Among Jews and Gentiles* (Philadelphia: Fortress, 1976), pp. 79, 82-87.
[6] Ibid., pp. 82-83.
[7] Ibid., p. 131.
[8] James D. G. Dunn, *The Theology of Paul the Apostle* (Grand Rapids: Eerdmans, 1998), p. 340.
[9] N. T. Wright, "The Paul of History and the Apostle of Faith," *Tyndale Bulletin* 29 (1978): 61-88 (on p. 71).

kind of proto-Pelagian pulling themselves up by their moral bootstraps" but rather "strikes against all attempts to demarcate membership in the people of God by anything other than faith in Jesus Christ; particularly . . . any claim to status before God based on race, class or gender."[10]

But what might the reformers say in response? How, as Stephen Westerholm imagines in the introduction to *Perspectives Old and New on Paul*, might Luther react to the following words from E. P. Sanders:

> Martin Luther, whose influence on subsequent interpreters has been enormous, made Paul's statements central to his own quite different theology. . . . Luther, plagued by guilt, read Paul's passages on "righteousness by faith" as meaning that God reckoned a Christian to be righteous even though he or she was a sinner. . . . Luther's emphasis on fictional, imputed righteousness, though it has often been shown to be an incorrect interpretation of Paul, has been influential because it corresponds to the sense of sinfulness which many people feel, and which is part and parcel of Western concepts of personhood, with their emphasis on individualism and introspection. Luther sought and found relief from guilt. But Luther's problems were not Paul's, and we misunderstand him if we see him through Luther's eyes.[11]

What Luther is likely to say is probably not appropriate for this genre, but perhaps we can risk one of his milder criticisms: "You are an excellent person, as skillful, clever, and versed in Holy Scripture as a cow in a walnut tree or a sow on a harp."[12] Such a comment is unlikely to further the dialogue, but it does bring a reformer into the conversation. And that, in fact, is the point of this book—to invite the reformers back into the discussion about Paul's texts and the theology they articulated as a reading of those texts.

While contemporary writing on Paul is littered with references to the "Lutheran Paul" or the "Paul of the Reformation," what is equally conspicuous is the absence of detailed engagement with the exegesis and theology of the reformers.[13] It is suggestive that one of the first Pauline scholars to use the

---

[10]N. T. Wright, *What Saint Paul Really Said: Was Paul of Tarsus the Real Founder of Christianity?* (Grand Rapids: Eerdmans, 1997), pp. 119, 160.

[11]E. P. Sanders, *Paul: A Very Short Introduction* (Oxford: Oxford University Press, 1991), pp. 53, 57-58. For Stephen Westerholm's well-documented tour of criticisms and defenses of Augustinian and Reformational readings of Paul, see *Perspectives Old and New on Paul: The "Lutheran" Paul and His Critics* (Grand Rapids: Eerdmans, 2004).

[12]"Against Hanswurst," LW 41:219.

[13]Stephen Chester's forthcoming *Paul Among the Reformers* and the now-appearing Reformation

label the "Lutheran Paul" later clarified that his critique was not of Luther himself but of "a figure derived from Luther but reinvented by the German Protestant biblical scholarship of the mid-twentieth century."[14] There is, it seems, a disconnect between the "Lutheran Paul" and the reader of Paul, Martin Luther. Schweitzer's claim, for example, that "the Reformation fought and conquered in the name of Paul," while true as far as it goes, forgets that Luther's recollection of his early exegetical experience was one of fighting against Paul and being conquered by the gospel of which the apostle was unashamed. Luther would be the first to admit that he "read [his] own ideas into Paul," but these ideas were a "philosophical" understanding of the Pauline phrase "the righteousness of God" that meant the "formal or active righteousness by which God is just and punishes unrighteous sinners."[15] The result of this reading was that Luther hated both "the phrase 'the righteousness of God'" and the "righteous God." This is what he read *into* Paul, but because he was "desperate and disturbed" he "persistently pounded upon Paul in this passage [i.e., Rom 1:16-17]" and "meditated day and night on the connection of the words" until a definition of God's righteousness came *out*: "the 'righteousness of God' is that by which the righteous lives by the gift of God"; it "refers to a passive righteousness by which the merciful God justifies us through faith." To borrow Schweitzer's metaphor, it was, as

---

Commentary on Scripture series will be notable exceptions, as is part one of Westerholm's *Perspectives Old and New*, though Westerholm's interaction with Luther and Calvin is more a summary of their (Pauline) theology than it is a tracing and evaluating of their actual acts of interpretation.

[14]Francis Watson, *Paul, Judaism, and the Gentiles: Beyond the New Perspective* (Grand Rapids: Eerdmans, 2007), p. 26. Watson observes the need for "a more nuanced account of what is and is not wrong with the type of reading that reflects the ongoing influence of Martin Luther" (p. xii) and adds that "to eliminate exegetical proposals on the grounds of a perceived proximity to a 'Lutheran Paul' is simply to succumb to prejudice and dogmatisms" (p. 25).

[15]This and the following quotations are from the 1545 *Preface to the Complete Edition of Luther's Latin Writings*, LW 34:336-37. Luther's "philosophical" understanding of the *iustitia Dei* is related to the so-called *via moderna*, which, following William of Ockham, understood justification in terms of a divine *pactum* (covenant) according to which God has promised to give the grace that justifies to the person who does *quod in se est* ("what lies within themselves"). As Stephen Chester has pointed out, that Luther was "reacting against a rather contractual understanding of justification" makes him an ironic target of Douglas Campbell's critique of the contractual framework of what he calls "justification theory." For Campbell's critique, see parts one through three of *The Deliverance of God: An Apocalyptic Rereading of Justification in Paul* (Grand Rapids: Eerdmans, 2009); for Chester's observation, see "It Is No Longer I Who Live: Justification by Faith and Participation in Christ in Martin Luther's Exegesis of Galatians," *New Testament Studies* 55 (2009): 315-37 (p. 333 n. 74).

Luther reminisced in 1545, reading Paul that broke the spell that "dogma" had lain on the apostle's text.

This, of course, is not to say that Luther's reading is a good one. That is a different kind of question, and one that will be asked by the Pauline scholars in this volume. But what it does recall is that the reformers were readers. Consider, for instance, Thomas Bilney, who in 1519 obtained an edition of Desiderius Erasmus's translation of the Bible in order to savor the eloquence of the Latin only to

> chance upon this sentence of St. Paul . . . in 1 Tim 1:15: "It is a true saying and worthy of all men to be embraced, that Christ Jesus came into the world to save sinners, of whom I am the chief and principal." This one sentence, through God's instruction . . . working inwardly in my heart, did so gladden it—which before was wounded by the awareness of my sins almost to the point of desperation—that immediately I felt a marvelous inner peace, so much so that my bruised bones leapt for joy.[16]

The result of this exegetical experience was, as Bilney remembers it, a desire to study the "Scripture [that] began to be more pleasant to me than honey or the honey comb."[17] Luther and Bilney tell a common sixteenth-century story: reading leading to Reformation.

It is the reformers as readers, and specifically the readings offered by the reformers of Paul's letters, that is the subject of this book. Pairing a text or texts of Paul with a reformer, this collection of essays will consider, in turn, Martin Luther and Galatians, Philipp Melanchthon and Romans, Martin Bucer and Ephesians, John Calvin and 1 & 2 Corinthians, and Thomas Cranmer and the *corpus Paulinum*. The hope is to catch the reformers in action as exegetes—to follow them as they move from Paul's texts to their own theological comments. By attending to the actual exegesis of the reformers, their interpretations of Paul's letters will be brought into focus, providing a vantage point from which to take some initial soundings of the relationship between the texts of Paul and the theology of the reformers that resulted from reading them. To facilitate this movement from historical

---

[16]John Fox, *Actes and Monuments* (London: John Day, 1570), pp. 1141-43. I am grateful to Ashley Null for alerting me to the two versions of Bilney's correspondence with Bishop Cuthbert Tunstall during his heresy trail in 1527 that contain this account.
[17]Ibid.

theological description to evaluation, the reading of each reformer will be considered twice, first in a descriptive mode by a historical theologian, and second by a Pauline scholar who will curate a conversation between the Pauline text(s) and their interpretation. The first essay will address issues like the editions of Paul's letters available to the reformer, their structural outline of the text, the way the subject matter or *argumentum* is summarized, and the basic content and contours of the letters' theology as expressed by the reformers' exegesis. The second essays are not responses to the first so much as they are interactions with the reading of the reformers. To borrow an image from Dane Ortlund's essay on Calvin and the Corinthian correspondence,

> Picture a table. At one end sits the scarred apostle, short, balding, with a penetrating gaze, but overall very unimpressive. . . . At the other end sits the pointy-bearded French reformer, gaunt, thin, rather emaciated and equally physically unimpressive. We will listen in as Calvin tells us about the apostle.

But as Ortlund adds, "the purpose" is not just to "listen in as Calvin tells us about the apostle" but to "facilitate a dialogue of sorts between Paul and Calvin in light of currents in New Testament study."

Together the essays, and thus this volume, hope (1) to understand the reformers' exegesis as authentic acts of interpretation—as readings of texts—and (2) to ask after the *quality* of the various interpretations of the reformers in relation to the Pauline texts they are reading. Wesley Hill provides a helpful index of questions that guides the first goal:

> What is there in the text that causes the reformer to start off in such-and-such a direction? What does the reformer see *here* that causes him to say *this*? Is what he says there simply a "ruminative overlay"—a comment affixed to the words of a text (Paul's) to which they bear little or no relation? Is this or that comment of a reformer an actualization of some of the text's own semantic potential or is it better described as a theological "performance" of a text that says nothing about what the reformer goes on to say by means of it? Above all, how is the reformer's exegesis explicable as a *reading* of a *text*?[18]

---

[18]This is adapted from Hill's contribution to this volume; for the original source of these questions, see Wesley A. Hill, "The Church as Israel and Israel as the Church: An Examination of Karl Barth's Exegesis of Romans 9.1-5 in the *Römerbrief* and *Church Dogmatics* II/2," *Journal of Theological Interpretation* 6, no. 1 (2012): 139-60 (on pp. 139-40).

These kinds of questions enable a form of exegetical eavesdropping, the chance to listen in as the reformers read Paul and move from his words to their own comments.

But suppose Paul's texts want to talk back? What if, having demonstrated how a reformer got from a first-century document to a sixteenth-century comment, there are philological, historical and theological details in the Pauline text that raise questions about the way they have been read? It is the commitment to ask these sorts of questions that creates the possibility of a conversation between Paul and his Reformational readers. But, as John Barclay asks in his essay on Luther and Galatians, how should one evaluate a reformer's reading of a Pauline text? Hill notes that "internal consistency" and contemporary usability can be seen as partial criteria of what counts as a "good" reading. Barclay adds that "philological precision, an accountability to the likely sense of the original Greek, constitutes a core requirement" of exegesis. None of our authors stops there, however. As Barclay writes, "exegesis always draws on an interpretation of the text as a whole" and so any evaluation of a Reformation reading of Paul has to ask what the reformer understood the "central subject matter" of the Pauline text to be—to ask not just what certain words or phrases "refer to (e.g., what 'law' Paul means when he speaks of 'works of the law') but also what the discussion is fundamentally about." Within this frame of evaluation, it is possible that, as Stephen Westerholm concludes his study, "the critics [of the reformers] have rightly defined the occasion that elicited the formulation of Paul's doctrine [of justification] and have reminded us of its first-century social and strategic significance" and that "the [reformers], for their part, rightly captured Paul's rationale and basic point."[19]

As this dialogue between Paul and the reformers is listened to—as both the *data* and the *Sache* of the Pauline letters converse with the comments and theology presented as their interpretation—there is, in every essay, compliment and criticism. But there is also a consensus that the reformers were readers, and that their readings are worth reading again (e.g., Mark Seifrid

---

[19]Westerholm, *Perspectives Old and New*, p. 445. For an essay that both understands this distinction and works to think through the theology that results from the interplay between the impact of the Christ event, Paul's Gentile mission and a continued interaction with Israel's scriptures, see John Barclay's contribution to this volume as well as his forthcoming *Paul and the Gift* (Grand Rapids: Eerdmans).

declares it "high time that we gave heed to the Preceptor [Melanchthon] and his interpretation of the apostle to the Gentiles," and Ortlund feels it right to "commend Calvin to Christians today, especially students and scholars of the apostle"). In this respect, Hill's comment about attending to Martin Bucer's interpretation of Ephesians could be applied to the exegesis of all the reformers considered in this book: "reading [a reformer] is not just a matter of seeing how one interpreter has learned or failed to learn from a text"—the evaluative direction here would then be exclusively "from more distant past (Paul) to more recent past" (reformer). Rather, "reading [a reformer] is also, or should be, a way of seeing how a commentary may lead one back into the text from which it originated"—a backwards move "from past commentator [reformer] to more distant past author (Paul)."

And this, finally, is the raison d'être for this collection. It is, or hopes to be, a hermeneutical tale—there and back again, you might say (with apologies to Bilbo Baggins). In his *Commentary on the Heidelberg Catechism*, Zacharias Ursinus insists that the reason we study doctrine is to be returned to Scripture as better readers, noting that as "doctrines . . . are taken out of the Scriptures, and are directed by them as their rule, so they again lead us, as it were, by the hand to the Scriptures."[20] A similar circularity is in play here: from Paul's letters to Reformation readings and back to Paul. The goal is not simply to establish Reformation exegesis as authentic acts of scriptural interpretation; the hope is, having engaged the reformers as readers, to invite them into the ongoing conversation about Paul's texts. Hill is again helpful: "a commentary generated by the Pauline text . . . may cast light retrospectively, as it were, illuminating features of the Pauline texts that elicited the commentary in the first place. . . . Paying attention to [the reformers'] exegetical moves . . . will remind us that *all* interpretation depends on such a to-and-fro, past-and-present spiral." The reformers would insist that the finish line of reading their interpretations of Paul's letters is not reading their commentaries; it is reading Paul's letters. Remember Luther's fear: "I'd rather that all my books would disappear and the Holy Scriptures alone would be read. Otherwise we'll rely on such writings and let the Bible go."[21] Perhaps, though, rather than distract

---

[20]Zacharias Ursinus, *Commentary on the Heidelberg Catechism*, trans. G. W. Williard (repr., Phillipsburg, NJ: P&R, 1852), p. 10.

[21]*Table Talk* no. 4075 (September 29, 1538), LW 54:311.

from Paul's letters, some Reformation readings of Paul can return us to his texts in deep and surprising ways.

For the reformers, Scripture is the "living and active" Word; it is the voice of the one who acts by speaking ("Let there be light"; "Little girl, get up") and is therefore less an object for us to interpret than it is the sound of the speaking God who interprets us. Understood this way, Scripture is God speaking, reading is listening, and helpful commentary is simply that which helps us hear. That, in the end, is the criterion the reformers would asked to be judged by: having heard them read Paul, are our ears more open to the gospel he proclaimed—the gospel the reformers, like Paul, were "unashamed" of because they, like Paul, confessed it to be "the power of God unto salvation" (Rom 1:16 KJV)?

Galatians *and* Martin Luther

MARTIN LUTHER'S READING of GALATIANS

David C. Fink

P AUL'S LETTER TO THE GALATIANS exercised a special fascination for Martin Luther, a fact recognized not only by generations of Luther scholars but also by the reformer himself. Often quoted in this connection is Luther's remark at the dinner table that he regarded himself as engaged to the "dear epistle"; regarding his own efforts at expounding the text, however, he was more ambivalent.[1] Responding (negatively) in 1538 to a proposal to reprint his collected works, Luther feared that the mere sight of so bloated a monstrosity as his commentary on Galatians would inspire nothing but disgust.[2] Eventually, however, Luther agreed to have the work reprinted, and by 1543 he seems to have regarded it as one of his few writings of any lasting value.[3]

Modern scholars have generally concurred in according a certain pride of place to Luther's exposition of Galatians (particularly his "commentary" of 1531/35) within his literary corpus, and for good reason.[4] To begin with,

---

[1] *Epistola ad Galatas ist mein epistelcha, der ich mit vertrawt hab. Ist mein Keth von Bor.* WATR 1:69 (no. 146).
[2] WATR 4:84-85 (no. 4025); LW 54:311-12.
[3] WATR 5:204 (no. 5511); LW 54:440.
[4] Landmark studies include Karin Bornkamm, *Luthers Auslegungen des Galaterbriefs von 1519 bis 1531: Ein Vergliech*, Arbeiten zur Kirchengeschichte 35 (Berlin: de Gruyter, 1963); Peter Manns, "Absolute and Incarnate Faith: Luther on Justification in the Galatians Commentary of 1531-35,"

Luther consistently ranked the epistle as one of the clearest distillations of the gospel within the canon of Scripture. For example, in his 1546 preface to the New Testament, he writes, "St. John's Gospel and his first epistle, St. Paul's epistles, especially Romans, Galatians, and Ephesians, and St. Peter's first epistle are the books that show you Christ and teach you all that is necessary and salvatory for you to know, even if you were never to see or hear any other book or doctrine."[5] Of the biblical books that make up Luther's "canon within the canon," however, it was Galatians to which he continually returned, publishing more on this one text than on all the rest combined.

My goal in this chapter is to trace out the distinctive features of Luther's interpretation of Paul in the letter to Galatians, beginning with an assessment of the place of this remarkable letter in Luther's career and body of work. Next, I offer analysis of Luther's exegetical methods and intentions, including a detailed discussion of his sources and interlocutors. Following this, I examine Luther's understanding of the argument and structure of the epistle, contrasting his approach with those of patristic and medieval exegetes. In the final section, I offer summary observations on three theological themes that set Luther's reading of Galatians apart from those of his predecessors. My aim in this chapter is not to defend Luther's exegesis against modern biblical scholarship but to facilitate a more fruitful engagement with his ideas by setting them in the context of the remarkably fecund period of intellectual ferment in which he lived, moved and had his being. Luther's reading of Galatians has proven enormously influential—indeed, it is probably not much of an overstatement to suggest no other reading has loomed larger over the text in the modern world, at least within Protestantism. For this reason, it is all the more imperative that any serious attempt to assess the merits of Luther's exegesis proceed from a careful understanding of his historical context, theological aims and exegetical practices.

---

in *Catholic Scholars Dialogue with Luther*, ed. Jared Wicks (Chicago: Loyola University Press, 1970), pp. 121-56; Kenneth Hagen, *Luther's Approach to Scripture as Seen in His "Commentaries" on Galatians* (Tübingen: Mohr, 1993); Juha Mikkonen, *Luther and Calvin on Paul's Epistle to the Galatians: An Analysis and Comparison of Substantial Concepts in Luther's 1531/35 and Calvin's 1546/48 Commentaries on Galatians* (Åbo: Åbo Akademi University Press, 2007).
[5]WADB 6:11; LW 35:362.

Luther's Exegesis of Galatians: A Syllabus

Luther was awarded the rank of *Doctor sacrae scripturae* in October 1512, the highest academic title in medieval Christendom. Luther's biographers often refer to him as a "professor of Holy Scripture" or as a "professor of Bible," yet this ought not to suggest that Luther was engaged in the more specialized (and modern) discipline of "biblical studies." Luther was a professor of theology, and he occupied the same teaching position as medieval luminaries such as Albert the Great and Thomas Aquinas.[6] Departing from the typical practice to a considerable extent, however, Luther focused his teaching energies almost exclusively on the Scriptures, lecturing on the Psalms (1513–1515), Romans (1515–1516), Galatians (1516–1517) and Hebrews (1517–1518) in the years leading up to his confrontation with the Roman curia over the matter of indulgences. Following the appointment of Philipp Melanchthon to the more specialized post of professor of Greek in the spring of 1518, Luther turned his focus in the classroom primarily to lecturing on the Old Testament.

Luther's lectures on Galatians from this early period survive in the form of student notes (*Nachschriften*).[7] These have been of enormous interest to modern scholars seeking to reconstruct Luther's early theology and thereby identify the exact moment of his "Reformation breakthrough," though gaps still remain in the notes themselves.[8] What is clear, however, is that these lectures—delivered immediately prior to the outbreak of the controversy over indulgences that inaugurated Luther's career as a reformer—served as the basis for Luther's first published commentary on Galatians in 1519.[9] Writing to his friend and mentor Johann von Staupitz in October of that year, Luther describes his work in the following mixed terms:

---

[6]Siegfried Raeder, "The Exegetical and Hermeneutical Work of Martin Luther," in *Hebrew Bible/Old Testament: The History of Its Interpretation II: From the Renaissance to the Enlightenment*, ed. Magne Sæbø (Göttingen: Vandenhoeck & Ruprecht, 2008), p. 365.
[7]WA 57:2.
[8]Hans Volz, "Eine neue studentische Nachschrift von Luthers erster Galaterbrief-vorlesung von 1516/17," *Zeitschrift für Kirchengeschichte* 46 (1954/55): 72-96.
[9]Luther, *In epistolam Pauli ad Galatas, F. Martini Lutheri Augustiniani, commentarius* (Leipzig: Melchior Lotther, 1519); WA 2:436-618; LW 27:153-410. Four years later the Wittenberg printer Johann Grünenberg issued a slightly abridged edition of the same work, the title now reflecting Luther's estrangement from his religious order: *In epistolam Pauli ad Galatas Martini Lutheri commentarius* (Wittenberg: Johann Grünenberg, 1523).

> I am sending you two copies, Reverend Father, of my foolish commentary. I am not so happy with it as I was at first, and I see that it might have been expounded more fully and clearly. But who can do everything at once? Indeed, who can manage to do very much for long? Nevertheless, I am confident that Paul is made clearer here than he has previously been by others, even though it is not yet quite to my liking.[10]

This remark highlights not only Luther's evolving perspective (no longer pleased with a work barely two years old) but also his aim in exposition: to clarify the mind of the apostle for a contemporary audience. In this regard, Luther's work is in keeping with the aims of many humanist scholars of his generation, including Desiderius Erasmus, whose influence looms large in this volume.[11]

Given Luther's ambivalence regarding his first effort at expounding Galatians, it comes as no surprise to find him returning to the letter once again in 1531. It is important to keep in mind, however, how much had changed for Luther in the intervening years. At the time he had given his first lectures on Galatians in 1516, Luther was an obscure friar, fresh out of graduate school, beginning his teaching career at a relatively new (and consequently not very prestigious) university on the margins of European intellectual life. Twelve years later, Luther had been excommunicated by the pope, declared an outlaw by the emperor, hailed as a prophet by his supporters and excoriated as a heresiarch by his detractors. He had translated the New Testament into German from the original language, and then broken publicly with Erasmus, the scholar whose retrieval of the Greek text had made this possible. And his voluminous popular writings had helped first to precipitate—and then to suppress—a small civil war. Over the course of this period, Luther and his followers had slowly shifted their stance from that of prophetic witness to apostolic mission—that is, they had gone from being loyal Catholics, calling the church back to its most ancient and authentic traditions, to becoming the founders of an alternate ecclesial polity in the face of intransigent opposition.[12]

---

[10]Epistle 162 (October 3, 1519), WABr 1:340.
[11]Johannes Kunze, *Erasmus und Luther: Der Einfluss des Erasmus auf die Kommentierung des Galaterbriefes und der Psalmen durch Luther 1519–1521* (Münster: LIT Verlag, 2000).
[12]David C. Steinmetz, "The Catholic Luther: A Critical Reappraisal," *Theology Today* 61, no. 2 (2004): 187-201.

All these developments came to a head in 1530, when representatives from the "Protestant" (as we must now call them) territories of the Holy Roman Empire sent representatives to the imperial diet meeting at Augsburg in hopes of persuading Charles V to side with them against Rome. The emperor declined, declaring instead his intention "to remain firmly faithful to the old, true, traditional Christian faith and religion, and [to] the honorable, praiseworthy ceremonies and usages which have always been performed in all the churches."[13] After nearly a decade of legal maneuvers following the Diet of Worms, Luther and his supporters were forced to confront the reality that the empire would not aid in reforming the church. Within five weeks after the end of the Diet, envoys from the Lutheran territories were meeting in the Thuringian village of Smalkalden to draft an agreement for mutual protection against their Catholic emperor.[14] If the gospel were to survive, it would have to be defended by force of arms, rather than by constitutional appeals.

All this serves to underscore the context in which Luther turned his attention to Paul's letter to the Galatians once more in July 1531—and to explain the note of urgency that runs throughout his exposition. When Luther prefaced his lectures in July 1531 with the warning that "there is a great and present danger that the devil may take away from us the pure doctrine of faith," he may have been indulging in polemical rhetoric, but the danger to his movement was real enough.[15] Nevertheless, Luther and his students worked their way through the epistle at a much more leisurely pace than in 1519, devoting six lectures to the first chapter (July 3–18, 1531), five to the second (July 24–Aug. 21), eleven to the third (Aug. 22–Oct. 10), six to the fourth (Oct. 17–Nov. 14), six to the fifth (Nov. 14–Dec. 4) and three to the sixth (Dec. 5–12). Again, student notes formed the basis for the later printed edition, which hit the presses with two editions in 1535, followed by a corrected reprint of the same material in 1538.[16] It is this

---

[13]Thomas A. Brady Jr., *German Histories in the Age of Reformations, 1400–1650* (New York: Cambridge University Press, 2009), p. 220.
[14]This brief summary of events follows the analysis in ibid.
[15]Luther, *Galatas* (1535), WA 40.1:39; LW 26:3.
[16]Luther, *In Epistolam S. Pauli ad Galatas commentarius ex praelectione D. Martini Lutheri collectus* (Wittenberg: Johannes Luft, 1535; Hagenau: Peter Brubach, 1535); *In epistolam S. Pauli ad Galatas commentarius ex praelectione D. Mart. Luth. collectus. Iam denuo diligenter recognitus, castigatus etc.* (Wittenberg: Luft, 1538); WA 40.1 and 40.2. The Weimar edition tracks variations between

"final" edition, often referred to as the "1531/35 edition," that would establish Luther as the preeminent commentator on Galatians in the sixteenth century, and perhaps of the early modern era.[17]

TEXTS AND TOOLS

Of what tools did Luther avail himself as he set about his work of expounding the text? What commentaries did he consult, and—above all—what text of the Bible itself? Owing in large part to his work as a translator, Luther's linguistic handling of the text has received nearly exhaustive treatment by modern scholars. Heinz Bluhm has demonstrated that Luther's translation of Galatians in the 1522 *Septembertestament* was based on the most up-to-date edition of the Greek text available in Germany at the time, Erasmus's 1519 *Novum Testamentum Omne*.[18] This edition was accompanied by Erasmus's own annotations on the Greek and a fresh Latin translation, which often departed from the Vulgate in ways that would prove jarring, even controversial.[19] Luther made full use of these tools, and his translation of Galatians into German gives evidence of discerning linguistic and literary judgment. This is evident, Bluhm argues, in the way Luther avoids a slavish, mechanical translation of the original, at times preferring the Vulgate's reading when it made better sense, and at times even anticipating some of the Greek readings of the Complutensian Polyglot, a superior text unavailable to Luther at the time of his early translation.[20]

There is no doubt but that Luther's exegesis of Galatians was rooted in a deep understanding of the Greek text, but what about his classroom practice? Despite his humanist conviction that sound exegesis of the New Testament must be rooted in the *graeca veritas* (the "Greek truth") and delivered to common folk in the common tongue, Luther and his colleagues maintained

---

these editions and reproduces the *Nachschriften* of Luther's student, Georg Rörer, on the upper half of the page.

[17] Robert Kolb, "The Influence of Luther's Galatians Commentary of 1535 on Later Sixteenth-Century Lutheran Commentaries on Galatians," *Archiv für Reformationsgeschichte* 84 (1993): 156-84. Luther's engagement with Galatians also extended to his work as a translator and preacher.

[18] Heinz Bluhm, "The Sources of Luther's *Septembertestament*: Galatians," in *Luther for an Ecumenical Age*, ed. Carl Meyer (St. Louis: Concordia, 1967), pp. 144-71.

[19] Robert Coogan, *Erasmus, Lee, and the Correction of the Vulgate: The Shaking of the Foundations* (Geneva: Librairie Droz, 1992).

[20] Bluhm, "Sources," p. 170.

the use of the Vulgate in the liturgy throughout this period, even publishing a revision of the venerable Latin translation in 1529, the so-called Wittenberg Vulgate. This may have been the text to which he referred in his classroom lectures, though the Latin text of Galatians supplied in the print edition beginning in 1535 does at times differ from this text.

Finally, who were Luther's interlocutors as he worked his way through the text? In his 1519 *Commentarius,* Luther explicitly cites exegetical works by Jerome,[21] Augustine,[22] "Ambrose,"[23] Nicholas of Lyra,[24] Erasmus[25] and Jacques Lefèvre d'Étaples.[26] In his later treatise *On the Councils and the Church* (1539), Luther would defend himself against the charge that his biblical exegesis was conducted in willful ignorance of patristic interpretation, remarking that he had actually felt compelled to keep his enthusiasm for the books of the fathers in check and identifying Jerome as his primary guide as

---

[21] Jerome, *Sancti Hieronymi Presbyteri Commentarius in Epistulam Pauli Apostoli ad Galatas* (CCSL 77A); ET, *Commentary on Galatians,* trans. Andrew Cain (FC 121).

[22] Eric Plummer, ed., *Augustine's Commentary on Galatians: Introduction, Text, Translation, and Notes* (New York: Oxford University Press, 2003).

[23] Luther follows universal medieval opinion in ascribing this text to the bishop of Milan. Erasmus is widely regarded as the first scholar to reject this view, though this is not quite accurate. In 1527 he published a four-volume edition of Ambrose (*Diui Ambrosii Episcopi Mediolanensis omnia opera...*) with the Basel printer Johannes Froben. Erasmus noted his concerns in this edition that the text had been corrupted, though he never rejected Ambrose's authorship outright, and in his later *Annotationes* on Romans, he cites the commentary as the work of Ambrose without qualification. According to Hoven, the name "Ambrosiaster" was coined by the editors of the later Benedictine edition of Ambrose's *Opera* (Paris, 1686–1890). René Hoven, "Saint Ambroise ou l'Ambrosiaster?," *L'antiquité classique* 38 (1969): 172-74. *Commentariae in XII epostolas beati Pauli* (CSEL 81); ET, *Commentaries on Galatians–Philemon,* trans. Gerald L. Bray (Downers Grove, IL: InterVarsity Press, 2009).

[24] Nicholas of Lyra, *Postilla super totam bibliam* (Strassburg, 1492; repr., Frankfurt am Main: Minerva, 1971).

[25] Luther draws on two exegetical tools produced by Erasmus during this period, the *Annotationes* and the *Paraphrases.* The former were a set of terse explanatory notes, mainly philological in nature, that accompanied the *Novum Instrumentum* beginning in 1516 and were subsequently expanded in 1519, 1523, 1527 and 1535. A critical edition of the Latin text has recently been published in the Amsterdam edition of Erasmus's works (ASD VI-9). Beginning with Romans in 1517, Erasmus also began publishing a set of *Paraphrases* on the New Testament. This project was motivated by "the pastoral necessity of simplifying the sacred text for less-educated Christians" (Jean-François Cottie, "Erasmus's Paraphrases: A 'New Kind of Commentary'?," in *The Unfolding of Words: Commentary in the Age of Erasmus,* ed. Judith Rice Henderson [Toronto: University of Toronto Press, 2012], p. 28). *In epistolam Pauli Apostoli ad Galatas paraphrasis* was not published until the spring of 1519, and so was unavailable to Luther during the composition of his first commentary. A modern critical edition of this work is not yet available, but for a serviceable English translation, see CWE 42.

[26] Jacques Lefèvre d'Étaples, *S. Pauli epistolae XIV ex vulgate: Adiecta intelligentia ex Graeco, cum commentariis* (Paris, 1512; repr., Stuttgart: Frommann, 1978).

he made his way through the text.[27] Both of these recollections are borne out by the pattern of Luther's citations in the first *Commentarius* (table 1). Indeed, if Luther can be accused of neglecting the exegetical tradition, it could only be the medieval tradition, with which he barely interacts at all.

Table 1. Exegetical citations in Luther's 1519 *Commentarius* on Galatians*

Commentator	Positive/Neutral	Negative	Total
Jerome	68	37	105
Augustine	18	7	25
Erasmus	23	1	24
"Ambrose"	4	2	6
Stapulensis	3	2	5
Lyra	0	1	1

*By "exegetical citations" I mean places in the text where Luther explicitly enters into dialogue with earlier interpreters in an effort to establish the basic meaning of the biblical text; thus, I exclude those instances where Luther interacts with anonymous exegetical lore, as well as anecdotes or historical references for which he gives an explicit reference. By "positive/neutral," I include those instances where Luther either clearly endorses a reading, or where he lets it stand as one possible (and, by implication, valid) reading, even if he goes on to elaborate a further meaning.

Jerome is by far the most important dialogue partner for Luther in the 1519 *Commentarius*; indeed, he cites Jerome's commentary more than all the other "secondary sources" at his disposal combined. Luther has high regard for Jerome's linguistic skill, and he relies heavily on "the saintly man" for a wealth of exegetical detail, from questions of historical context to textual criticism and the etymology of Greek and Hebrew words.[28] Nevertheless, Luther is not shy in demurring from Jerome's conclusions when he finds them objectionable on exegetical or theological grounds, as he does on several occasions: for example, on the conflict between Peter and Paul (Gal 2:11-13), on Christ's having become a "curse" (Gal 3:13) and on the distinction between spirit and flesh (Gal 5:17).[29] Most significant, however, is Luther's critique of the way in which Jerome parses Paul's language of law, and the resulting contrast between justification by faith and that by works (on which, more anon). Luther regards this as a major blind spot in Jerome's

---

[27] WA 50:519; LW 41:9.
[28] WA 2:561; LW 27:327.
[29] For Luther's take on the famous argument between Jerome and Augustine over Gal 2:11, see Kenneth Hagen, "Did Peter Err? The Text Is the Best Judge: Luther on Galatians (1519-1538)," in *Augustine, the Harvest, and Theology (1300-1650): Essays Dedicated to Heiko Augustinus Oberman in Honor of His Sixtieth Birthday*, ed. Kenneth Hagen (Leiden: Brill, 1991), pp. 110-26.

reading of Paul; however, his esteem for Jerome is so high that in several places he explains away the latter's misjudgment by blaming it on Origen. Augustine is also a major source for Luther's theological exegesis of the letter, especially on the core (from Luther's point of view) matter of justification and the law, though Luther is well aware of his limitations as an exegete of the Greek text. For this, Luther is heavily dependent on Erasmus, "that excellent man," whom he cites with an almost boyish admiration.[30]

In the 1531/35 *Commentarius*, Luther's interaction with the exegetical literature has changed dramatically, as has his attitude toward Jerome and Erasmus. Most apparently, the latter commentary reads much less like a scholarly work of textual exegesis and something more like a set of sermons or a polemical treatise. Whereas in the 1519 edition Luther had tethered his discussion more tightly to the lexical and syntactical details of Paul's text, considering the best of patristic and Renaissance scholarship with a workmanlike consistency, his style in the 1535 edition is much more freewheeling, with scant reference to the scholars with whose exegetical judgments he is interacting. Despite the fact that the latter edition is nearly three times the length of the former, explicit references to the works cited in 1519 are far fewer: for example, Jerome's commentary is cited 105 times in 1519, but only 20 times in 1535; Augustine's is cited 25 times in 1519, but only 3 times in 1535; and Ambrosiaster, Lyra and Stauplensis are neglected entirely. Nor, so far as I can tell, does Luther interact with any new exegesis between the time of his first and second commentaries.[31]

Moreover, when he does refer to ancient and contemporary exegetes in the 1535 edition, it is almost always to disagree with them. Jerome, who has now become Luther's exegetical whipping boy, is cited positively only four times, and never in a way that suggests he has made any real contribution to Luther's understanding of the text. In 1519, Luther tended to maintain a respectful tone when discussing Jerome's opinions, even when he disagreed with them; in 1535, his contempt is undisguised.[32] In conversation

---

[30] WA 2:553; LW 27:315.

[31] This despite the fact that several significant works of Pauline exegesis were published during this period: Johannes Bugenhagen (1525), Kaspar Megander (1533), Johannes Campensis (1534) and Heinrich Bullinger (1535), as well as a Latin translation by Erasmus of a commentary by John Chrysostom (1527) and the aforementioned *Paraphrases*.

[32] For example, Jerome "speaks foolishly" (WA 2:170; LW 26:92); he "made awkward and inept al-

during this period, Luther remarked, "I cannot think of a doctor whom I have come to detest so much, and yet I have loved him and read him with the utmost ardor."[33] The same is true, though to a lesser degree, with Erasmus, who in 1535 is cited almost exclusively as a theological foil, not as a philological authority. During the intervening years, Luther's theology had undergone considerable development, and his changing attitude to these two exegetes should serve to alert us not to expect a mere restatement of Luther's early theology in the later commentary.

In concluding this section, a word must be said regarding the genre of Luther's writings on Galatians. Much has been made of Luther's comment in the dedication (1519) that he regarded the work as "not so much a commentary as a testimony of my faith in Christ."[34] Kenneth Hagen argues trenchantly against the notion that Luther wrote "commentaries," arguing instead for the Latin term *enarratio*, a word with no direct English equivalent.[35] Hagen's concern is to ensure that we do not confuse Luther's writings with the work of nineteenth-century exegetes working with a subject-object dichotomy. To be sure, Luther could be quite scathing in his critique of academic exegetes who read the Bible "solely for the purpose of intellectual knowledge, as if it were a historical writing."[36] But this does not imply that Luther regarded his work as an exercise in pure subjectivity, and neither that he entirely collapsed the distance between past and present. On the contrary, Christian piety must be grounded in a clear apprehension of the text, for only in this way could God's authoritative message for humanity be distinguished from the later accretions of human tradition. To put the matter in more contemporary terms, for Luther theological exegesis involves more

---

legories out of the simplest statements of Scripture" (WA 2:653; LW 26:433); he "was so deceived by his precious Origen that he understood almost nothing in Paul" (WA 2:430; LW 26:275), etc.

[33]*Ergo nullum doctorem scie, quem aeque oderim, cum tamen ardentissime eum amaverim et legerim* (WATR 1:194 [no. 445]). See Joseph Lössl, "Martin Luther's Jerome: New Evidence for a Changing Attitude," in *Jerome of Stridon: His Life, Writings, and Legacy*, ed. Andrew J. Cain and Josef Lössl (Burlington, VT: Ashgate, 2009), pp. 237-51.

[34]*Nec tam commentarium quam testimonium meae in Christo fidei* (WA 2:449; LW 27:159).

[35]"The term 'enarratio' is very old. It goes back to Augustine, to the Psalter (c. 18), and to Isaiah (c. 53)—in medieval Latin translations of the Bible. It is to set forth in the public arena praise to the glory of God" (Hagen, *Luther's Approach to Scripture*, p. 51).

[36]Martin Brecht, *Martin Luther: His Road to Reformation, 1483-1521*, trans. James L. Schaaf (Minneapolis: Fortress, 1985), p. 84.

than mere historical reconstruction, but it certainly does not involve less.[37] Once this point is grasped, there is no need to quibble over categories like *commentarius* and *enarratio*, terms that Luther appears to have used more or less interchangeably.[38] Both versions of Luther's *Commentary* on Galatians contain the sort of rigorous grammatico-historical analysis of the biblical text we are accustomed to look for in biblical commentaries today, and both versions apply the results of that exegesis to a wide range of social, political and theological issues confronting Luther in his day. Luther showed himself by turns both generous and scathing with earlier interpreters, but he never pulled his punches: when advances in textual, linguistic and historical understanding discomfited traditional readings, Luther showed no hesitation in setting aside the views of Jerome, Erasmus or even Augustine. If we take him at his word, there is no reason to think

---

[37]"While grammatical and historical study formed the basis of an edifying interpretation of the text, Luther was unwilling to make the sharp distinction encouraged by modern criticism between what the text meant and what it means. He did not ignore this distinction and could leave the meaning of a text at the level of historical or theological analysis. At the same time, he often utilized personal experience and his diagnosis of the contemporary church to make the text speak immediately to his own day and thus to reveal its meaning" (Scott H. Hendrix, "Luther Against the Background of the History of Biblical Interpretation," *Interpretation* 37, no. 3 [1983]: 229-39; quote on p. 238).

[38]Hagen states pointedly that "the word that Luther used instead of 'commentary' is the verb 'enarrare' or the noun 'enarratio'" (*Luther's Approach to Scripture*, p. 50), but the texts he cites do not support this conclusion—indeed the reverse. In the 1519 *Commentarius*, Luther explains (with the help of Erasmus) a figure of speech in Gal 1:9 by means of a Latin analogue: *Virgilium lego, Hieronymum enarro* ("I read Vergil; I comment on Jerome"); WA 2:463; LW 27:179. Here Luther is obviously using the term in the more restrictive, or "academic" sense, rather than in the sense elaborated by Hagen. In the 1535 *Commentarius*, Luther simply quotes the Vulgate text of Ps 18:1 (MT 19:1): *coeli enarrant gloriam Dei*. In neither context does he make any reference to the genre of his own writing. Nor is it the case that Luther "distinguished his work from the 'Commentaries' of Erasmus" on this basis, as Hagen claims. In the dedication of 1519, Luther offers a sort of apology for publishing "this slight thing," remarking that he "would certainly have preferred to wait for the commentaries (*commentarios*) promised long ago by Erasmus, a man preeminent in theology and impervious to envy. But since he is postponing this (God grant that it may not be for long), the situation which you see forces me to come before the public" (WA 2:450; LW 27:159-60). This hardly seems like an attempt to introduce a distinction between his own work and that of Erasmus by appealing to a difference in genre. To be sure, Luther begins his lectures (and the printed edition of his commentary in 1535) with the words *Suscipimus denuo enarrare in nomine Domini epistolam Pauli ad Galatas* (WA 40.1:39), but it is also the case that each of the successive works Luther published on Galatians was titled *commentarius*, not *enarratio*. Hagen rightly points out that sixteenth-century titles were often supplied by publishers, but I find it hard to imagine that so forceful a personality as Luther—particularly later in his career—could not have carried the point if it really mattered to him. The fact that he was willing to let successive editions of his *Commentary* on Galatians proceed so titled ought rather to alert us to the breadth of this genre in the sixteenth century. For more on this last point, see the helpful discussion in Cottie, "Erasmus's *Paraphrases*."

he would not expect the same handling from modern exegetes today.

ARGUMENT AND STRUCTURE

Luther follows patristic and medieval custom by prefacing his commentary with a summary of what he takes to be the *argumentum* of the epistle as a whole, and here his departure from traditional exegesis is apparent, even in the earliest edition.

Traditional exegesis. For Jerome, Paul's letter to the Galatians (like the letter to the Romans) is concerned especially with establishing the "cessation of the old Law and the introduction of the new Law."[39] Here, the relationship is clearly one of promise and fulfillment, whereby the fullness of evangelical grace renders obsolete the burdens of Jewish custom.[40] The uniqueness of Galatians lies in the fact that Paul is not, as in Romans, addressing Jewish believers who were still clinging to the rites of their forefathers, but Gentile converts who had been intimidated into observing Jewish practices by the authority of "certain people who claimed that Peter, James, and all the churches of Judea were conflating the Gospel of Christ with the old Law." In response to this crisis, "Paul proceeds cautiously, steering a middle course between two extremes so as neither to betray the grace of the Gospel . . . nor to detract from his [Jewish] forefathers in his preaching of grace."[41] For Jerome, therefore, the letter to the Galatians must be read as addressing a very specific historical context, and Paul's rhetoric must be interpreted accordingly. The letter does not set out a straightforward description of universal theological themes in the manner of a philosophical treatise; rather, it "makes a stealthy approach, as if going by a secret passageway."[42] This allows Jerome

---

[39]*In his autem duabus, ut dixi, epistolis, specialiter antiquae legis cessatio, et nouae introductio continetur* (PL 26:334; FC 121:59).

[40]"In everything that the Apostle wrote or said in person, he tirelessly taught that the burdensome obligations [*onera deposita*] of the old Law have been abolished and that everything that had preceded in types and symbols [*typis et imaginibus*] (the Sabbath rest, injurious circumcision, the recurring cycle of new moons and of the three annual feasts, the dietary laws, and the daily ablution, after which one would become defiled again) ceased to have validity with the arrival of evangelical grace, which is fulfilled by the faith of the believing soul [*fides animae credentis impleret*] and not by the blood of animal sacrifices" (PL 26:334; FC 121:58-59).

[41]*Quamobrem ita caute inter utrumque et medius incedit, ut nec euangelii prodat gratiam, pressus pondere et auctoritate maiorum, nec praecessoribus faciat iniuriam, dum assertor est gratiae* (PL 26:334; FC 121:59).

[42]*Oblique uero et quasi per cuniculos latenter incedens* (PL 26:334; FC 121:59).

to explain (away) the apparent conflict between Peter and Paul, a source of some embarrassment for Christian intellectuals ever since the publication of Porphyry's *Adversus Christianos* and a major worry for Jerome.[43]

For Augustine, Galatians is ultimately concerned not with a contrast between old law and new law, between Jewish customs and evangelical grace, but with the nature of grace itself. The reality of the grace revealed in the gospel has not yet dawned on some, and Paul writes to make explicit the underlying logic of grace, a logic that makes sense of both the law and faith:

> The reason the Apostle writes to the Galatians is so they may understand what it is that God's grace accomplishes for them: they are no longer under the law. For though the grace of the gospel had been preached to them, there were some from the circumcision who still did not grasp the real benefit of grace. Despite being called Christians, they still wanted to be under the burdens of the law—burdens that the Lord God had imposed not on those serving righteousness but on those serving sin. That is, he had given a righteous law to unrighteous people to point out their sins, not take them away. He takes away sins only by the grace of faith, which works through love (Gal. 5:6).[44]

"Law," for Augustine, is not limited to the ceremonial functions regarded by Jerome as mere "types and symbols." Rather, law in this context is a comprehensive category embracing all the commands of God revealed under the old dispensation—what in the later tradition would be distinguished under the tripartite headings of "moral," "ceremonial" and "civil" law.[45] While Augustine agrees with Jerome that many of the typological functions of the Mosaic law have been fulfilled, and therefore rendered nonbinding for Christians—though he never goes so far as Jerome in regarding them as "abolished"—the primary contrast is not between Jewish law and Christian grace but between law and faith as complementary movements within God's overarching economy of grace. Formulating the issue with striking clarity

---

[43]See Robert M. Grant, "Porphyry Among the Early Christians," in *Romanitas et Christianitas: Studia Iano Henrico Waszink oblata*, ed. Willem den Boer et al. (Amsterdam: North Holland, 1973), pp. 181-87.
[44]Augustine, *Expositio Epistolae ad Galatas* 1.1; ET, Plummer, *Augustine's Commentary on Galatians*, p. 125.
[45]On the development of this typology in Thomas Aquinas, see the discussion in Matthew Levering, *Christ's Fulfillment of Torah and Temple: Salvation According to Thomas Aquinas* (South Bend, IN: University of Notre Dame Press, 2002), pp. 22-30.

during the early stages of the Pelagian controversy, Augustine would write in his treatise *On the Spirit and the Letter* that "by the law of works God says: Do what I command! By the law of faith we say to God: Give what you command!"[46] Faith, for Augustine, thus provides the power for fulfillment of the law's moral demands, not the abrogation of those demands.

As I have already shown, Luther's primary interlocutors in his exegesis of Galatians were patristic commentators and humanist scholars, with scant heed paid to the roughly thousand years of interpretive tradition between the two. Nevertheless, it will be helpful briefly to sketch out the approach of at least one medieval interpreter with whom Luther was *not* in explicit dialogue, in order to further highlight the distinctiveness of Luther's own approach. Thomas Aquinas is typical of many medieval interpreters in that he seeks to synthesize patristic opinion rather than pit one source against another. Thus it is unsurprising that we see themes from both Jerome and Augustine harmonized without any sense that his sources might be in tension. Although modern scholars have consistently demonstrated Thomas's profound debts to Augustine, particularly on the questions of grace, faith and works so central to Galatians,[47] when it came to making sense of Galatians on its own terms, Thomas's work bears a much heavier impress from Jerome. Taking Leviticus 26:10 as an epigram for the entire epistle ("The new coming on, you shall cast away the old"), Thomas explains,

> The Apostle writes the Galatians this epistle in which he shows that with the coming of the grace of the New Testament, the Old Testament should be cast out, so that with the fulfillment of the truth, the figure may be abandoned, and with the attainment of these two, namely, grace and truth, one may arrive at the truth of justice [*iustitiae*] and glory.[48]

According to Thomas, all the other books of the Pauline corpus treat grace as it exists in the church in light of the "newness of the doctrine of Christ," but Galatians is concerned with refuting "oldness." This *vetustas* is fourfold:

---

[46]Augustine, *De Spiritu et littera* 22, CSEL 60:174. Cf. *Confessions* 10.31.45: "Give what you command, and command what you will."

[47]See, for example, Daniel A. Keating, "Justification, Sanctification, and Divinization in Thomas Aquinas," in *Aquinas on Doctrine: A Critical Introduction*, ed. Thomas Weinandy et al. (Edinburgh: T&T Clark, 2004), pp. 139-58.

[48]Thomas Aquinas, *Super Epistolas S. Pauli lectura*, vol. 1, *Super Epistolam ad Galatas lectura*, ed. Busa (Stuttgart-Bad Cannstadt: Frommann-Hoolzbog, 1980), p. 181.

(1) the "oldness of error" (Is 26:3); (2) the "oldness of figure" (Heb 8:8); (3) the "oldness of guilt" (Ps 31:3); and (4) the "oldness of punishment" (Lam 3:4).[49] This oldness, Thomas argues, stands in sharp contrast to the newness of grace made manifest in Christ.

So far as the structure of the epistle is concerned, Thomas provides a detailed analysis of the flow of Paul's argument. After a brief *salutatio* (Gal 1:1-5), the rest of the letter is taken up with the *narratio epistularis*, which consists of two parts: first, Paul refutes the Galatians' error on the authority of the gospel (Gal 1:6–2:21) and on that of the Old Testament (Gal 3:1–4:31); second, he admonishes them with regard to doctrine and morals (Gal 5:1–6:18). The first part of the *admonitio* (*quantum ad divina*) is thus for Thomas the climax of the letter, with its twofold charge to "stand firm" and "do not submit to a yoke of slavery" (Gal 5:1). This twofold construction is reiterated in Galatians 5:6, where Thomas focuses on the contrast between circumcision as a sign of the "oldness" that enslaves, and "faith working through love" as the empowering "newness" that saves. For Thomas, therefore, faith is at the center of Paul's argument in Galatians, but understood here in the Augustinian sense as the power that liberates the will to perform works of love. Thus construed, Galatians becomes a key text for reconciling the theology of Paul with that of James.

Luther. Luther is having none of this. His exposition of Galatians departs radically from his predecessors both in his apprehension of the epistle's argument and its structure. In his summary of the epistle's *argumentum*, Luther sets out as clearly as anywhere else in his corpus his distinctive understanding of the *iustitia Dei* so central to his mature theology.[50] At the heart of this insight is the sharp distinction Luther draws between active and passive righteousness, a "breakthrough" he would later describe as the turning point in his understanding of the Christian gospel.[51] In 1519, the

---

[49]Ibid.
[50]The secondary literature on this subject is massive, but for a basic overview of Luther's development during this period, see Bernhard Lohse, *Martin Luther's Theology: Its Historical and Systematic Development*, trans. Roy A. Harrisville (Minneapolis: Fortress, 1999), pp. 85-95, 258-66.
[51]See the famous account in the *Vorrede zum ersten Bande der Gesamtausgaben seiner lateinischen Schriften* (1545), WA 54:185-86; LW 34:336-38. Scholars continue to disagree about the dating and theological significance of Luther's so-called Reformation discovery. I have examined the issues in some detail in chapter four of my doctoral dissertation, "Divided by Faith: The Protestant Doctrine of Justification and the Confessionalization of Biblical Exegesis" (Duke University, 2010). Luther

distinction is implicit: "Although the Galatians had first been taught . . . to trust in Jesus Christ alone, not in their own righteousnesses [*iusticias*] or in those of the Law, later on they were again turned away by the false apostles and led to trust in works of legalistic righteousness [*legalis iusticiae*]."[52] Here careful attention to Luther's language is critical: the plural *iusticias* points to what would become a characteristically Lutheran way of speaking of the various types of human righteousness, against which is set the righteousness of God (*iustitia Dei*). In 1535, Luther picks up this term and unpacks it more fully: "The argument is this: Paul wants to establish the doctrine of faith, grace, the forgiveness of sins or Christian righteousness, so that we may have a perfect knowledge and know the difference between Christian righteousness and all other kinds of righteousness."[53] In contrast with this "Christian righteousness" (*iustitia Christiana*), Luther enumerates a sweeping range of *iustitiae*: there is "political righteousness" (*iustitia politica*), "which the emperor, the princes of the world, philosophers, and lawyers consider." So also there is "ceremonial righteousness" (*iustitia ceremonialis*), a righteousness grounded in "human traditions," ranging from the traditions of the pope to practices of moral discipline employed by parents. Finally there is the righteousness of the law, or the Ten Commandments (*iustitia legalis seu decalogi*), taught by Moses.[54]

Luther argues that the primary aim of Paul's letter to the Galatians is to contrast these various forms of active righteousness with the passive righteousness of the gospel. His description of this contrast is well known but worth quoting here at length:

---

was clearly using the language of *iustitia passiva* as early as his lectures on Romans in 1515, though I argue that the revolutionary implications of this terminological shift dawned on Luther's consciousness much more gradually than his own later account suggests.

[52]*Galatae primum ab Apostolo sanam fidem, id est in solum Iesum Chistum, non in suas aut legis iusticias fidere, docti post per pseudoapostolos rursum deturbati sunt in fiduciam operum legalis iustitiae*. . . . (Galatas [1519], WA 2:451; LW 27:161).

[53]Luther, *Galatas* (1535), WA 40.1:40; LW 26:4. The Latin word *iustitia* is notoriously difficult to translate into English, carrying with it a much richer set of associations than either of the terms most frequently used, "righteousness" and "justice." For this reason, I have opted to retain the Latin in the text whenever possible.

[54]It is important to point out here that despite the similarity in terms, Luther is not referring to the well-known distinction in Western theology between civil, ceremonial and moral law. This distinction was developed in order to parse the various dimensions of the law given by God to the Jews under the Mosaic dispensation. Luther's terminology, however, is much broader, embracing laws of both human and divine origin.

Over and above all these there is the righteousness of faith or Christian righteousness, which is to be distinguished most carefully from all the others. For they are all contrary to this righteousness, both because they proceed from the laws of emperors, the traditions of the pope, and the commandments of God, and because they consist in our works and can be achieved by us with "purely natural endowments" [*ex puris naturalibus*] as the scholastics teach, or from a gift of God. For these kinds of the righteousness of works, too, are gifts of God, as are all the things we have. But this most excellent righteousness, the righteousness of faith, which God imputes to us through Christ without works, is neither political nor ceremonial nor legal nor work-righteousness but is quite the opposite; it is a merely passive righteousness, while all the others, listed above, are active. For here we work nothing, render nothing to God; we only receive and permit someone else to work in us, namely, God. Therefore it is appropriate to call the righteousness of faith or Christian righteousness "passive." This is a righteousness hidden in a mystery, which the world does not understand.[55]

This passage signals not only a break with the "semi-Pelagianism" of late medieval theologians, such as Gabriel Biel, who taught that human beings could merit the gift of grace *ex puris naturalibus*, but also with the broader Augustinian tradition, which saw God's gift of inner grace as the transformative power that freed the Christian from sin and empowered her to fulfill the righteous demands of the law.[56] As Augustine himself put it, in a dictum that had become axiomatic in Western theology, "when God crowns our merits, he does nothing but reward his own gifts."[57] Luther, of course, does not deny the transformative power of this inner grace. Like the legislation of a wise prince, the rites of a holy pontiff or the moral injunctions of divine law, this inner habit of grace is a gift of God. But like all these gifts, it is a *human activity*, something we do in response to the more fundamental gift of God's creative word, which stands prior to all else.

For Luther, Paul's letter addresses a concrete historical situation, and it must be read in light of that situation: the Galatian Christians, a pre-

---

[55] Luther, *Galatas* (1535), WA 40.1:40-41; LW 26:4.
[56] On Biel's theology, see Heiko A. Oberman, *The Harvest of Medieval Theology: Gabriel Biel and Late Medieval Nominalism* (Cambridge, MA: Harvard University Press, 1963), pp. 47-48. Luther opposed this notion from as early as 1515, when he lectured on Paul's epistle to the Romans (WA 56:360).
[57] Augustine, *Epistle* 194.5; CSEL 57:190.

dominantly Gentile group, have responded in faith to the preaching of Paul's gospel, but after a promising beginning, they have lapsed back into a sub-Christian faith, putting their confidence in "works of legalistic righteousness."[58] The problem, as Luther sees it, is not that these works are obsolete, as Jerome had thought, or that they are impotent, as Augustine had thought. The problem is that the Galatians have failed to recognize the gratuitous nature of the *iustitia Dei* as the gift that stands prior to all human response. This failure jeopardizes the Galatians' very identity in Christ and thus calls forth Paul's most strenuous response.

Luther's exposition of Galatians differs from modern biblical commentaries in that he does not offer an explicit outline of the text. In this he differs also from many of his medieval predecessors, who often provided careful analyses of rhetorical and dialectical structure. Luther seems to have had little use for such interpretive tools, but this does not mean that he paid no attention to the structure of the argument, as is seen from several key passages in the commentary itself. Because Luther recognizes in Paul a fellow warrior of the gospel, his attention is riveted by Paul's polemical rhetoric to the near exclusion of any explicit analysis of the flow of Paul's thought within the epistle or of the place of the epistle within the apostle's wider corpus. In fact, it is not until the end of Galatians 4—at the close of what Luther regards as the positive argument of the epistle—that a rough sketch of its structure is given, and this only in passing.

As he enters on his treatment of the allegory of Sarah and Hagar beginning at Galatians 4:24, Luther notes that Paul had already proven his central argument, the righteousness of faith against that of works, by arguments based on experience (Gal 1–2), on the story of Abraham (Gal 3:1-9) and on the evidence of Scripture (Gal 3:10-22), and by a series of analogies (Gal 3:23–4:7). The story of Abraham's two sons is then added as "a kind of ornament."[59] Thus the substance of Paul's positive argument ends at Galatians 4:7 with the declaration, "so through God you are no longer a slave but a son." Then, in Galatians 4:8-9, when Paul asks the Galatians how it is that they could abandon such benefits and return in slavery to "weak and beggarly elements," Luther

---

[58] Luther, *Galatas* (1519), WA 2:451; LW 27:161.
[59] Luther, *Galatas* (1535), WA 40.1:657; LW 26:436.

discerns the conclusion of Paul's main line of thought.[60]

For Luther, therefore, the core of Paul's argument in Galatians is front-loaded in the first two chapters of the epistle; everything else merely expands on this central point and reinforces it. The "scolding" and moral admonition that come in the final two chapters of the letter represent not the climax of Paul's argumentation, as it is for Thomas, but a set of derivative considerations flowing from the *argumentum*. For Thomas, the central thrust of the epistle reaches its climax with "faith working through love" (Gal 5:6); for Luther, this is simply an outworking of the more fundamental insight that "a man is not justified by works of the law, but by faith in Jesus Christ" (Gal 2:16). This shift in how the argument and structure of the epistle are construed has important theological consequences, three of which I will now highlight.

THEOLOGICAL THEMES

Anti-asceticism. Luther's rejection of all forms of *iustitia activa*, as he describes it in the *argumentum*, carries radical consequences for how he views "religion." In commenting on Galatians 1:4, Luther regards Paul's statement that Christ delivers us "from the present evil world" as a summary statement of the epistle as a whole. "Paul is correct in calling it the evil world; for when it is at its best, then it is at its worst. The world is at its best in men who are religious, wise, and learned; yet in them it is actually evil twice over."[61] In medieval Latin, the term *religion* (*religio*) had come to refer very narrowly to life in the monastery—that is, life governed by a *regula*, a "rule," and this is clearly the meaning Luther has primarily in mind.[62] And yet, more broadly, Luther equates "religion" not so much with the institutional form of monasticism itself, but rather with the mindset of *askesis*, the notion that human beings are transformed through practice "from the outside in," and that this transformative process can ultimately lead to salvation.[63] This notion, as it

---

[60]Luther, *Galatas* (1535), WA 40.1:600; LW 26:394.
[61]Luther, *Galatas* (1535), WA 40.1:95; LW 26:40.
[62]John Bossy, "Some Elementary Forms of Durkheim," *Past and Present* 95 (May 1982): 4. The student notes on this text record his words as follows: *In monachis est optimus, in ingeniosis hominibus, sapientibus, philosophis, et ibi dupliciter malus, Invidiam, avaritiam, furtum, wie gisstig die leut sind, vides* (WA 40.1:95).
[63]Jennifer A. Herdt, *Putting on Virtue: The Legacy of the Splendid Vices* (Chicago: University of Chicago Press, 2008), p. 180. Despite widespread scholarly consensus that "asceticism" is virtually universal in all human cultures, the term has proven notoriously difficult to define. For my pur-

developed in early Christianity, rested on an essentially optimistic assessment of the human condition (despite the often spectacular austerities of ascetic practice): "Men and women are not slaves to the habitual, but can cultivate extraordinary forms of human existence."[64]

Luther attacks this notion relentlessly throughout both commentaries, arguing that ascetic practice makes Christ useless. The problem, for Luther, is not the intensity of the discipline. Despite caricatures that have persisted since his own lifetime, Luther was not a libertine: he is clear that the Christian life is arduous, and not for the faint of heart.[65] The problem is rather the orientation of means to ends, of practice in relation to soteriology. Commenting on Galatians 5:2, Luther reads Paul's objection to the circumcision of Gentile converts as a summary rejection of all ascetic practice:

> This passage is a terrible thunderbolt against the entire kingdom of the pope. To speak only of the best among them, all the priests, monks, and hermits did not trust in Christ, . . . they trusted in their own works, righteousnesses, vows, and merits. Hence they hear their judgment in this passage, namely, that Christ is of no use to them. For if they are able to abolish sins and to merit the forgiveness of sins and eternal life by their own righteousness and ascetic life (*austeritate vitae*), what good does it do them that Christ was born, suffered, shed His blood, was raised, conquered sin, death, and the devil, when they themselves can overcome these monsters by their own powers?[66]

Luther rejects this more optimistic anthropology, but what makes his polemic so extraordinary is the way in which he identifies this ascetic impulse with the essence of religion itself. The gospel, for Luther, is something that stands in opposition to "religion."[67] To be sure, Luther is not entirely consistent with his language: at times he uses the term *religio* in a positive sense

---

poses here, the two key elements are self-discipline/self-denial and its goal—that is, disciplined practice aimed at achieving salvation.

[64]Elizabeth A. Clark, *Reading Renunciation: Asceticism and Scripture in Early Christianity* (Princeton, NJ: Princeton University Press, 1999), p. 17.

[65]In his comments on Gal 5:7, for example, he remarks that "the life of the devout is strenuous running" (Luther, *Galatas* [1535], WA 40.2:39; LW 27:32).

[66]Luther, *Galatas* (1535), WA 40.2:10; LW 27:10.

[67]In his comments on the very first verse of the epistle, for example, he writes that "the Gospel is a doctrine that teaches something far more sublime than the wisdom, righteousness and religion of the world" (WA 40.1:52; LW 26:13). See also his comments (1535) on Gal 1:10; 2:16, 21; 3:1; 4:9, 14; 6:14.

(i.e., "true religion" vs. "false religion"), but even in these instances it is clear that what is in view is the proclamation of the Word (received passively by faith), over against human wisdom and practice (active righteousness). By equating *religio* (or at least *religio falsa*) with "active righteousness" (*iustitia activa*), therefore, it would seem that Luther is very close to Émile Durkheim's insight that asceticism is one of the "elementary forms" of religious life.[68] This explains the ease with which Luther can lump together all forms of religious practice in opposition to the "righteousness of God" (*iustitia Dei*): "Those in the world who do not teach it are either Jews or Turks or papists or sectarians."[69]

In one sense, Luther pays a certain backhanded tribute, both to the Jews and to the monks, when he equates them with each other: both represent the very best of what human beings are capable of achieving through *askesis*. The problem, for Luther, is not that the virtues produced thereby are not real.[70] The problem is that human beings seem driven by a psychological necessity to regard these virtues as currency in an economy of divine exchange. When this happens, the good becomes the enemy of the perfect, and "all the gifts of body and mind that you enjoy—wisdom, righteousness, holiness, eloquence, power, beauty, or wealth—are only the instruments of the devil's infernal tyranny."[71]

Law and the "presumption of religion." Luther would also have agreed with Durkheim's judgment that the source of ascetic practice is law, since all religious practice is grounded in a "system of interdicts." Luther is operating not with the generalized categories of a social theorist but with the biblical categories of law and gospel: all human beings have some access to natural law, however dimly discerned, and all human religions are attempts to respond to the law's demands in ways deemed appropriate to human reason.[72]

---

[68] According to Durkheim, "asceticism is not a rare, exceptional and nearly abnormal fruit of the religious life, as some have supposed it to be; on the contrary, it is one of its essential elements." In *The Elementary Forms of the Religious Life*, trans. Joseph W. Swain (New York: Free Press, 1947), p. 311.

[69] Luther, *Galatas* (1535), WA 40.1:48; LW 26:9.

[70] See, for example, Luther's remarks on the virtues of "noble Pagans," such as Cicero and Pomponius, in WA 40.1:219.

[71] Luther, *Galatas* (1535), WA 40.1:95; LW 26:40.

[72] Luther writes in another context: "All by nature have a certain knowledge of the law, though it is very weak and hazy. Hence it was and is necessary to hand on to them that knowledge of the law so that they may recognize the magnitude of their sin, the wrath of God, etc." 1. *Antinomerdispu-*

The real purpose of the Mosaic law, in Luther's view, is not to replace or even to supplement the law of nature, but to make it explicit with the aim of unmasking the ascetic impulse for the presumption he takes it to be:

> To curb and crush this monster and raging beast, that is, the presumption of religion [*opinionem scilicet religionis*], God is obliged, on Mt. Sinai, to give a new Law with such pomp and with such an awesome spectacle that the entire people is crushed with fear. For since reason becomes haughty with this human presumption of righteousness and imagines that on account of this it is pleasing to God, therefore God has to send some Hercules, namely, the Law, to attack, subdue, and destroy this monster with full force. Therefore the Law is intent only on this beast, not on any other.[73]

The law of Moses (i.e., Sinai) is not aimed at destroying sin per se, but the human presumption, implicit in ascetic practice (and thus, by extension, in all religious activity), that any human activity can do so.

The problem, as Luther sees it, stems not from the form of the law but from its content: the law commands that we love God with all our heart, soul, mind and strength, and that we love our neighbors as ourselves. "But from this it does not follow: 'this is written, and therefore it is done; the Law commands love, and therefore we love.'"[74] Augustine had solved this problem with his distinction between the letter and the spirit: the former demands that we love God and neighbor; the latter enables us to do so. For Luther, however, this solution overlooks the plain fact (or so he regards it) that nobody actually does: "You cannot produce anyone on earth who loves God and his neighbor as the Law requires." In the life to come, Luther explains, we will be fully empowered to love God in the manner commanded by the Law, but in the meantime "such purity is hindered by our flesh, to which sin

---

tation (1537), WA 39.1:361; quoted in Lohse, *Martin Luther's Theology*, p. 273.

[73]Luther, *Galatas* (1535), WA 40.1:219; LW 26:123. In WA, the sentence is rendered thus: *Ut ergo Deus compescat et contundat monstrum et bestiam istam furentem, Opinionem scilicet religionis, coactus est ferre in monte Syna novam legem tanta pompa et tam horribili specie, ut totus populous pavore concussus sit etc.* The 1538 printed version, however, reads as follows: *Ut autem compescat & contundat Deus monstrum & bestiam illam furentem (opinionem iusticiae seu religionis) quae naturaliter instat & superbire facit homines, ut putent propter eam se placere Deo, oportuit eum mittere aliquem Herculem, qui monstrum istud toto impetu adoriretur, prosterneret & conficeret, ho est, coactus est ferre in monte Syna legem, tanta pompa & tam horribili specie, ut totus populous pavore concussus sit.* This reading makes even more explicit Luther's equation of "religion" with the "presumption of righteousness."

[74]Luther, *Galatas* (1535), WA 40.2:79; LW 27:63.

will cling as long as we live."⁷⁵ Faith *does* empower us to respond to God and our neighbor in love, but never so as to stand as the basis for our acceptance into fellowship with God—either at the beginning of the Christian life or at its end.

Faith, love and the gift. Luther's mature theology of justification cannot be explained away in terms of his psychology or his personal "quest for a merciful God." It is a serious attempt to grapple with the great commandment of Scripture: "You shall love the Lord your God with all your heart, and with all your soul, and with all your strength, and with all your mind; and your neighbor as yourself" (Lk 10:27 NRSV).⁷⁶ Medieval theologians, building on Augustine's central distinction between the letter and the spirit in his anti-Pelagian writings, had reconciled Paul's language of justification by faith with the love command of Christ by a metaphysical distinction in causation. Faith was seen as the material cause of salvation; love as the formal cause. This love, infused by God's grace, is thus the *forma*, the divine reality which "(in-)forms" faith, giving it tangible reality. Love thus changes faith from a "dead," formless void to something living and active, a "colorful" knowing. This understanding was summarized by the expression "faith formed by love" (*fides charitate formata*).⁷⁷

To say that Luther rejects this notion would be an understatement: he regards it as a "wicked and destructive gloss" and a "hellish poison."⁷⁸ The reason for this is apparent once we recall the biblical insistence that love itself is the content of the law: to say that faith is dead unless "formed" or "colored" by love is, from Luther's point of view, simply another way of saying that faith is dead unless formed by the law, since love is what the law commands. Thus is Christ made into a lawgiver, a charge Luther hurls at his Roman opponents with relentless fury throughout the commentary.

Luther's solution to this problem is to introduce a temporal diremption between faith (*fides*) and love (*charitas*) as a way of isolating the latter from

---

⁷⁵Luther, *Galatas* (1535), WA 40.2:79; LW 27:64.
⁷⁶Simo Peura, "What God Gives Man Receives: Luther on Salvation," in *Union with Christ: The New Finnish Interpretation of Luther*, ed. Carl E. Braaten and Robert W. Jenson (Grand Rapids: Eerdmans, 1998), p. 76.
⁷⁷Tuomo Mannermaa, *Christ Present in Faith: Luther's View of Justification*, ed. Kirsi Stjerna (Minneapolis: Fortress, 2005), p. 24. Cf. Thomas Aquinas, *Super Epistolam ad Galatas lectura* 5.2.
⁷⁸Luther, *Galatas* (1535), WA 40.1:239-40; LW 26:136-37.

any implication in justification or the believer's union with Christ. Faith thus becomes the unitive force: it "takes hold of Christ and has Him present, enclosing Him as the ring encloses a gem."[79] But even though faith unites the believer to Christ, faith is distinct from love and in fact precedes it: "Because you have taken hold of Christ by faith, through whom you are righteous, you should now go and love God and your neighbor."[80] So insistent is Luther on distinguishing faith from love as the basis of union with Christ that he adds a new twist on his spousal metaphor for justification to drive the point home: "This Bridegroom, Christ, must be alone with His bride in His private chamber, and all the family and household must be shunted away. But later on, when the Bridegroom opens the door and comes out, then let the servants return to take care of them and serve them food and drink. Then let works and love begin."[81]

Many of Luther's most incisive critics have noted his tendency, despite the most insistent rhetoric to the contrary, to collapse love back into faith—after all, if faith is a unitive act, it is difficult to see how it can exist absent any element of desire.[82] The analogy quoted above might seem to support such a critique—can it really be that Luther is celebrating "a spousal union without spousal love"?[83] Rather than chalk this up to bad temper or Luther's "Nominalist philosophical formation,"[84] we would do well to remember that early modern notions of marriage were rather different from our own. The

---

[79] *Fides enim apprehendit Christum et habet eum praesentem includitque eum annulus gemmam, Et qui fuerit inventus cum tali fide apprehensi Christi in corde, illum reputat Deus iustum* (Luther, *Galatas* [1535], WA 40.1:233; LW 26:132).

[80] *Quia apprehendisti fide Christum per quem iustuts es, nunc eas et diligas Deum et proximum* (Luther, *Galatas* [1535], WA 40.1:234; LW 26:133).

[81] Luther, *Galatas* (1535), WA 40.1:241; LW 26:137. Spousal metaphors for the believer's union with Christ do not figure especially large in Luther's commentaries on Galatians, perhaps because the imagery is not present in the biblical text itself. Luther had deployed this metaphor most famously in his 1520 treatise *On the Freedom of a Christian*, and he returned to it frequently over the course of his long career.

[82] The most formidable of these critics remains, in my view, John Henry Newman, who pointed out the tendency in Luther and his followers to blur the line between faith and love: "At all times they have indulged in descriptions of faith as an adhering to Christ, a delighting and rejoicing in Him, and a giving oneself up to Him; all which seem to be nothing more or less than properties of love" (*Lectures on the Doctrine of Justification*, 3rd ed. [Eugene, OR: Wipf and Stock, 2001], p. 9).

[83] Michael Waldstein, "The Trinitarian, Spousal, and Ecclesial Logic of Justification," in *Reading Romans with St Thomas Aquinas*, ed. Matthew Levering and Michael Dauphinais (Washington, DC: Catholic University of America Press, 2012), p. 281.

[84] Ibid.

evangelical reformers viewed marriage as a social arrangement ordered for the promotion of mutual support, the procreation of children and the avoidance of sexual sin.[85] There was no assumption that sexual congress was an expression of genuine love, and Luther warned against confusing the two. It was easy enough to take a wife in the heat of infatuation, but abiding love could only arise from the union of habits and character, not merely of bodies.[86] Seen in this light, Luther's conjugal analogy makes a bit more sense: both in the marriage union and the believer's union with Christ, genuine love arises only in the context of a relationship constituted by mutual trust and fidelity.

This spousal imagery sheds further light on a topic that has been of considerable interest to recent scholars, Luther's theology of gift/giving.[87] Although Luther's distinctive understanding of justification by faith alone has often been described in terms of a unilateral gift, allowing for no reciprocity, this must be carefully qualified. On the one hand, the dialectic between law and gospel would seem to rule out any notion of human beings offering anything to God: "Now demanding [i.e., law] and granting [i.e., gospel], receiving and offering, are exact opposites and cannot exist together. For that which is granted, I receive; but that which I grant, I do not receive but offer to someone else."[88] But even this cannot be taken as an absolute contrast, as Luther's language in this very context makes clear: "The Gospel, on the contrary, *does not demand*; it grants freely; *it commands* us to hold out our hands and to receive what is being offered."[89] For Luther, this passive reception of faith is itself the "gift" we give God in return: it is "the supreme

---

[85] John Witte Jr., *Law and Protestantism: The Legal Teachings of the Lutheran Reformation* (New York: Cambridge University Press, 2004), p. 201.
[86] WATR 5:214 (no. 5524); ET in *Luther on Women: A Sourcebook*, ed. Susan C. Karant-Nunn and Merry E. Wiesner-Hanks (New York: Cambridge University Press, 2003), p. 133.
[87] See Simo Puera, "Christ as Favor and Gift: The Challenge of Luther's Understanding of Justification," in Braaten and Jenson, *Union with Christ*, pp. 42-69; Bo Kristian Holm, "Luther's Theology of the Gift," in *The Gift of Grace: The Future of Lutheran Theology*, ed. Niels Henrik Gregersen et al. (Minneapolis: Fortress, 2004), pp. 78-86; Holm, *Gabe und Geben bei Luther: Das Verhaltnis zwischen Reziprozitat und Reformatorischer Rechtfertigungslehre* (Berlin: Walter de Gruyter, 2006); Oswald Bayer, "The Ethics of Gift," *Lutheran Quarterly* 24, no. 4 (2010): 447-68; and the essays collected in *Word-Being-Gift: Justification-Economy-Ontology*, ed. Bo Kristian Holm and Peter Widmann (Tübingen: Mohr Siebeck, 2009).
[88] Luther, *Galatas* (1535), WA 40.1:337; LW 26:208-9.
[89] *Contra Evangelium non exigit, sed donat gratis et iubet nos porrectis manibus oblata accipere* (ibid., emphasis mine).

worship, the supreme allegiance, the supreme obedience, and the supreme sacrifice." Its "omnipotent" power lies in the fact that it acknowledges God as "the Author and Donor of every good." In so doing, faith "consummates the Deity; and, if I may put it this way, it is the creator of the Deity, not in the substance of God but in us."[90] As Oswald Bayer summarizes this remarkable passage, "The passivity of receiving the gift does not exclude a certain form of activity, but instead empowers and liberates us to that activity."[91] First consummation—"then let works and love begin."

Conclusion

Luther's engagement with Galatians was, for all its creative brilliance, a product of its time. He was one of the first Western exegetes in more than a thousand years to wrestle with the text in something like its original form—that is, in Greek, rather than in Latin—and this gives his exposition a sense of freshness, of discovery. Moreover, he was writing at a time of fierce theological controversy, when the central claims of the Christian faith were being renegotiated at the most fundamental level. Luther's commentaries on Galatians represent a serious effort to reframe the grammar and vocabulary of Christian theology more closely on the language of the Bible. In so doing, he attacked many of the dominant theological paradigms of his day and traced their errors (as he saw them) back to their patristic sources, especially Origen and Jerome. This adds a certain irony to the observation that Luther has himself come to represent an analogous interpretive orthodoxy in the minds of many biblical scholars, one that must now be displaced in order to understand Paul more fully. I am not so sure Luther would be entirely surprised by this. In the dedication to his first commentary in 1519, Luther hopes that through his effort "those who have heard me interpreting the letters of the apostle may find Paul clearer and may happily surpass me. But even if I have not achieved this, well, I shall still have wasted this labor gladly; it remains an attempt by which I have wanted to kindle the interest of others in Paul's theology; and this no good man will charge against me as a fault."[92] None indeed.

---

[90]Luther, *Galatas* (1535), WA 40.1:360; LW 26:226-27.
[91]Bayer, "Ethics of Gift," p. 459.
[92]Luther, *Galatas* (1519), WA 2:449; LW 27:160.

2

The Text of Galatians and the Theology of Luther

John M. G. Barclay

How should one evaluate Martin Luther's famous reading of Galatians? Like any reading, it is accountable to the evidence of the text, but what this means in practice is less obvious than might appear. To be sure, philological precision, an accountability to the likely sense of the original Greek, constitutes a core requirement. As Fink points out in the previous chapter, Luther was the first for many centuries in the West to provide a full exegesis of the *Greek* text of Galatians, and there are moments when this really counted: that the last phrase of Galatians 5:6 (πίστις δι' ἀγάπης ἐνεργουμένη) is likely to mean "faith working through love" (middle voice) rather than "faith formed by love" (passive, as in the Latin, *fides charitate formata*) was of great significance for Luther's reading of the letter and for Reformation theology as a whole. An accurate understanding of Paul's Greek is thus a sine qua non for any responsible reading; on this criterion, Luther scores well, even if one could question his construal of individual words and phrases at certain points.[1] But detailed exegesis

---

[1]Luther took the image of the παιδαγωγός (Gal 3:24-25) to suggest that the law was a "schoolmaster" to bring us to Christ (by making us aware of our sinfulness). Modern exegesis would insist that the term refers to a role that is more "child-minder" than "schoolmaster," and that the prepositional phrase εἰς Χριστόν is likely to mean "until Christ" (cf. Gal 3:23) rather than "to bring us to Christ." But Luther's reading of this phrase is not just a linguistic decision but part of his com-

always draws on an interpretation of the text as a whole, a reading of the meaning and the coherence of its central themes. Thus to evaluate Luther's interpretation of Galatians requires one to ask what the letter is really about. Did Luther grasp its central subject matter? Did he see what Paul was fighting against and arguing for?

To raise questions at that level takes us deeper than mere linguistic competence. Our tools for analysis would need to be exegetical (investigating the content and unifying threads of the text) and historical (examining its original context and purpose). But we would also need to evaluate both Luther's reading and our own construal of the letter as exercises in *hermeneutics*. To ask about the subject matter of Galatians is to ask not only *what it refers to* (e.g., what "law" Paul means when he speaks of "works of the law") but also *what the discussion is fundamentally about*. Any answer to that question is bound to enlist interpreters themselves in the act of making sense of the text. If we merely repeat the language of Paul (and even translation is no mere repetition), we have yet to *understand* it, but as soon as we introduce our own language and our own interpretative categories, we inevitably (and properly) bring ourselves into the hermeneutical circle.

For Luther, Galatians is fundamentally about the difference between "active" and "passive" righteousness (see below). Paul himself does not use the categories "active" and "passive," but Luther is perfectly entitled to sum up the issue in his own terms. Modern exegetes might say that Paul is "defending the rights of Gentiles" to be heirs of God's promises to Israel, but the language of "rights" has also been brought to the text from elsewhere.[2] According to Luther, Paul directs this letter against "all such as will work for their salvation" (*operarii*); according to one "new perspective" interpreter, he opposes "Jewish ideological and nationalistic imperialism."[3] Neither of these is a mere *description* of the text: both are *hermeneutical constructs*. Although modern construals of Galatians have a pronounced interest in the

---

prehensive construal of the relationship between law and gospel.

[2] See K. Stendahl, *Paul Among Jews and Gentiles* (London: SCM Press, 1977), pp. 2, 130-31; M. Barth, "Jews and Gentiles: The Social Character of Justification," *Journal of Ecumenical Studies* 5 (1968): 241-61, esp. p. 246.

[3] J. D. G. Dunn, *The Epistle to the Galatians*, Black's New Testament Commentaries (London: A & C Black, 1993), p. 267.

circumstances of its origin, they too "frame" its subject matter in order to render it meaningful. Like Luther, they are required to undertake some hermeneutical work.

Luther himself was quite conscious of this necessity. He knew that the text concerns circumcision and other Jewish practices under dispute in Paul's day. But he wanted to know why Paul should be so worked up about these things and why he should consider the gospel itself to be at stake. Luther's answer to that question inevitably reflects the issues of his own day, not least because he understood the exegete's task (as a *Doctor Sacrae Scripturae*) to include more than mere historical reconstruction of the past: it was necessary to make Paul "clear" and therefore relevant to his contemporaries. As Fink reminds us, Luther discerned in his day the outbreak of an apocalyptic war between the gospel and its counterfeit, and he was bound to reconceptualize Paul's polemics in contemporary terms.[4] Thus the question we should ask is not whether Luther got Galatians "right"—as if interpretation involved nothing more than the discovery of a single and original meaning—but something rather more complex. To evaluate Luther's reading of Galatians from our own vantage point is to ask *both* how well he responded to the text, in all its parts and dimensions (literary and historical), *and* whether his reading should be supplemented or superseded by readings that are responsive to our own context(s). Whatever we decide on these matters, we cannot fault Luther for engaging with Galatians in terms relevant to his context, unless we wish to question altogether the possibility or the value of theological hermeneutics.

In what follows I will draw attention to some of Luther's central hermeneutical moves before surveying some of the ways in which Pauline scholarship of the last fifty years has attempted to discredit his reading. I will then return to the text of Galatians to suggest how themes rightly identified by Luther as central to the letter might be differently construed today, both because of the ways we now relate Paul's argument to its original historical context and because we inevitably (and properly) bring our own twenty-first-century selves into the hermeneutical circle.

---

[4]See H. A. Oberman, *Luther: Man Between God and the Devil* (New Haven, CT: Yale University Press, 1989).

Luther and the Subject Matter of the Text

As Fink has noted, Luther opens his 1531 lectures on Galatians with a statement on "the argument" of Galatians ("the issue with which Paul deals in this epistle").[5] Here he summarizes the subject of the letter by means of a macro-antithesis between various kinds of "active righteousness" (forms of obedience to God in the civic, social and "ceremonial" spheres) and a "passive righteousness" that we merely *receive* "without our work or merit," "when God the Father grants it to us through Jesus Christ."[6] This construal of the letter suggests the centrality of the language of "justification" ("righteousness") and of gift, and the pivotal significance of the antitheses between (works of the) law, on the one hand, and faith, grace or Christ, on the other (Gal 2:15-16, 21; 3:2-5, 19-25; 5:2-6). Luther's very extensive exegesis of Galatians 2:15-21 sets out the contrast between a soteriology of works and a soteriology of faith-in-Christ, the former (in Luther's view) integral to the theological tradition in which he was reared, the latter expressing the Pauline gospel. In Luther's reading, the "works of the law" were problematic to Paul not because they were Jewish "ceremonies" (here, as Fink notes, Luther sides with Augustine against Origen and Jerome) but because they embody a false understanding of salvation. What matters is not their content or their cultural heritage, but the understanding that is operative in their performance, and this is composed of three conjoined elements: a faulty interpretation of these works as a necessary means to salvation, an irreligious motivation that attends their performance (a desire to gain salvation from one's own resources, in effect to supplant God), and an arrogant presumption (or, by turns, anxious self-doubt) that arises from relying on oneself.

Luther knew that Paul was referring in this letter to the Mosaic law, and because Galatians speaks sometimes of "works of the law" and sometimes simply of "law" (e.g., Gal 2:16-21; 3:10-12; 5:4) he took him to be speaking about the performance of *any part* of the law (including the Decalogue) and not just specific elements within it. But Paul would hardly object to compliance with the holy law of God unless there were something wrong

---

[5]LW 26:4-12. All translations are taken from LW vols. 26-27: *Lectures on Galatians 1535*. The original text may be found in WA vol. 40. I focus throughout on the 1531 lectures, revised and published in 1535, rather than the earlier lectures on this text (1516–1517, published in 1519).
[6]LW 26:6.

in the *attitude* of those who observed it. And that attitude was present in the performance of any works *for the sake of salvation*, whether by Jews, Muslims or Christians (including "enthusiasts," advocates of the radical Reformation). Thus anyone who thinks that they are justified other than by faith alone are "our Jews" (in relation to *Papistae*): Luther is quite explicit on the hermeneutical connection between Paul's context and his own.[7] "Law" is therefore a category capable of wide generalization. If Paul attacks those who seek justification by means of God's perfect law, the pursuit of the same goal through any lesser law (including the rules of the church) is surely included in the same condemnation.

On the opposite side of the Pauline antithesis is "faith in Christ" (so Luther, like his contemporaries, read the phrase πίστις Χριστοῦ),[8] which is important less for its reference to faith (since everyone trusts in something) than for its reference to Christ, the ground and source of salvation. "It takes hold of Christ in such a way that Christ is the object of faith, or rather not the object but, so to speak, the One who is present in the faith itself."[9] Held by faith, like the precious jewel clasped in the wedding ring, Christ provides all that is necessary for salvation. He is to be received in faith not as the lawgiver who demands obedience and threatens judgment but as the Savior and High Priest who intercedes for us, as the *Giver* whose self-gift we have only to receive. While works will follow, like fruit from a fruit tree (Gal 5:22-23), and love will proceed from faith (Gal 5:6), it must be clear that the faith that justifies is prior (and in that sense "alone"), "without and before love."[10] Otherwise the regime of law and the good news of the gospel will be disastrously confused, and our consciences will be terrified in awareness of our inadequacies before God. Luther thus advocates a careful distinction between law and gospel: the law is not evil or irrelevant for the Christian, but its purpose is limited and strictly confined. It plays its role in controlling the flesh and in making us aware of how sinful we are, but that is

---

[7]LW 26:207.
[8]The genitive phrase could also be taken to mean "the faith of Christ" or "the faithfulness of Christ," as some modern scholars now prefer (see below).
[9]LW 26:129.
[10]LW 26:137. *Haec fides sine et ante charitatem iustificat* (WA 40.1:240.16). "First there must be a tree, then the fruit. For apples do not make a tree, but a tree makes apples. So faith first makes a person, who afterwards performs works" (LW 26:255; WA 40.1:402.15-17).

only for the sake of the gospel, to drive us to Christ.[11] Justification or salvation is the business of the gospel, in the sphere of faith; and in that realm law has no role at all.

What is characteristic of Luther is that this dialectical relation between law and gospel is played out not in a once-off transition to faith, but repeatedly, even daily, in the life of the believer. Inasmuch as believers live in the flesh, in bodies liable to sin, they need the law to discipline them and to highlight their sinfulness; but in the sphere of the conscience and in the spirit they live in Christ and therefore are free from the demands of the law. Luther here responds to the flesh-spirit antithesis that runs through Galatians (Gal 3:3; 4:29; 5:13–6:10), which he takes to describe not the boundary between the past and the present of the believer but a dialectical relation between simultaneous dimensions of the Christian's life. That is a notion he derives from Galatians 2:20 ("It is no longer I who live, but Christ who lives in me; but the life I now live in the flesh . . . ") and Galatians 5:17 ("the flesh desires against the Spirit, and the Spirit against the flesh"), the latter read in the light of Romans 7 (as interpreted by Augustine).[12]

This notion of a permanent, existential dialectic in the Christian life leads Luther to read Paul's salvation-historical statements about the "coming" of faith (Gal 3:23-25) on two levels. When Paul speaks of a time "before faith came" (Gal 3:23) and then of a time "when faith came" (Gal 3:25), he speaks, on the one hand ("literally"), of the periods before and after the Christ event in the history of the world. But on the other hand ("spiritually" or "theologically"), he speaks of the place of the law, whose role is continually to frighten us in its conviction of sin *until* the gospel is announced, which assures us of grace, peace and forgiveness in Christ.[13] This dialectic is a constant feature of

---

[11]See Luther's extensive discussion of "the double use of the law" in expounding Gal 3:19. The civil use (to restrain sin) is supplemented by the "theological" use, to reveal sin. For the latter, Luther interprets "for the sake of transgressions" (Gal 3:19) with the aid of Rom 3:20; 4:15; 5:20; 7:7-25—an exegetical move that would be supported by many exegetes today but contested by others.
[12]Unless otherwise noted, Scripture quotations are my translation.
[13]LW 26:317, 328-29, 338-43, 349-51. "Therefore the Christian is divided this way into two times. To the extent that he is flesh, he is under the Law; to the extent that he is spirit, he is under the Gospel" (LW 26:342). Luther speaks therefore of a "daily coming of Christ" (LW 26:349): "Christ came once for all at a set time, and faith came once for all when the apostles preached the Gospel throughout the world. In addition, Christ comes spiritually (*spiritualiter*) every day; through the Word of the Gospel faith also comes every day" (LW 26:351; WA 40.1:538.29-31).

the experience of the believer, who is stationed perpetually on the front between law and gospel, and thus must continually return to baptism as the assurance of God's grace in Christ.[14]

The appropriate application of gospel or law to the believer, who is simultaneously the "new man" in Christ and the "old man" in the flesh (in other terms, *simul iustus et peccator* ["at the same time justified and a sinner"]), is a delicate task, but Luther's greatest fear was that believers might tragically fail to find release and comfort in the gospel. In other words, what gave Luther's reading of Galatians its enduring power was not only that it updated the letter, finding deep resonance between Paul's battles and those of the Reformation, and not only that it generalized Paul's message, finding the same conflict between faith and "works of the law" wherever good works are made a condition of salvation, but that it brought Paul's gospel truths into the daily life of the individual believer, providing assurance to the troubled consciences of Christians who were acutely aware of their moral and spiritual failings.[15]

RECENT CHALLENGES TO LUTHER'S READING

Luther's reading of Galatians, encountered either directly through his commentary or indirectly through Rudolf Bultmann, Ernst Käsemann or others in the Lutheran tradition, has come under sustained attack in the last fifty years of Pauline scholarship.[16] The "new perspective on Paul" has characteristically emphasized the historical specificity of Paul's theology, which was hammered out in Galatians not just *in the context* of his mission to the Gentiles (as if his response to Galatian issues merely illustrated his broader theological principles) but *for the specific purpose* of defending and promoting that mission. Paul's opening statement in Galatians focuses on his calling as apostle to the Gentiles (Gal 1:11-17), and the issues he depicts as

---

[14]For the Christian life as "nothing else than a daily baptism," see Luther's *Large Catechism*, Holy Baptism, 65 (WA 30.1:218-20). For discussion, see J. D. Trigg, *Baptism in the Theology of Martin Luther* (Leiden: Brill, 1994). Note the characteristic appeal to baptism ("For I am baptized") when the conscience is oppressed by the accusations of the law (LW 26:11).

[15]The pastoral significance of Luther's reading is already clear at the end of his discussion of the "argument" of Galatians (LW 26:10-12).

[16]For survey and analysis, see S. Westerholm, *Perspectives Old and New on Paul: The "Lutheran" Paul and His Critics* (Grand Rapids: Eerdmans, 2004); J. M. G. Barclay, *Paul and the Gift* (Grand Rapids: Eerdmans, forthcoming), chap. 3.

disputed in Jerusalem (Gal 2:1-10) and in Antioch (Gal 2:11-14) concern the terms on which Gentiles are admitted into Christian fellowship. Thus "the centre of gravity in Paul's theological work is related to the fact that he knew himself to be called to be the Apostle to the Gentiles."[17] As Krister Stendahl puts it, "The doctrine of justification by faith was hammered out by Paul for the very specific and limited purpose of defending the rights of Gentile converts to be full and genuine heirs to the promises of God to Israel."[18] On this reading, Paul's concerns are those of the first generation of Christianity and are irreducibly particular: they cannot be presumed to apply outside that situation, let alone across time. At the same time, scholarship has reacted strongly, in a postexistentialist era, against individualizing interpretations of Paul and, in a post-Holocaust context, against readings that express or imply a negative evaluation of Judaism. Both of these trends have encouraged the repudiation of the "Lutheran" tradition as known and received in modern times.

If the presenting issue of Galatians is whether male Gentile converts need to be circumcised (Gal 2:1-10; 5:2-12; 6:12-15), and if this represents a dispute about whether Gentile believers need to adopt a specifically Jewish identity, one may resist Luther's reading of "works" and "law" in a far more general sense. The law in question is the Mosaic law (the Torah), and Paul has nothing other than that in view. The "works of the law" are Torah practices, and on some readings particularly the "badges" of Jewish identity, or the "boundary markers" that distinguished Jews from Gentiles in the first-century world: circumcision (Gal 6:12-15), food laws (Gal 2:11-14), and perhaps Sabbaths and Jewish festivals (Gal 4:10) constitute what Paul means by "works of the law."[19] On this reading, Paul is not attacking a view of works as a necessary means toward salvation: the issue is not a faulty soteriology but an erroneous judgment about the social and cultural requirements for belonging to the people of God in the era after Christ.[20]

---

[17]Stendahl, *Paul Among Jews*, p. 15.
[18]Ibid., p. 2. A theology designed not just *in* but *for* the Gentile mission can also be described, in functionalist terms, as its legitimating ideology; see F. Watson, *Paul, Judaism, and the Gentiles: Beyond the New Perspective*, 2nd ed. (Grand Rapids: Eerdmans, 2007), pp. 21, 51.
[19]See N. T. Wright, "The Paul of History and the Apostle of Faith," *Tyndale Bulletin* 29 (1978): 61-88, repr. in *Pauline Perspectives: Essays on Paul, 1978-2013* (London: SPCK, 2013), pp. 3-20; J. D. G. Dunn, *The New Perspective on Paul: Collected Essays* (Tübingen: Mohr Siebeck, 2005).
[20]N. T. Wright speaks of the present era of scholarship as "trying to repent of projecting late-medieval or

It is important to be clear about what is at issue here. Luther and his modern critics agree that Paul is referring in Galatians to the Mosaic law. The question is whether Paul's critical comments regarding justification through (works of) the law concern the role of this law *in defining Jewish identity* or an understanding of its observance *as providing a means toward salvation*. In the one case, the issue in Galatians is the cultural and social identity of early Christianity: Paul appeals to Abraham (Gal 3:6-29) to show that God's promises extend "to all the nations" (Gal 3:8), and since faith is available to both Jews and non-Jews (Gal 3:26-28), the latter should not be pressurized into "Judaizing" (Gal 2:14). In the other, the issue is whether salvation is received as a gift through faith alone, or whether "works" are a necessary means toward salvation: Abraham is important as the original and prime example of faith (Gal 3:6, 9), and since salvation by faith is unconditioned by works (Gal 2:16; 3:10-12), no one has grounds for "boasting" except in Christ (Gal 6:12-14). Both readings attend to the exegetical details of the text. The difference lies at the deeper level of determining what is truly at stake in Galatians and what is the issue to which Paul's theology is addressed.

Because Luther read the letter as addressing the question of the conditions for salvation, he felt entitled to draw out the relevance of Paul's answer to other contexts, including his own. Because the issue itself is general, the letter is readily generalized. Luther's critics in the "new perspective" insist on the historical particularity of the issue, and some are inclined to leave this letter as a witness to a once-central but now-outdated issue in the history of Christianity.[21] For others, however, the cultural and historical issues addressed by Paul have contemporary resonance. For Francis Watson, Paul's letter grounds a decision about the relationship of the Christian movement to the Old Testament and to Judaism, which is of continuing significance as a historical and nonnegotiable facet of Christian identity.[22] For other interpreters, it evokes contemporary social and political issues analogous to Paul's, both in the churches and in society at large.[23] For still

---

Reformational soteriological categories back onto [Paul]" (*Paul and the Faithfulness of God* [London: SPCK, 2013], p. 43). Luther, of course, saw himself as continuing a tradition going back at least as far as Augustine.

[21]See, e.g., E. P. Sanders, *Paul* (Oxford: Oxford University Press, 1991).

[22]Watson, *Paul, Judaism, and the Gentiles*, pp. 351-69.

[23]See, e.g., Dunn, *New Perspective*, p. 199, on contemporary ecclesial divisions and on racial/ethnic

others, the correct reading of Galatians is crucial for determining the extent to which Paul did *not* turn against Judaism, with a view to the fraught relationship between Christianity and Judaism in which Paul has always played a disputed role.[24] Thus to insist on the historical and cultural particularity of Galatians is not necessarily to consign it to irrelevance, but the kinds of connections it has to the present are very different from those envisaged by Luther. Luther, of course, would want to know why Paul thought *the gospel* was at stake (Gal 1:6-9; 2:5, 14).

To place the letter fully in its original historical context does not exclude the possibility that Paul *interpreted* the Galatian issues in terms that are of wide, even of universal, theological significance. Thus, for instance, J. L. Martyn offers a very precise reconstruction of the issues between Paul and "the Teachers" (Paul's opponents) in Galatia, fully recognizing the specificity of the Jewish traditions under debate.[25] But Paul, he insists, places these matters within an "apocalyptic" frame in which the Christ event constitutes God's invasion of the "present evil age" (Gal 1:4) and inaugurates the "new creation" (Gal 6:15). From this perspective, Paul takes the Teachers' appeal to the Galatian converts to transfer by Torah observance into the realm of salvation as a perversion of the gospel, which concerns not human initiative but God's prior action in Christ and the Spirit's presence and power in the response of believers.[26] On this reading, the letter is simultaneously about a decision whether to adopt the Jewish law *and* about the structure of relations between God and humanity. There are similarities between the hermeneutical strategies of Martyn and Luther, even if Martyn's emphasis on *agency* sets him at one point against Luther. Martyn insists that πίστις Χριστοῦ means not "faith in Christ" (a human act) but "the faithfulness of Christ" (a divine act in the death of Christ); only so, Martyn holds, can the

---

conflicts around the globe. B. Kahl relates Galatians to an ethical critique of "imperial" power in *Galatians Reimagined: Reading with the Eyes of the Vanquished* (Minneapolis: Fortress, 2010).

[24]M. D. Nanos, *The Irony of Galatians: Paul's Letter in First-Century Context* (Minneapolis: Fortress, 2002).

[25]J. L. Martyn, *Galatians: A New Translation with Introduction and Commentary*, Anchor Bible 33A (New York: Doubleday, 1997).

[26]Ibid., pp. 36-41, 97-105, using a Barth-inspired antithesis between "apocalyptic" and "religion." See also M. C. de Boer, *Galatians: A Commentary*, New Testament Library (Louisville: Westminster John Knox, 2011).

phrase stand as a true alternative to "works of the law" (Gal 2:16).[27] Whatever one decides on this matter (and in the debate, Luther's understanding of faith is rarely well represented or understood),[28] Martyn's reading makes clear that a minute analysis of the original circumstances of this letter, conducted with all the modern historical tools, can be incorporated into a theological hermeneutic that reads Paul's response to the Galatian crisis as of wide-ranging, and contemporary, significance.

THE CONTOURS OF THE TEXT

As we have seen, the key hermeneutical decisions regarding Galatians concern not so much what Paul is referring to in this letter as what Paul takes (and what we take) to be its most fundamental issue. There is wide agreement that Paul is discussing the circumcision of his male Gentile converts and probably other matters of acculturation into the Jewish tradition (Gal 2:1-14; 4:8-10; 5:2-12; 6:12-15). Our historical knowledge of the first generation of the Christian movement and of first-century Judaism, together with Paul's own comments about the history of the law (Gal 3:15-21), makes clear that by "law" (νόμος) Paul means the Mosaic Torah, and not "law" in general.[29] The question then is whether Paul sets the observance of the Torah in some wider frame (for Luther, in the soteriological antithesis between working and receipt by faith; for Martyn in the apocalyptic antinomy between human and divine initiative).

A good place to start is to see what else Paul associates with circumcision, and here one can note that twice he relativizes not only circumcision but also its opposite, uncircumcision, the unmarked state of the male (Gal 5:6; 6:15). According to Paul, "neither circumcision nor uncircumcision counts for anything" (τι ἰσχύει, Gal 5:6 NRSV); it seems that the issue is not human achievement or self-reliance but the counting of worth, what makes a person valued or honored according to prevailing norms. Uncircumcision

---

[27]Martyn, *Galatians*, pp. 263-75; cf. Martyn, "The Apocalyptic Gospel in Galatians," *Interpretation* 54 (2000): 246-66.
[28]See, however, for a well-informed contribution, J. A. Linebaugh, "The Christo-Centrism of Faith in Christ: Martin Luther's Reading of Galatians 2.16, 19-20," *New Testament Studies* 59 (2013): 535-44.
[29]Gal 5:23; 6:2 are possible exceptions.

is a natural human state, and not the result of a "work" or achievement.[30] In fact, here as elsewhere (e.g., Gal 2:6-9) "circumcision" and "uncircumcision" stand for Jewish and non-Jewish identity, respectively, so it seems that it is the value or worth of these ethnic identities that may be at stake. Elsewhere Jew and Greek are put alongside other status indicators (also conveying differential worth): in Christ there is neither Jew nor Greek, neither slave nor free, no male and female (Gal 3:28). Even wider than that, Paul indicates that God shows no interest in a person's established honor (God shows no partiality, Gal 2:6). The Galatians rightly disregarded his despicable condition when he came into Galatia (Gal 4:12-20) and are encouraged now to resist taking part in the honor-competition characteristic of Greco-Roman culture (Gal 5:15, 26; 6:1-5).[31] In fact, Paul says, he refuses to boast by the outward criteria that his opponents apply (Gal 6:12-13) or to appeal to human standards of judgment: the gospel he preaches is not according to human criteria (οὐκ ἔστιν κατὰ ἄνθρωπον, Gal 1:11). The breadth of scope is enormous: in his final appeal, Paul insists that "the world has been crucified to me, and I to the world" (Gal 6:14 NRSV). So if he has been crucified in relation to the law of Moses (Gal 2:19) and in relation to the flesh (Gal 5:24), this is related to a comprehensive break with "the world," as effected in the cross of Christ.

What seems to be at stake here is not the achievement of good works, or of the merit by which salvation is attained, but, more basically, the criteria by which worth is measured, that is, what God does, or does not, count as worth in his calling of those he saves. Paul's gospel does not recognize ethnic worth, or the worth of gender or social status (cf. 1 Cor 1:26-31), because the Christ event and the "new creation" it founds (Gal 6:15) do not operate by such criteria. Paul has no anxiety about "working" as such: the faith that works through love (Gal 5:6) and the good works that arise from the fruit of the Spirit (Gal 5:22-23; 6:8-10) are the modes of practice that

---

[30]Luther associates "uncircumcision" with "some of our followers [e.g., Karlstadt?], who . . . regard freedom from the traditions of the pope as something so necessary that they are afraid of committing sin if they do not violate or abolish all of them immediately" (LW 27:138). He takes this antithesis to signal Paul's opposition to making trivial things significant.

[31]For the exegesis of these texts, see Barclay, *Paul and the Gift*, chaps. 12-14. Cf. J. M. G. Barclay, "Grace and the Countercultural Reckoning of Worth: Community Construction in Galatians 5-6," in M. W. Elliott, S. J. Hafemann, N. T. Wright and J. Frederick, eds., *Galatians and Christian Theology* (Grand Rapids: Baker Academic, 2014), pp. 306-17.

characterize the new community of faith that is created and sustained by the act of God in Christ. In fact, such practices seem to be integral to the Christ-founded community, because they embody and display the difference between the life of the Spirit and the life of the flesh (Gal 5:13-25). These represent the differing patterns of life characteristic of those within or outside the community of faith, not two different dimensions of the Christian life; there is no good reason to read Galatians 5:17 as expressing a tussle in the inner life of a believer. Paul's concern was not that people erroneously imagine that they need to work to gain salvation; the letter finishes with strong ethical appeals, including a threat that if they sow to their flesh they will reap destruction (Gal 6:8). What was at stake in the Antioch dispute, in which Paul took issue with Peter (Gal 2:11-14), was not that Peter was leading Gentile believers to work for their salvation, but that he gave the impression that to "walk in line with the truth of the gospel" was to adopt the criteria of the Jewish tradition ("to judaize," Gal 2:14). Peter was confusing his own, inherited criteria of worth with the criteria established by the gospel.

However, Luther was right to affirm that a central theme of Galatians is that the Christ event constituted the definitive divine *gift*; the language of grace is indeed prominent in this letter and seems to have load-bearing significance. Quite apart from the references to grace in the epistolary greeting and concluding prayer (Gal 1:3; 6:18), Paul refers to the Galatians' conversion as their "calling in grace" (Gal 1:6) and proceeds to describe his own calling in similar terms, attributing it to God, "who set me apart from my mother's womb and called me through his grace" (Gal 1:15). In narrating this event, Paul makes clear that this calling bore no relation to his previous worth (his ethnicity, his zeal or his excellence), which had been invested in the persecution of the church: his "calling in grace" means, in particular, a calling without regard to preexistent criteria of worth.[32] Because of such grace, Paul was in no way superior to the Gentiles, despite their former idolatry and ignorance of God (Gal 4:8-10), and in no way inferior to the other apostles, whatever their biographical advantages (Gal 2:6-9). Because the Christ gift is given without regard to worth, it recognizes no necessity to

---

[32]See J. M. G. Barclay, "Paul's Story: Theology as Testimony," in B. W. Longenecker, ed., *Narrative Dynamics in Paul* (Louisville: Westminster John Knox, 2002), pp. 133-56.

conform the believers' life in the Spirit to the preformed criteria established by the practice of the Mosaic law. Conversely, if "righteousness" (that is, worth before God) is defined in Torah terms, this would be tantamount to rejecting the grace of God (Gal 2:21). As Paul puts it in Galatians 5:4, those who look for righteousness in the terms of the Torah are cut off from Christ and have fallen from grace. That is not because they are substituting their own works for the grace of God in Christ, but because the gospel stands or falls on the fact that the gift of Christ is unconditioned (without prior conditions of worth) and cannot be packaged in some other criteria of value without losing its meaning and its revolutionary impact.

On this reading of the letter, Paul's initial statement about justification by faith (Gal 2:15-21) is to be read in close conjunction with the preceding account of the Antioch dispute (Gal 2:11-14), in which Peter's behavior had pressured Gentile believers to live like Jews. But believers recognize, Paul says, that Torah observance ("the works of the law") is not the criterion of worth ("righteousness") that counts before God. All that counts is faith in Christ,[33] that is, the recognition, elicited by the gospel, that the Christ gift is the foundation and core of salvation. To consider "the works of the law" the criterion of worth (i.e., "righteousness") is to assume the validity of a symbolic capital that has been shown to count for nothing before God. To make the Gentiles "judaize" is to invest in that symbolic capital (Gal 2:14), but "we know" in Christ that this is not what God considers valuable (Gal 2:15-16). In other words, to take "the works of the law" as the measure of value is to bank on an outdated currency—like collecting French francs when the currency has switched to the euro. The old currency is dead, because the Christ gift has rendered it no longer of value; in fact, as Scripture shows, it was never the currency some had taken it to be (cf. Gal 3:10-12, 21). So what is the new currency? It is hardly some other human capacity or some inherent token of worth, but "faith in Christ"—the acknowledgment that the only thing of value is Christ himself. Faith is a declaration of bank-

---

[33] I agree with Luther, against his modern critics, that πίστις Χριστοῦ means faith based on and directed to Christ (not "the faithfulness of Christ"); Paul takes care to disambiguate this shorthand phrase as soon as he uses it: "we have believed in Jesus Christ" (Gal 2:16). The modern dispute on this matter is wide-ranging, and there may be less at stake in this matter for the interpretation of the letter than Martyn and others have claimed; see M. Bird and P. M. Sprinkle, eds., *The Faith of Jesus Christ: Exegetical, Biblical, and Theological Studies* (Milton Keynes, UK: Paternoster, 2009).

ruptcy, a radical and shattering recognition that the only capital in God's economy is the gift of Christ crucified and risen (Gal 2:19-20).

On this reading, Paul's theology of gift (or grace) is given a twist different from that adopted by Luther. What is at issue is not a straightforward contrast between working and receiving, between achieving merit or being given all that is necessary for salvation already and once for all in Christ. Paul does indeed declare that the gift has already been given, and everything he says about the life and work of believers depends completely on that: they live "by faith in the Son of God who loved me and *gave himself* for me" (Gal 2:20; cf. 1:4). But what is radical about this gift is not only that God gave it, or that he gave it *before* any initiative on the part of the believer, or that the gift itself effects or at least enables the believer's response. What is especially significant is that the gift is *incongruous*, given without regard for worth. Luther rightly saw, following Augustine, that the gift of Christ paid no regard to prior merit, and (unlike Augustine) he would not allow any talk of human "merit," even that which might arise from faith. But what he did not draw out fully, and what was crucial for Paul in his original context, was that this definitive and incongruous gift subverted the criteria of value by which it was common to evaluate worth.[34] In Paul's day, divine gifts were normally (and reasonably) assumed, by both Jews and non-Jews, to be distributed according to the worth of the recipients: otherwise the cosmos appeared arbitrary or unfair.[35] But if God gave without regard to worth, it was impossible to keep sacrosanct any previous system of norms. In this sense, Paul has been "crucified to the Torah" (Gal 2:19), which is no longer his unquestioned standard of value (Gal 2:17-18); and in this sense, more broadly, he has been "crucified to the world" (Gal 6:14), because there are no standards of value that count except those that derive from the Christ event itself.

Paul, as apostle to the Gentiles (Gal 1:16-17), founded innovative com-

---

[34]In certain respects one may say that Luther *did* draw out this conclusion: by contesting the salvific value of good works, he subverted the special evaluation of the clerical and monastic life, with its "higher" standards of holiness. By "horizontalizing" good works, which concern our relationship to our neighbors and not an ongoing transaction with God, Luther equalized every vocation and instituted a revolution in attitudes to marriage and everyday work. See his *Treatise on Good Works* (1520), and Oberman, *Luther*, pp. 80, 179, 192.

[35]For further detail, see Barclay, *Paul and the Gift*. The point is well illustrated by the contrast between *Wisdom of Solomon* and Paul drawn out by J. A. Linebaugh, *God, Grace, and Righteousness in Wisdom of Solomon and Paul's Letter to the Romans: Texts in Conversation* (Leiden: Brill, 2013).

munities that crossed the ethnic and cultural boundary between Jew and Greek (and slave and free, male and female, Gal 3:28) in the name of a gift event that was not only hypergenerous but also "blind" to the normal standards of superior worth. Because there were no applicable qualifications, the gift could be given *to all*. Both the scope of Paul's mission (to Gentiles) and the terms on which it was conducted (without requiring them to "judaize") reflect the unconditioned character of the gift of Christ, whose purpose is to construct crosscultural communities of faith, beholden to no other law than "the law of Christ" (Gal 6:2). The Christ gift could not take effect in the Galatian churches if it did not enjoy sole and supreme authority in shaping their lives. To the extent that it found expression in new communities, who sat loose to both Jewish and non-Jewish traditions of value, it was constituted in their midst as the unconditioned gift.

If the issue of the law in Galatians is not law-as-demand or law-as-means-to-salvation, we are able to appreciate in a new way the place within the book of Galatians 5–6, which indicate that *communal practice is integral to the expression of the good news*. Luther's placement of justification by faith "before and without love" created a dichotomy that made it difficult for many in the subsequent Lutheran tradition to integrate "faith" with "ethics" in Pauline theology; it runs the risk of making faith merely an interior, individual phenomenon.[36] But if "faith in Christ" is the mark of those whose lives have begun anew in the death and resurrection of Christ, "living by faith" is necessarily expressed in new patterns of loyalty and behavior in the life of the Spirit, which cut across the normal patterns of fleshly existence. As a community founded on and shaped by the incongruous gift of Christ, this "new creation" is evident precisely in (and not independently of) reordered patterns of social and personal behavior. Without such difference, it is hard to see how the gift of Christ differs from a reward for socially conformist behavior: but for Paul the gospel stands or falls on its announcement of an unconditioned gift.

In Galatians 3–4, Paul traces how the Christ gift fulfills the promise ini-

---

[36]Luther himself, responding to sharp criticism of his theology, worked extremely hard in the Galatians lectures to emphasize that works *will follow* faith, even if faith alone is significant for justification: "It is true that faith alone justifies, without works; but I am speaking about genuine faith, which, after it has justified, will not go to sleep but is active through love" (LW 27:30). Thus Luther has no problems with "works" as such, so long as they are given no *soteriological* significance.

tially given to Abraham (who responded in faith) but is *not* conditioned by the practice of the Torah, which was "added" after the promise and for a time-limited period, until the coming of Christ. The Torah is not the frame within which the Christ event is to be understood: it had a temporary role now finished. At the same time, Paul makes clear that the Torah provided no platform of worth to be rewarded by divine beneficence. Everything was imprisoned "under sin" (Gal 3:22) and "under a curse" (Gal 3:13), indeed "under the elements of the cosmos" (Gal 4:3, 8-9), so that even those who could be considered "heirs" required not a natural process of maturation but a dramatic and liberating intervention by God (Gal 4:1-7). Thus Paul locates the Christ event on a (reconfigured) map of history, and what he finds there is the same incongruity between divine act and human worth that he could trace in his own life (Gal 1:10-17) and in the experience of his Gentile converts (Gal 3:1-5; 4:8-10). The offspring of Abraham are miraculous products, children of the promise (Gal 4:21-31), brought into existence by a grace that does not correspond to any inherent quality, inherited or achieved.

CONCLUSIONS

Luther can rightly be acclaimed as rediscovering the unsettling and even explosive force of Galatians, while reviving Paul's capacity to break with the normal conventions of thought and practice. But in so doing he altered the focus of the letter (on the reading sketched above) in significant ways. In its original context, Paul's theology reflected and supported his mission in the formation of unconventional communities: intervening at the very outset of the Christian movement, it served to disjoin converts from their previous standards of worth, scoring a line between their past and their present, between insiders and outsiders. After this initial generation and within Christian communities whose boundaries were already established, this same theology was bound to play a different role and to acquire a different focus. The language of grace, of divine gift to the undeserving, that had once served to destabilize systems of worth and thus to detach new communities from their previous cultural allegiances, was now applied to believers with little or no consciousness of a break with their past (since their primary socialization was already as Christians), and to communities whose external boundaries were either nonexistent (in a solidly Christian culture) or already obvious. Their criteria of worth (what counted as honorable or righteous) were already strongly "Christianized," and the Christ gift could hardly unsettle those.

In such contexts Paul's theology of grace became a tool for the inner reform of the Christian tradition, its critical edge turned against believers themselves in order to undermine not their pre-Christian criteria of worth but their pride or purpose in gaining Christian worth. Grace remained the means of access to the community, but the critical dissolution of preconstituted norms ("what accords with human values," Gal 1:11) became an attack on the believer's confidence or independence in adhering to Christian norms. In a context where "the law," once passed through Christian filters, was granted full authority as divine law, it was impossible to imagine that the believer should challenge its authority as Paul had challenged the normative role of "the law" as Mosaic Torah. It was far more likely that he intended to criticize a deficiency in the believer, either in measuring up to the law or in construing its intention.

The shift that takes place in Luther (and to some degree before him) is not, as is sometimes thought, from the specific to the universal: Paul himself covers both, working from the particularity of the Christ event to its universal implications, in the believer's crucifixion to "the world" (Gal 6:14). Neither does Luther move entirely from the concrete to the abstract: like Paul, he had specific targets in view, real people with practical programs of action and belief. Nor again is there is a straightforward shift from the communal to the individual: Paul's own theology concerned the reconstitution of the individual (Gal 2:19-20) as well the construction of novel communities. What changes, rather, is the social context. The critical theology of a new social movement, by which it formulated its identity and clarified its boundaries, becomes the self-critical theology of an established tradition: even where it is still involved in mission, its subversive missionary theology is turned inward on the church.

The first signs of this contextual shift may be traced in the deutero-Pauline letters, where "works" are refocused as moral achievements (Eph 2:8-10; 2 Tim 1:9; Tit 3:5) and "boasting" indicates not the cultural confidence of the Jew in the Torah (or of the Greek in wisdom) but pride in achievement (Eph 2:9). In the Augustinian tradition, Paul's theology of grace is taken to subvert not the standard human *criteria of worth* but the human tendency to self-congratulation in the *attainment of worth*. The critical edge of Paul's theology is directed against Christian construals of virtue acquisition. The distinction between life "in the flesh" and new life "in the Spirit" (Rom 7–8)—a contrast for Paul between the former and the present life of a convert—is taken to represent the inner duality of the believer. To speak of grace is to speak of the believer's dependence on the agency of God.

The achievement of Luther was to translate Paul's missionary theology into an urgent and perpetual *inward mission*, directed to the church, but especially to the heart of each believer.[37] Luther recaptured both the incongruity of grace in Paul and its origin in the *event* of Jesus Christ; his achievement was to make this significant in communities of believers long socialized in the Christian tradition. The subversive dynamic of Paul's theology is directed against a new target—not the old normative systems that believers are struggling to shed, but a faulty understanding of their own good works as necessary means to gain God's favor. As we have seen, Paul's theology of gift is repreached by Luther to effect the *perpetual conversion* of believers, who need to learn over and again to receive the gift of God and to banish both despair at their sin and the false opinion that their works will merit salvation. Although the gospel of grace applies across the church's boundaries to nonbelievers, Luther's focus is on the church itself. Here the gospel founds a mission to the self and a daily return to baptism, since the old nature persists in its sin and in its tendency to arrogant self-sufficiency and must be alternately assuaged or rebuked by reminders that Christ has already given all. Thus grace here scores a line through the life of the Christian, and Paul's polemics against "works of the law" are taken to be directed not against an external (and no longer valid) definition of worth (Torah practice) but against the subjective evaluation of one's own good works as effective for salvation. This change in focus fostered a regrettable tendency to figure "Jews" as examplars of self-righteousness, but it consti-

---

[37] I owe this insight to conversations with Michael Wolter, who interprets Luther as repristinating Paul's missionary theology in order to render every believer a convert. For his application to early Christianity of the sociological distinction between a "Bekehrungsreligion" (conversion-religion) and a "Traditionsreligion" (tradition-based religion), see "Die Entwicklung des paulinishen Christentums von einer Bekehrungsreligion zu einer Traditionsreligion," *Early Christianity* 1 (2010): 15-40.

tuted a brilliant recontextualization of Pauline theology in the conditions of the sixteenth-century church.

It was suggested above that if a reading of Galatians is to compete with Luther's on anything like his terms, it would have to be responsive both to the textual and historical particularity of the letter and to the concerns of our own contemporary context. What I have offered above is self-consciously written in that mode. Because the christological event of grace is both highly particular and has an impact on *any* criteria of worth that are not derived from the good news itself, Paul's theology does not remain encased within its first-century context. One does not have to find "timeless principles" by extracting general truths from particular historical debates: Paul himself saw the universal relevance of a theology that reconfigured the map of reality (Gal 6:14-15). As we have seen, that theology fitted its original context of an inaugural mission and is necessarily refocused when used in the reform of an established Christian tradition.

Today, however, the Christian tradition is anything but stable and established. In fact, one can hardly miss the *similarities* between Paul's missional context and the social context of many churches today.[38] Not only in pioneer mission, but even (in fact, especially) in a pluralist or secularizing context, churches now find themselves needing to rediscover their social, political and cultural identity and to reground that identity in the gospel itself. Taken-for-granted criteria of value regarding age, ethnicity, social status, education, gender, health or wealth become in such circumstances the object of critical reevaluation, and churches are required to identify anew what it is about the good news that makes them socially and ideologically distinctive. This new missional context makes Paul's theology in Galatians relevant not only in the recontextualized forms in which it has become familiar (as a theology of individualized grace), but also in its *original* dynamic, which accompanied the creation of innovative, countercultural communities of faith. By starting from the Christ event, and by clarifying with radical sharpness the unconditioned grace that was given in Christ, Paul promotes the dissolution of preformed assumptions and the construction of boundary-erasing communities.

---

[38]This is not to suggest that this is the first such point of similarity. Paul's mission theology has resonated in many missionary contexts and wherever the recipients of his message have been presumed to require *conversion* to Christianity (e.g., in Methodist evangelism).

That theology could prove vital for churches as they renegotiate their identities in cultures where what it means to be "church" has become radically uncertain. Luther's reading of Paul retains its theological richness, while offering a model of how to recontextualize the theology of Galatians. But his reading is hardly definitive, as he was the first to say.[39] And the best way to be true to his legacy would not be to repeat what he said five centuries ago, but to reread Paul's letter to the Galatians and to match Luther's deep theological engagement with this letter in order to communicate its good news in our own very different historical context.

---

[39]See the citation from the 1519 commentary at the very end of chapter one.

Romans *and* Philipp Melanchthon

3

Philipp Melanchthon's Reading *of* Romans

Robert Kolb

Martin Luther praised Paul's epistle to the Romans as "the most important part of the New Testament," "indeed the purest gospel," and counseled readers of his translation of the New Testament to memorize it word-for-word and study it every day "as the daily bread of the soul."¹ Before he wrote these words for the publication of his translation in 1522, he had been deeply engaged with his colleague Philipp Melanchthon in the preparation of the latter's *Loci communes theologici*. In connection with his lectures on the Greek text of Romans, Melanchthon had prepared this work as a handbook for reading the letter, and actually all of Scripture, organized by the topics that the apostle presents in this letter.² As a "biblical humanist" dedicated to effective delivery of the message, he wished to concentrate his instruction on teaching the text for future use by his students.

In Wittenberg it was no longer exegesis as usual by 1522. Luther wrote in 1518 that his Galatians commentary was not a traditional commentary but a "testimony."³ Together Luther and Melanchthon came to the conviction that

---

¹LW 35:365; WADB 7:2/3, 3-4.
²Timothy J. Wengert, "The Rhetorical Paul: Philipp Melanchthon's Interpretation of the Pauline Epistles," in *A Companion to Paul in the Reformation*, ed. R. Ward Holder (Leiden: Brill, 2009), p. 140.
³LW 27:159; WA 2:449.18-19.

medieval Christianity had falsely defined what it means to be Christian by focusing the attention of the pious on their own approach to God, particularly through sacred works and activities designed to win or confirm his giving them grace. They rejected the belief that the sacraments bestowed spiritual benefit apart from faith, *ex opere operato*, a view, they perceived, that popular piety cultivated. Wittenberg theology rejected this definition of Christianity, asserting instead that it is God who approaches sinners and does so in his Word. God initiates conversation and community with his chosen people through the proclamation of his Word on the basis of his giving it to humankind in Scripture. Thus the two Wittenberg theologians and their colleagues took most seriously the proper interpretation of Scripture and its salutary delivery to God's people. What Melanchthon sought in his published commentaries was not a careful verse-by-verse exposition of a biblical book but rather the preparation of its readers for preaching and teaching the message of repentance and forgiveness of sins that he believed brought life and salvation, faith and new obedience, to sinners. His commentaries must be evaluated on this basis; all are dialogues with the medieval system of religion that he was trying to reform. He believed such reform could only be accomplished through the power of God's Word.

In 1522 Luther also absconded with Melanchthon's recent lecture notes on Romans and arranged for their publication. This exegetical interpretation presented simply the reverse image of the *Loci communes*, the latter a doctrinal summary arising from the biblical text, the former a comment on the text focusing on the topics to be taught from it. Luther's preface to this work admitted to this theft but excused it by labeling Melanchthon's failure to present his insights to the public a greater sin.[4] By that time Luther had turned his attention as a university lecturer away from Romans; his lectures on the letter in 1515–1516 reveal that he was still very much in the process of his evangelical maturation at that time.[5] Luther went on to treat other biblical books, but he entrusted instruction on Romans to his colleague Philipp. Among the most wide-reaching, long-lasting sources, among many, of Melanchthon's impact on the Christian church, his biblical

---

[4] Melanchthon, *Annotationes Philippi Melanchthonis in Epistolas Pauli ad Rhomanos et Corinthios* (Nuremberg: Johannes Stuch, 1522), p. A2a.
[5] WA 56; LW 25; cf. WA 57.

interpretation stands out. He presented no other biblical book to students as often as Romans.[6]

MELANCHTHON'S TREATMENTS OF ROMANS

Melanchthon engaged Romans in lectures and print.[7] In addition to the 1521 handbook to reading the epistle, the *Loci*, he conducted lectures for his students at least eight times during his career (and probably even more frequently); four lecture courses between 1522 and 1556 were published, the first without his consent. He sketched an outline of the epistle—a *dispositio*—presenting Paul's rhetorical method and providing short chapter summaries (1529).

Melanchthon, Luther and their other Wittenberg colleagues believed that, as Melanchthon asserted, Paul's epistle to the Romans offered the "method of heavenly teaching and sheds light on all the other parts of the prophetic and apostolic Scriptures," presenting "Paul's true and simple meaning" so that it can be easily understood.[8] In 1533, under Melanchthon's leadership, the Wittenberg theological faculty adopted a new curriculum that placed Romans, along with John's Gospel, the Psalms, Genesis and Isaiah, as well as lectures on Augustine's *De spiritu et littera*, at the heart of what Wittenberg students of theology were to study.[9] This reflects Melanchthon's own conception of how theological learning should proceed. In a plan for theological study composed for an anonymous inquirer in 1529, the Preceptor advised beginning with the reading of Romans since it contained a *methodus totius scripturae*—a method for reading all of Scripture—centered on topics such as the justification of the sinner, the use of the law, and the proper distinction of law and gospel, "the most important topics of Christian

---

[6]See Timothy J. Wengert, "The Biblical Commentaries of Philipp Melanchthon," in Irene Dingel, Robert Kolb, Nicole Kuropka and Timothy J. Wengert, *Philipp Melanchthon: Theologian in Classroom, Confession, and Controversy* (Göttingen: Vandenhoeck & Ruprecht, 2012), pp. 43-76.
[7]Wengert, "Biblical Commentaries," pp. 62-67.
[8]Melanchthon, *Commentarii in Epistolam Pavli ad Romanos* (Wittenberg: 1532; Marburg: Franz Rhode, 1533), pp. A5a-b; the modern editions of this work are found in MO 15:495-796 and MWA 5. See also *Commentarii in Epistolam Pavli ad Romanos*... (1540; Wittenberg: Josef Klug, 1541), pp. IIIb-IIIIa; ET, Philipp Melanchthon, *Commentary on Romans*, trans. Fred Kramer, 2nd ed. (St. Louis: Concordia, 2010).
[9]Walther Friedensburg, ed., *Urkundenbuch der Universität Wittenberg* (Magdeburg: Historische Kommission, 1926), 1:155.

teaching."[10] It is sometimes said that Melanchthon's strong focus on Romans created "a canon within a canon," but Timothy Wengert more accurately observes that Melanchthon never believed that "he could thereby ignore or distort other books through his single-minded interest" in this epistle. Instead, he regarded it as a hermeneutical tool, "a key to the entire Bible, providing the exegete with both the goal (*scopus*) of the Scripture and the proper method for interpretation."[11]

Melanchthon's early work on Romans refocused the exegetical conversation of the time from the epistle's later, ethically oriented chapters to the central question of the Wittenberg Reformation, that regarding the status of the sinner who trusts in Christ in the sight of, or in relation to, God. His fundamental hermeneutical presupposition rested on his conviction that Paul sought to bring all readers before God's judgment throne for their failure to trust in him and that the apostle sought to convince Jew and Gentile alike that God had sent his Son Jesus Christ to die and rise for the forgiveness of sins and new life for them. By distinguishing the law's call to repentance from the gospel's promise of forgiveness and life, contemporary preachers could carry out the task Paul set before them.

Melanchthon's Rhetorical Exegesis

Melanchthon highlighted the apostle's rhetorical patterns of argument; his practice of exegesis pioneered the use of the Wittenberg humanist's rhetorical analysis of biblical texts.[12] The rhetorical ruminations of Rudolf Agricola and Desiderius Erasmus had helped propel Melanchthon into ancient rhetorical theory—Aristotle's, Demosthenes's, Cicero's and others'—ever more deeply.[13] Melanchthon's comments on Romans developed as his rhetorical theory was maturing, and his several approaches to the epistle reflect his concern that the apostle's message reach its sixteenth-century audience.

Melanchthon's rhetorical approach embraced, above all, his cultivation of

---

[10]MBW *Texte* 3:670.
[11]Wengert, "Biblical Commentaries," p. 67. Cf. *Dispositio orationis, in Epistola Pauli ad Romanos* (1529; Wittenberg: Georg Rhau, 1530), p. A2b (the modern edition of this work is found in MO 15:443-92).
[12]See Wengert, "Rhetorical Paul," pp. 134-36; Wengert, "Biblical Commentaries," pp. 64-67.
[13]Cf. Carl Joachim Classen, *Rhetorical Criticism of the New Testament* (Tübingen: Mohr Siebeck, 2000), pp. 99-177; Olaf Berwald, *Philipp Melanchthons Sicht der Rhetorik* (Wiesbaden: Harrassowitz, 1994).

topical thinking, conducive both to the students' learning and organizing the meaning of texts in their own minds and to their future preaching and teaching on the basis of biblical materials compiled by topic for practical application in their hearers' lives. Alongside this organization and classification of individual passages by topic, the *locus communis* or τόπος, the Preceptor clarified the text and the course of its line of reasoning through careful attention to the rhetorical development of the apostle's argument. He did so through analysis according to the three traditional genres of persuasion—deliberative, judicial and demonstrative—and his own invention, the didactic genus. All this served to deliver the apostolic message clearly and move hearers to trust God's Word and live a Christian life.[14]

Melanchthon's concerns for improved rhetoric and increased attention to original sources had met and meshed with Luther's theological concerns when the two became colleagues in 1518.[15] Thus it was natural that the younger colleague's lectures strove to equip students to use God's Word in Scripture for practical effect. He sought to guide the proclamation of the biblical message to its goal of calling sinners to repentance and then bestowing on them the forgiveness of sins (Lk 24:45-49) through the proper distinction of law and gospel. Early in his career in Wittenberg, Melanchthon learned this distinction of God's kinds of speech-act from Luther, taking it as the guiding hermeneutical principle for the interpreting of both text and hearer and the application of the text to the hearer.[16]

Among the elements Melanchthon adapted from Aristotelian logic in his blending of rhetoric and dialectic, syllogistic reasoning seems most prominent. For instance, he explains the distinction of "law" and "promise" in commenting on Abraham's trust in God's promise through syllogistic exploration of the conditional nature of the former and the unconditional nature

---

[14]Fuller treatment is found in Wengert, "Rhetorical Paul," pp. 132-38, and Wengert, "Philipp Melanchthon's 1522 Annotations on Romans and the Lutheran Origins of Rhetorical Criticism," in *Biblical Interpretation in the Era of the Reformation: Essays Presented to David C. Steinmetz in Honor of His Sixtieth Birthday*, ed. Richard A. Muller and John L. Thompson (Grand Rapids: Eerdmans, 1996), pp. 118-40.

[15]Helmar Junghans, "Martin Luthers Einfluß auf die Wittenberger Universitätsreform," in Irene Dingel and Günther Wartenberg, eds., *Die Theologische Fakultät Wittenberg 1502 bis 1602. Beiträge zur 500. Wiederkehr des Gründungsjahres der Leucorea* (Leipzig: Evangelische Verlagsanstalt, 2002), p. 70.

[16]Melanchthon's 1543 oration written for Christoph Jonas, "De Paulo apostolo" (MO 11:624), highlighted the law/gospel distinction and joined it to two kinds of righteousness.

of the latter.¹⁷ Aristotle's schema of "factors" (*causae*) also guided the Preceptor's explanations of terms and actions. On Romans 5:17-21 he explained that the efficient cause of grace is God's will that Christ become the sacrificial victim for sinners. The instrumental factor, God's Word, produces faith, the chief effect of grace.¹⁸

For all of Melanchthon's emphasis on reading texts in the original, his commentaries on Romans contain relatively few references to or discussions of Greek vocabulary or usage. He did discuss Greek words for sin and unrighteousness at Romans 1:29.¹⁹ He also refers to "Hebraisms" in the Greek text; for instance, "he condemned sin" (Rom 8:3) is the Hebrew way of saying that he abolished, destroyed and voided sin in Christ.²⁰ His early *Annotations* reveal that Melanchthon worked text-critically, identifying Paul's source for the quotation from Isaiah (Is 10:22-23) at Romans 9:27-28 as the Septuagint and showing that the apostle had abbreviated the prophet's statement.²¹

All biblical commentary takes place in conversation with earlier exegetes.²² Although Melanchthon championed use of the fathers,²³ particularly in exegesis, his Romans commentaries show relatively little direct citation of or engagement with their works (Augustine most often, Ambrose, Anselm, Gerson occasionally; Origen won frequent criticism²⁴). Melanchthon also had read contemporary interpreters, and these conversations were not always friendly. His exegesis often employed polemic against his opponents, especially Roman Catholics, Zwingli (especially in 1532) and

---

[17]Melanchthon, *Commentarii* 1540, pp. CXXVIIa-CXXXa; *Commentary on Romans*, pp. 114-17.
[18]Melanchthon, *Commentarii* 1540, p. CLVIIa; *Commentary on Romans*, p. 140. On Melanchthon's more elaborate discussion of *causae* in his 1556 critique of Andreas Osiander's doctrine of justification, see Timothy J. Wengert, *Defending Faith: Lutheran Responses to Andreas Osiander's Doctrine of Justification, 1551–1559* (Tübingen: Mohr Siebeck, 2012), pp. 344-46.
[19]Melanchthon, *Commentarii* 1540, pp. XCIb-XCIIIb; *Commentary on Romans*, pp. 82-84.
[20]Melanchthon, *Commentarii* 1540, p. CLXXXVa-b; *Commentary on Romans*, p. 166. Cf. his discussion of Hebrew meanings behind Greek words; *Commentarii* 1540, p. CCLXXa-b; *Commentary on Romans*, p. 289.
[21]Melanchthon, *Annotationes*, pp. H4a-b.
[22]Timothy J. Wengert, *Philipp Melanchthon's* Annotationes in Johannem *in Relation to Its Predecessors and Contemporaries* (Geneva: Droz, 1987), pp. 17-19.
[23]Peter Fraenkel, *Testimonia Patrum: The Function of Patristic Argument in the Theology of Philipp Melanchthon* (Geneva: Droz, 1961).
[24]Melanchthon, *Dispositio*, pp. D8a-b; *Commentarii* 1532, pp. S8a-T1a.

Anabaptists, to whom he often attributed "spiritualizing" positions.[25] He repudiated those who wished to find a voice within themselves rather than look to Scripture.[26] He also rejected the *ex opere operato* interpretations, which he regarded as superstitious.[27]

Melanchthon's rhetorical analyses presumed that readers could determine the *argumentum* or *scopus* of the work, its purpose and manner of pursuing the purpose. In his printed Romans commentaries he acquainted readers immediately with the *argumentum* and outfitted them with necessary definitions of terms to expedite their understanding of the epistle. He saw the epistle as a single literary unit and believed, in a larger sense, that all of Scripture, in its many facets and forms, contained a unified message from its ultimate author, the Holy Spirit. Thus he drew from throughout the Bible to illuminate the Romans text.

Two factors colored his defining fundamental biblical concepts. Melanchthon's philological expertise, combined with this comprehensive command of Scripture, equipped him to marshal insights from the usage of a variety of biblical authors, whom he regarded as agents of the Holy Spirit's revelation of the single message of prophets and apostles alike. It is important to note that he understood words not only from what they meant in themselves but also from their effect or impact (*effectus*). Second, his experiences as an ecclesiastical diplomat in frequent conversation with Roman Catholic critics made him sensitive to using traditional language even when he altered or expanded its definitions. He did so often as he implemented the Wittenberg alteration of the fundamental understanding of Christianity. This Wittenberg redefinition of being Christian—that reconciliation comes at God's initiative through his living, active Word, authoritatively placed in Scripture, on the basis of trust in God through Christ's work—framed the reading of the text that Melanchthon's commentaries aimed to cultivate. That obviated the necessity of treating Paul's words

---

[25] E.g., he named specifically five Roman Catholic foes who had perverted the interpretation of Romans, along with Anabaptists in general, Servetus and Schwenkfeld, in his preface to *Epistolae Pavli Scriptae ad Romanos, Enarratio* ... (Wittenberg: Veit Creutzer, 1556), pp. A8a-b (the modern edition of this work is found in MO 15:797-1052).

[26] Melanchthon, *Commentarii* 1540, p. CCLXVIIIa-b; *Commentary on Romans*, p. 287.

[27] E.g., Melanchthon, *Commentarii* 1540, pp. CCXXXIXb, CCLXXIIIIa; *Commentary on Romans*, pp. 215, 293.

phrase by phrase, as most exegetes of the time did, but instead enabled the commentator to pursue the threads that were carrying and conveying the *argumentum*—although he did allow himself the privilege of offering clarification of Paul's rhetorical moves and his vocabulary, grammar and syntax.[28]

Like Luther, Melanchthon never ceased experimenting with the expression of his ideas, but his theology came into its fundamental form quite early. As with Luther, shifting emphases emerged in Melanchthon's interpretation as new concerns within Wittenberg reform as well as fresh criticisms and challenges from a variety of opponents arose, while his fundamental convictions remained largely unchanged.[29]

The *Argumentum* of Romans

The *argumentum* of the 1522 commentary filled one quarto page. With attendant discussion of "justification by faith and other terms," the *argumentum* grew to 10 percent of the total pages in 1532 and to nearly 20 percent in 1540; by 1556 it had fallen back to 10 percent of the work.

In 1522 Melanchthon defined the *argumentum* or *scopus* of Romans as knowing Christ, adding that "no one knows him apart from knowing his benefits." Knowing Christ's benefits eliminates all reliance on one's own works. The first eight chapters elaborate this point by treating "grace, the law, sin." These topics had provided the outline for the *Loci communes* and present the *status causae*. Melanchthon compared the *status* to the architect's design or structure. He elaborated his understanding of the *status* as justification by faith or "Christian righteousness," that is, trust in Christ as redeemer and propitiator.[30] His subsequent published comment on the epistle continued this focus, expanding the discussion without altering the emphasis on the work of Christ on behalf of sinners and their appropriation of the benefits of that work through trust in him. The *Dispositio* expressed this cluster of ideas through a wider anthropological definition of the two kinds of human righteousness that enable readers to understand this message. Political or civil righteousness, the righteousness of human good works, is clear

---

[28]Wengert, "Rhetorical Paul," p. 138.
[29]This chapter marshals evidence from Melanchthon's four printed commentaries and his *Dispositio*. When possible, the 1540 commentary is used because it is available for English-only readers in translation.
[30]Melanchthon, *Annotationes*, p. A3a; *Dispositio*, pp. B5a-b.

to human reason. It cannot justify sinners before God. Trust in God constitutes justifying righteousness: "The gospel teaches that Christ, God's Son, was given for us, that righteousness before God is to believe that our sins are forgiven for Christ's sake, or that for Christ's sake we are received into God's grace."[31] The 1556 *argumentum* began, "God wants his Son to be known as the mediator and desires no other way to free human beings from sin and eternal death than calling on the Son."[32] Implicit throughout and often explicit is Melanchthon's reliance on the distinction of law, which speaks of the human performance God expects, and gospel, which proclaims God's work for deliverance of sinners through Christ.[33]

Thus Melanchthon's abiding orientation for reading the epistle centered on Jesus Christ and what he had done to accomplish the restoration of righteousness in God's sight to the faithful who trust in him and his word of forgiveness. This replicates the approach of the *Loci communes* of 1521, composed as a handbook for reading Romans, by beginning with the topics "human powers, specifically the free will," "sin" and "the law"—reflecting Romans 1:1–3:20. He proceeded into Romans 3:21–5:21 by treating "the gospel," "grace" and "justification and faith," with related subtopics. Paul's words on baptism in Romans 6 gave occasion to treat "signs" along with "baptism," which flowed into "penance" or "repentance." Romans 12–16 gave reason for exposition of "love," "magistrates" and "offense." A series of related subtopics, in part reflecting the *Sententiae* of Peter Lombard, show Melanchthon's intention of replacing Lombard with his handbook to reading Romans as the foundation of theological study.

In the 1532 and 1540 commentaries Melanchthon sketched the *argumentum* of Romans again by dividing the epistle into a first part, "a long disputation," and a latter part concerning moral behavior. The former he labeled with the designation of the instructional method that Wittenberg had reintroduced in 1533 as an examination of competence and qualification for academic degrees and as a formal medium for defining the truth and refining the expression of the truth. The "disputation" of the epistle "distin-

---

[31]Melanchthon, *Dispositio*, pp. A4b-A5a.
[32]Melanchthon, *Enarratio*, p. 2a.
[33]E.g., Melanchthon sketched a *disputatio* on the distinction in commenting on Romans 4; *Commentarii* 1532, pp. M2a-M5a.

guishes the gospel from the law and from philosophy," and presents the "benefits of Christ, the gracious remission of sins, liberation from eternal death, the imputation of righteousness, the gift of the Holy Spirit, and eternal life," interconnected topics of Paul's teaching.[34] Key to understanding these topics was the corruption of human nature, which in sin cannot satisfy God's law but doubts God, a key anthropological presupposition to the Wittenberg conception of the redemption of sinners. For "the proper benefit of Christ is to take away sins," as—Melanchthon pointed out—Isaiah 53:12, John 1:29, Romans 3:21 and John 1:17 state. This 1540 commentary added to its *argumentum* a *summa* of the biblical teaching of justification. Since the law demands perfect obedience, which sinners cannot perform, God revealed another righteousness, which Christ has produced. This righteousness is bestowed through his people's proclamation of repentance and the remission of sins in his name. This preaching creates "trust in the promised mercy because of Christ; it gives assent to the divine promise."[35]

Like Luther, Melanchthon, though thoroughly trinitarian in his biblical interpretation, placed Christ at the existential center of attention of the reader of Romans. Like Luther, he focused particularly on Jesus' death and resurrection.[36] Faith in the promise must "embrace the mediator." Commenting on Romans 4:25, he writes that faith "apprehends Christ's death in order to hold fast to the sacrificial victim, it declares to be the sure ransom of our sins because God willed that there be a sacrifice for sin." This demonstrates both God's wrath that demanded the death of his Son and his infinite mercy. It is also necessary for faith to grasp Jesus as the risen high priest, who efficaciously intercedes for sinners, "truly gives life, gives the Holy Spirit, helps us, frees us from eternal death, will raise the dead, and will give new and everlasting life, wisdom, and righteousness."[37] Although Melanchthon did not ignore Christ's resurrection, he emphasized the Lamb's "propitiatory sacrifice" that satisfies the law's demand for the sinner's death.[38]

---

[34]Melanchthon, *Commentarii* 1532, pp. A5a-b; *Commentarii* 1540, pp. B1a-b; translated as *Commentary on Romans*, p. 11.
[35]Melanchthon, *Commentarii* 1540, pp. Xb-XVIIb; *Commentary on Romans*, pp. 12-18.
[36]Robert Kolb, "Resurrection and Justification: Luther's Use of Romans 4,25," *Lutherjahrbuch* 78 (2011): 39-60.
[37]Melanchthon, *Commentarii* 1540, pp. CXXXIIIIa-CXXXVa; *Commentary on Romans*, pp. 120-21.
[38]E.g., Melanchthon, *Commentarii* 1540, pp. CLXXXIIIa-CLXXXVIa; *Commentary on Romans*, pp. 164-67.

The repetition of proper definition of terms, injected at various points as the text demanded, reinforced the *argumentum* throughout. In 1540 Melanchthon elaborated his *argumentum* by defining the adverb *gratis* and related *particulae exclusivae*, adding to it some pages later a definition of the noun *gratia* and its usage in some six other biblical passages, which illumine the specific Hebrew and Greek ways of thinking of the term.[39]

At the heart of Melanchthon's rhetorical-theological hermeneutics lay the distinction between law and gospel, a hermeneutical tool given him by Luther. In 1540 he defined the law as "the teaching in which God prescribes what manner of persons we should be and what things are to be done and what things avoided." It demands perfect obedience.[40] The law is "the highest gift for bodily life"; its first use, political or pedagogical, preserves discipline in those not sanctified. This use, commanded by God, trains people to keep peace and order through rewards and punishments so that society functions well. It trains sanctified believers to distinguish the righteousness of faith from its fruits, an idea akin to the third use of the law that Melanchthon had already begun to discuss but did not employ at this point in his commentary.[41] The law's "second and chief use" is "to accuse and terrify consciences when it judges and condemns sin." This may provoke some to sin all the more, but it moves others to repentance.[42]

Later in this commentary, Melanchthon treated the use of the law according to his tripartite division for the law's role in the Christian life: it coerces the remaining "fleshly" desires, calls to repentance and the mortification of those remnants of sin, and teaches the righteous "what works please God" and "arouses spiritual impulses."[43] The gospel, on the contrary, "proclaims repentance and the promise of grace and eternal life." The "inexpressible" "greatness of this benefit, which God imparts to us through his Son, our Lord Jesus Christ," is that it erases sin and destroys death "so that we may enjoy the vision of God in eternal life, righteousness, and joy."[44]

---

[39]Melanchthon, *Commentarii* 1540, pp. XVIIb-XXIa, XXVIb-XXVIIIa; *Commentary on Romans*, pp. 18-21, 26-28.

[40]Melanchthon, *Commentarii* 1540, pp. XXIa-XXIIa; *Commentary on Romans*, pp. 21-22.

[41]Timothy J. Wengert, *Law and Gospel: Philipp Melanchthon's Debate with John Agricola of Eisleben over Poenitentia* (Grand Rapids: Baker Academic, 1997), pp. 177-210.

[42]Melanchthon, *Commentarii* 1540, pp. CLVIIIb-CLIXb; *Commentary on Romans*, pp. 141-42.

[43]Melanchthon, *Commentarii* 1540, p. CCXXXIIa-b; *Commentary on Romans*, p. 209.

[44]Melanchthon, *Commentarii* 1540, pp. XXIIb-XXIIIa; *Commentary on Romans*, p. 22. However,

Melanchthon defined grace in 1522 as "God's favor" attained through Christ's work,[45] and in 1540 as "unconditional mercy," which demonstrates itself in "forgiveness of sins and unconditional acceptance . . . through Christ." He distinguished grace from the gift that grace gives, "the Holy Spirit, who begins the new and eternal life in the mind and excites new impulses." Explicitly rejecting scholastic definitions that interpret grace as a quality in believers, *charitas* or new obedience, Melanchthon insisted that "by grace" be understood "relationally, as unconditional acceptance" of sinners by God.[46] This distinction became even more important in the Osiandrian controversy; in 1556 Melanchthon insisted that God's indwelling as gift resulted from, and did not constitute, righteousness in his sight.[47]

Melanchthon's definition of "sin" echoed Luther's First Commandment focus: the "immense weakness with which we are born," original sin, is most serious. "For darkness and doubting whether God cares about human affairs, whether he punishes, nourishes, gives aid, or grants people's prayers are not trivial evils. Likewise, to lack fear and love for God, to love ourselves while neglecting God's love, to admire our own wisdom, to play with opinions which flee from God" are great evils.[48] Treating Romans 5 in 1556, he defined Adam's sin as "doubt of God's Word," loss of faith, seeking other wisdom than the Word's, pride, contempt for God, preferring the devil over God, ingratitude, and murdering himself and his posterity through the fall.[49]

"Justification" lay at the center of Wittenberg theology. Melanchthon defined it as the action of God: his pronouncement or consideration that rendered a person righteous in God's judgment. He indeed understood justification, like Luther, as forensic, that is, an action of God's Word, the same speaker who spoke the entire creation into existence in Genesis 1.[50] God's

---

Melanchthon can say that the gospel rebukes unbelief and the law shows other sins (p. 145).
[45]Melanchthon, *Annotationes*, p. F3b.
[46]Melanchthon, *Commentarii* 1540, pp. CLIa-CLIIIIb; *Commentary on Romans*, pp. 135-38, on Rom 5:15.
[47]Melanchthon, *Enarratio*, pp. h3b-h4a.
[48]Melanchthon, *Commentarii* 1540, pp. XXIIIIb-XXVa; *Commentary on Romans*, pp. 24-25. Melanchthon repeated key elements in this definition in commenting on Rom 5:12-17 (pp. 132-34).
[49]Melanchthon, *Enarratio*, pp. b6a-b.
[50]Luther's and Melanchthon's understandings of justification varied very minimally, even though Albrecht Ritschl and others tried to drive a wedge between the two. See Mark Mattes, "Luther on Justification as Forensic and Effective," in *The Oxford Handbook of Martin Luther's Theology*, ed. Robert Kolb, Irene Dingel and L'ubomi'r Batka (Oxford: Oxford University Press, 2014), pp. 264-73.

regard for a person, in the Wittenberg view, determined reality. The Creator and Re-Creator, who acts, as always, through his Word, creates the reality of a new creature when he speaks his justifying Word, whether in oral, written or sacramental form. Therefore, God's imputation of righteousness, his acceptance of the sinner as his own, changed the reality of the situation, the status and the very essence of the person. "Righteous" is thus "understood relationally as acceptance to eternal life; . . . in the forgiveness of sins there is given at the same time the Holy Spirit." The Holy Spirit initiates faith and produces "fear and love of God, love of the truth, chastity, patience, proper action toward the neighbor." Melanchthon added the caution: "These virtues do not merit forgiveness of sins." His concern was for the terrified conscience, which cannot rely on its own virtues.[51] The anthropology that framed this understanding of justification replicated Luther's distinction of the two elements or aspects of being human, passive righteousness—the bestowal of identity as God's child that generates trust in him—and active righteousness—the performance of God's expectations for those whom he has made his children. Melanchthon termed them the righteousness of faith and the righteousness of the law.[52]

Throughout his life Melanchthon demonstrated his passion for the proper understanding of faith or trust in God as the heart of the biblical teaching on the relationship with a God who approaches human beings through his promise and who created and re-creates them to trust that promise as the orienting and motivating dominant of life. In Melanchthon's view, the church had lost almost completely a true sense of what faith means. It "signifies not only knowledge of history but trust in the mercy promised because of Christ or assent to the promise of grace." "This impulse of faith in our minds is not an idle cogitation, but it wrestles with the terrors of sin and death. It fights with the devil, who attacks weak minds in dreadful ways in order to drive them either to contempt of God or to despair." Melanchthon placed faith in Christ squarely in the midst of the eschatological battle between God's truth and Satan's lie. He supported his position by citing eleven Scripture passages that confirmed his understanding of faith, and he added

---

[51]Melanchthon, *Commentarii* 1540, pp. XXVa-XVIa; *Commentary on Romans*, pp. 25-26.
[52]Melanchthon, *Commentarii* 1540, pp. CXIXa-CXXa; *Commentary on Romans*, p. 108.

confirmation from Augustine, John Chrysostom and Bernard of Clairvaux.[53]

Faith led Melanchthon to the inseparable topic of good works, the inevitable product of trusting Christ. God's Word alone defines what works are good. Freed from the law, believers "receive the Holy Spirit in order that the new obedience, light, and life eternal may begin in them." That begins with the first table of the Commandments, first faith and then the works that proceed from faith in praise of God and love for others.[54] The commentary addressed the mystery of the continuation of sin and evil in the faith with more than a dozen biblical passages that spoke of the remnants of sin in believers. Such sins can always be forgiven, but Melanchthon insisted, in his distinction of law and gospel, that the call to repentance also always contains the threat that one may fall from faith through unrepentant sinfulness.[55]

MELANCHTHON'S COMMENTS ON THE TEXT

Romans 1:16-17. The Wittenberg reformers found Romans 1:16-17 important for their understanding both of the power of God's Word and of saving faith. In 1522 Melanchthon echoed Luther's Heidelberg Theses on the foolishness and impotence of the word from the cross in the view of mortal sinners and its serving as the instrument of God's power and wisdom; the gospel or promise bestows salvation on believers (1 Cor 1–2; 2 Thess 2:13). For the gospel, as God's instrument, creates the righteousness given to sinners, a righteousness not of works but of faith.[56] This interpretation appeared in extended form in later commentaries, emphasizing that the Word is efficacious and bestows the Holy Spirit on those who trust God's mercy through his use of that Word.[57]

Throughout his 1540 commentary Melanchthon presumed that the Holy Spirit was at work when God's Word comes from Scripture into the hearts and minds of hearers.[58] There he affirmed that ministry of the Word, which is the gospel's bestowal of the remission of sins, the Holy Spirit's illumining

---

[53]Melanchthon, *Commentarii* 1540, pp. XXVIIIa-XXXVIIa; *Commentary on Romans*, pp. 28-35.
[54]Melanchthon, *Commentarii* 1540, pp. XXXVIIa-XLIIb; *Commentary on Romans*, pp. 35-40.
[55]Melanchthon, *Commentarii* 1540, pp. XLIIb-LVa; *Commentary on Romans*, pp. 40-51.
[56]Melanchthon, *Annotationes*, pp. B1a-B2b.
[57]Melanchthon, *Commentarii* 1532, pp. D4b-D8a.
[58]Melanchthon, *Commentarii* 1540, pp. LXXVIa-LXXVIIb, cf. pp. CXLIIIa-CXLIIIIb, CLXXXIIa-b, CXCIIIa-b, CCIa-CCIIb; cf. *Commentary on Romans*, pp. 69-71, cf. pp. 129, 164, 174, 180.

of Scripture, and the beginning of eternal life through the human being's hearing, reading and pondering it. The Word of forgiveness is the instrument through which God works and through which the Holy Spirit enters the life of God's people.[59] The gospel reveals God's righteousness, which is his acceptance "by which God is now certainly propitious toward you, forgives your sins, and accounts you righteous," a righteousness imputed by God's mercy, accepted by faith, which justifies and makes the justified person alive.[60]

Romans 1:18-20. In 1522 Melanchthon briefly used Paul's judgment on human unrighteousness to demonstrate that righteousness can only come through faith in Christ. The law of nature—the light of nature (*acumen ingenii naturale*)—led to knowledge of both God and sin.[61] By 1532 and 1540 the professor's focus on the inadequacy of both Jewish and Gentile keeping of the law as a means of establishing righteousness had become progressively clearer. Formal presence within the Mosaic covenant was not the point for the apostle, according to Melanchthon, much less partial obedience to God's commands. Trusting in him above all else, especially one's own works, was Paul's concern. "Impiety signified . . . contempt and hatred for God, . . . not only outward crimes but natural impurity in the heart, which annuls fear of God, trust in God, love of God, etc."[62] "Impiety properly signifies the vices that militate against the first table: ignorance of God, being without fear, love, and trust in God, harboring fleshly security and contempt for God, anger and raging against God in afflictions, confidence in one's own wisdom, righteousness or health . . ."[63]

In both his 1532 and 1540 commentaries, especially the latter, Melanchthon expanded his evaluation of the Gentiles with an appeal to natural law, positing that the sinful mind acknowledges that God exists when it views creation, for God has left his footprints on nature. Conscience, the natural ability to distinguish the honorable and the shameful, is impressed on the human mind; atrocious crimes arouse fear in all that God will punish. The order in creation also points to God's existence, as does the natural

---

[59]Melanchthon, *Commentarii* 1540, pp. LXXVIa-LXXVIIa; *Commentary on Romans*, p. 69.
[60]Melanchthon, *Commentarii* 1540, pp. LXXVIIb-LXXIXa; *Commentary on Romans*, pp. 70-71.
[61]Melanchthon, *Annotationes*, pp. B2b-B3b.
[62]Melanchthon, *Commentarii* 1532, pp. E1b.
[63]Melanchthon, *Commentarii* 1540, pp. LXXXIb-LXXXIIIa; *Commentary on Romans*, p. 74.

emergence of social or political order. Indications of the future, in the stars or "inferior [heavenly] bodies," as well as prophecies that come true, point to his existence, as does the chain of causes (the necessity of an ultimate cause for reality).[64] Melanchthon summarized his views of natural law more succinctly in the 1556 commentary.[65]

Romans 3:20-31. At Romans 3:20, Melanchthon had arrived at the epistle's critical point, the restoration of human righteousness to sinners through Christ. His *Dispositio* called the chapter the *status* of the entire epistle.[66] His commentary of 1522 had traced the *occupationes*—counterarguments—of his own opponents and Paul's for justification through keeping the law. Melanchthon knew that his opponents all recognized the necessity of some role for divine grace in the system of salvation and that the Jews of Paul's time knew they were heirs of God's unconditioned choosing of Abraham and his descendants as his people. Critical for the Wittenberg professor, however, were the practical answers to questions of the ultimate key to salvation and to what believers should look for comfort when doubts afflicted their consciences. God gave the law to reveal sin, Paul said (Rom 3:20). "The chief point of this text and the status of the disputation is: righteousness is through faith in Christ." Pointing in passing to the "types and figures" of propitiation in the Old Testament, Melanchthon did not treat Christ's atoning work but simply emphasized that trust creates the present-day foundation for assurance of salvation. God's own righteousness consists of remitting sinners' sins (Rom 3:25-26).[67]

"God's righteousness signified the acceptation by which God accepts us," the 1532 commentary defined. "To be justified simply and properly signifies 'righteous,' that is, to be regarded as, or pronounced, acceptable." Faith means "not historical knowledge but trust in certain mercy." Implicitly

---

[64]Melanchthon, *Commentarii* 1532, esp. pp. E2a-E6a; *Commentarii* 1540, pp. LXXXIIIb-XCIIb; *Commentary on Romans*, pp. 76-79; on natural knowledge of God, see also *Commentarii* 1532, pp. F4a-F5a; *Commentarii* 1540, pp. XCVIIIb-C1a; *Commentary on Romans*, pp. 89-90. On Melanchthon's deep interest in the natural sciences, see Sachiko Kusukawa, *The Transformation of Natural Philosophy: The Case of Philipp Melanchthon* (Cambridge: Cambridge University Press, 1995) and *Melanchthon und die Naturwissenschaften seiner Zeit*, ed. Günther Frank and Stefan Rhein (Sigmaringen: Thorbecke, 1998).

[65]Melanchthon, *Enarratio*, pp. 34b-36a; cf. pp. 48a-49a.

[66]Melanchthon, *Dispositio*, pp. B5a-B8a.

[67]Melanchthon, *Annotationes*, pp. C3a-C4b.

countering late medieval definitions of faith still employed by his opponents, Melanchthon emphasized the mercy that this trust grasps on the basis of Christ's work, accentuating the certainty that God's promise in Christ delivers—reflecting the Wittenberg concern for pastoral care and the consolation of consciences.[68] Arguing explicitly against Charles V's theologians who authored the Confutation of the Augsburg Confession two years earlier, Melanchthon stressed that Christ alone can serve as mediator and propitiator for sinners; he alone has abolished sin and death. Thus "we are accepted and righteous not because of our renewal but through his mercy, which cannot be accepted except by faith," apart from the works of the law.[69]

While recognizing that God's moral law prescribes the standards of civil righteousness and external morals and coerces sinners to behave publicly, the 1540 commentary also emphatically ruled out any role in the human being's relationship with God for that use of the law and the works it might produce. In that dimension the law accuses and terrifies; it kills the conscience.[70] To meet that terror required absolute clarity in setting forth the "benefits of Christ," God's justification of sinners through the remission of sins and the imputation of righteousness.[71] Justification takes place on the basis of Christ's serving as propitiator, as sacrificial victim, a teaching that, Melanchthon again repeated, "our adversaries" change and corrupt, as he outlined medieval scholastic teaching on the necessity of works completing what God's grace enables. In 1540 Melanchthon noted also that God justifies himself by promising and delivering "a new righteousness, a new and eternal life, that he will renew the human race by abolishing sin and death." Here Melanchthon quite consistently joins forgiveness and the presence of the Holy Spirit.[72]

By far the longest of Melanchthon's treatments of Romans 3:20-31 appears in the 1556 commentary, with its sharp critique of the view of justification advanced by Andreas Osiander a half decade earlier.[73] His teaching that the

---

[68]Melanchthon, *Commentarii* 1532, pp. G6b-H3a.
[69]Ibid., pp. H5a–I5a.
[70]Melanchthon, *Commentarii* 1540, pp. CVIIb-CVIIIb; *Commentary on Romans*, pp. 97-98.
[71]Melanchthon, *Commentarii* 1540, pp. CVIIIb-CXa; *Commentary on Romans*, pp. 98-99.
[72]Melanchthon, *Commentarii* 1540, pp. CXVb-CXVb; *Commentary on Romans*, pp. 100-103.
[73]Wengert, *Defending Faith*, pp. 317-51, and Wengert, "Commentary as Polemic: Philipp Melanchthon's 1556 *Enarratio ad Romanos* Against Andreas Osiander," in Torbjörn Johansson et al., eds., *Hermeneutica Sacra: Studies of the Interpretation of Holy Scripture in the Sixteenth and Seventeenth Centuries* (Berlin: de Gruyter, 2010), pp. 147-63.

righteousness of sinners consists of the indwelling essential righteousness of Christ's divine nature—indeed grasped through faith—had aroused the ire of Melanchthon and almost every other theologian in the Wittenberg circle. They had several grounds for criticism. Melanchthon presumed the Wittenberg ontology of the Word and rejected Osiander's presupposition that God's "forensic" pronouncement of the sinner's righteousness constituted a legal fiction. God's Word creates reality. Melanchthon's chief worry concerned the disconsolate conscience's being directed to search inwardly for the presence of righteousness, demonstrable, according to many medieval theologies, in good works. The renewal of new obedience that flowed from God's pronouncement of righteousness and the faith it produced had to be distinguished from God's absolving Word and this trust.[74]

Romans 4 and 5. The treatment of Romans 4 in Melanchthon's 1522 comments focused especially on rhetorical analysis, showing students how Paul had constructed his argument, describing the apostle's rejection of works as a basis for the patriarch's receiving righteousness before God as a *confirmatio* of the *status disputationis*. The *Dispositio* and the commentaries of 1532, 1540 and 1556 continued this rhetorical analysis in similar fashion, sometimes adding extensive detail. For example, from 1532 on Melanchthon analyzed Paul's argument for justification by grace through faith, employing five elements in Abraham's story. Abraham's example demonstrates that trust in God's mercy, not human virtues, justifies. Second and third, the definitions of justification as "the gratuitous imputation of righteousness" and "the remission of sins" support this understanding. Fourth, justification is the effect of Abraham's faith, not its cause. Finally, the promise of the law is uncertain, dependent on human performance, and therefore the promise of the gospel must be accepted by faith.[75]

In 1522 Paul's mention of circumcision as the "sign" of God's promise (Rom 4:9-12) gave Melanchthon the occasion to explain his view of the sacraments. They may seem like "hallucinations" if their biblical use is not noted, he explained. These signs, addressing the senses, function as re-

---

[74]Melanchthon, *Enarratio*, pp. a2a-c6b.
[75]Melanchthon, *Commentarii* 1532, pp. I8a-K6b; *Commentarii* 1540, pp. CXVIIa-CXXVIIa; *Commentary on Romans*, pp. 106-14; *Enarratio*, pp. e1a-f6b.

minders and confirmation of God's promise.[76] This discussion expanded in 1532 with polemic against an *ex opere operato* conception of sacramental bestowal of grace apart from faith and against the Anabaptist claim that baptism and the Lord's Supper are reminders of the works Christians are committed to perform.[77] This excursus on the nature of the sacraments as instruments of the promise disappeared in 1540 and 1556.

The Osiandrian debate made Melanchthon more sensitive to the importance of treating Christ's atoning work; in 1556 he stated that "the total obedience of Christ is the payment for our sins and the propitiation which placates God's wrath. Christ rose, nevertheless, and because he is victor over death, he reigns and applies his merits to us and bestows on us life and eternal righteousness." Faith in his work brings remission of sins, justification, reconciliation and the gift of the Holy Spirit. Therein one recognizes the consummation of his benefits.[78]

Receiving righteousness in God's sight leads, according to Romans 5:1 (the "epilogue," Melanchthon noted), not to being peaceable toward other human beings, as Origen wrongly asserted, but receiving the consolation and assurance that sets the conscience at peace.[79] Melanchthon also rejected the contention that distinguished the remission of guilt and of eternal punishment. God's justifying action banishes both, bestowing peace.[80]

Paul's observation that Christians glory in affliction (Rom 5:3-4) returned Melanchthon to the subject of trust, which makes this possible, in 1522;[81] by 1532 he found here an application of one element of Luther's theology of the cross, the placing of Christian living into the context of the eschatological battle waged at the level of personal mortification of the flesh and other suffering. God punishes through afflictions to call believers to repentance and thereby exercises and cultivates faith, prayer and hope. Believers remember that God submits them to suffering not to destroy them

---

[76]Melanchthon, *Annotationes*, pp. C4b-D1b.
[77]Melanchthon, *Commentarii* 1532, pp. L2b-L4a.
[78]Melanchthon, *Enarratio*, pp. g1a-b.
[79]Cf. Melanchthon's introductory comments on chapter twelve for the relationship between the reception of righteousness and good works (see below).
[80]Melanchthon, *Commentarii* 1540, pp. CXXXVa-CXXXVIIb; *Commentary on Romans*, pp. 122-23, repeating generally the earlier comments in *Annotationes*, pp. D4a-b; *Commentarii* 1532, pp. N1a-N3b; cf. *Enarrtio*, pp. g2a-g3a.
[81]Melanchthon, *Annotationes*, pp. D4b-E1a.

but to save them.⁸² In 1556, with controversy over the bondage of the will brewing in the Wittenberg ranks, Melanchthon's remarks concentrated on rejecting the idea that God could be the origin of evil, insisting that it proceeds from the fall into sin and the devil.⁸³

Romans 6. In 1522 Melanchthon called attention to the power of baptism, "a sign by which our death becomes Christ's death," which means that "we have been raised." This reveals that "baptism is not the origin of being Christian but its fruit" (*non esse principium tantum Christianismi, sed eius fructus*), pertaining chiefly to the death of the old creature (a view that Luther would not have shared), and gives the dying assurance of victory over death. That launched a discussion of the struggle of the old and new creature, continuing into Romans 7, where Melanchthon distinguished three types of human being: those who apart from grace have a secure conscience, those who feel the affliction of their troubled consciences, and those whom God consoles and sets at peace.⁸⁴

The *Dispositio*'s treatment of Romans 6 ignored baptism, concentrating on the reasons that faith produces good works. Arguing with syllogistic examinations of other conclusions, Melanchthon demonstrated that those who have died with Christ produce good works.⁸⁵ In 1532 and 1540, he used Paul's baptismal discussion here to focus solely on the mortification of sinful desires and the vivification of the sinner as a faith-filled believer. Melanchthon rejected the accusation of Johannes Cochlaeus and other sycophants and sophists that the "Lutherans" denied the necessity of good works, demonstrating, in 1532, with syllogisms in detail that the *vivificatio* here described arises from "trust in God's mercy, by which we know certainly that our sins are remitted because of Christ, not because of our own contrition and good works."⁸⁶ "Conversion"—daily repentance—results from the gift of the Holy Spirit, who puts sinful natures to death and initiates the new nature, by imputation of righteousness and by moving the new nature to new obedience. The tomb of the cross, through which the devil "troubles

---

⁸²Melanchthon, *Commentarii* 1532, pp. N4b-N7a; *Commentarii* 1540, pp. CXLa-CXLIIIIb; *Commentary on Romans*, pp. 125-29; cf. similar arguments on Rom 8:26-27, pp. 180-81.
⁸³Melanchthon, *Enarratio*, pp. g3b-g5b.
⁸⁴Melanchthon, *Annotationes*, pp. E2b-F4b.
⁸⁵Melanchthon, *Dispositio*, pp. D1a-D4b.
⁸⁶Melanchthon, *Commentarii* 1532, pp. Q6b, R1b (Q5b-S3b).

and persecutes the godly in horrible ways," is countered by the Spirit's giving "new light and new impulses" for the godly life.[87] The 1556 commentary did not mention the sacrament; it recommended distinguishing law and gospel as the key to the chapter's interpretation and employed Aristotle's "causal" structure to demonstrate that the Holy Spirit is the "effecting" factor, killing the old nature and creating a new nature by his ruling the converted heart in order to attain the goal, the final factor, obedience to "God's immovable order" (*ordo Dei immotus*), expressed in good works.[88]

Romans 7–8. Melanchthon viewed Romans 7 as a description of the struggle that goes on because believers are *simul justus et peccator*, in Luther's seldom-used expression in the eschatological battle, which both Wittenberg professors frequently treat.[89] The mystery of the continuation of sin and evil in the lives of the faithful stood at the heart of Wittenberg perceptions of the Christian life, expressed in the concept of the necessity of daily dying to sin and being raised up to new life in Christ. In 1522 Melanchthon used Romans 7:14-20 to criticize those scholastics who did not view concupiscence as sinful desires. In the midst of that struggle, Romans 8:1 reminds believers that Christ has satisfied the law and that God does not impute their sins to them.[90] The dispute over concupiscence played a lesser role in the 1532 commentary, though Melanchthon continued to use these verses to emphasize the believer's need for continuing repentance in the battle against sin. The initial verses of chapter 8 provided occasion for a longer treatment of Christ's role as mediator for sinners, who are to recognize that the law's goal is to bring them to faith in Christ, not to terrorize them. Faith, however, produces good works.[91]

The 1540 commentary on Romans 7–8 also treats the sinner's struggle, describing it as the "soldiering and captivity," "powerful words... indicating the virulence of the impulses" in this struggle between the Holy Spirit and Satan, between "true fear and true trust" in Christ and sinful impulses. The only answer to Paul's agonized question, "Who can deliver me?" is Christ himself, for those who walk in him are not condemned (Rom 8:1). Here

---

[87]Melanchthon, *Commentarii* 1540, pp. CLXb-CLXIXa; *Commentary on Romans*, pp. 144-51.
[88]Melanchthon, *Enarratio*, pp. 69a-73.
[89]Rudolf Hermann, *Luthers These, 'Gerecht und Sünder zugleich'* (Gütersloh: Bertelsmann, 1930).
[90]Melanchthon, *Annotationes*, pp. F3a-F4a.
[91]Melanchthon, *Commentarii* 1532, pp. S5a-V1a.

Melanchthon also highlighted the destruction of sin by Christ as a sacrificial victim, who became a "curse" (Gal 3:13) to abolish or destroy his people's sin.[92] To aid comprehension of this battle, Melanchthon explained what Paul meant by "flesh" and "spirit," following Luther in defining "flesh" as all that transpires in a person apart from the Holy Spirit, including those things that are good when serving bodily life but misplaced and misused when used to assert one's goodness apart from the Spirit. This carnality is hostile to God and doubts him. Those caught in this "flesh" are dead. The battle against the "flesh" is aided by the afflictions felt by the saints, as discipline, not as a way of earning merit before God.[93]

Romans 9-16. The second half of Romans provided Melanchthon with material for discussing a number of doctrinal and ethical issues important to him. As examples, this chapter focuses on limited portions of his detailed treatment of these chapters. Melanchthon's treatment of Romans 9-11, especially Romans 9, changed significantly between 1522 and 1556, reflecting his retreat from full-blown support of Luther's views of necessity as a philosophical category to explain God's lordship over all things to a more nuanced view of contingency. His criticism of Erasmus's position on the freedom of the will, however, remained strong, and his emphasis on salvation by grace alone never wavered. This shift deserves a study in itself and has been discussed elsewhere, at least in part.[94]

The instruction for Christian living found in Romans 12-16 was certainly important for Melanchthon, commanding roughly its "fair share" of comment in Melanchthon's treatments: one-eighth (1522, 1529), one-fourth (1532), one-third (1540) and one-fifth (1556). Although his chief concern, reflecting Paul's, he believed, centered on consolation of troubled consciences after bringing them to repentance, Melanchthon also wished to give

---

[92]Melanchthon, *Commentarii* 1540, pp. CLXXVIIIb-CXCIb; *Commentary on Romans*, pp. 160-72.
[93]Melanchthon, *Commentarii* 1540, pp. CLXXXVIb-CXCVb; *Commentary on Romans*, pp. 167-75.
[94]Melanchthon, *Annotationes*, pp. H1a-H4b. On Melanchthon's critique of Erasmus on the subject, see Wengert, *Human Freedom, Christian Righteousness: Philipp Melanchthon's Exegetical Dispute with Erasmus of Rotterdam* (New York: Oxford University Press, 1998), esp. pp. 67-109; cf. Robert Kolb, *Bound Choice, Election, and Wittenberg Theological Method from Martin Luther to the Formula of Concord* (Grand Rapids: Eerdmans, 2005), pp. 70-102; and Kolb, "Melanchthon's Influence on the Exegesis of His Students: The Case of Romans 9," in *Philipp Melanchthon (1497-1560) and the Commentary*, ed. M. Patrick Graham and Timothy J. Wengert (Sheffield: Sheffield Academic Press, 1997), pp. 198-217.

readers aid in cultivating Christian virtues and in preaching on the majority of ethical lessons in the pericopes of the church year, which came from the latter chapters. He made clear that Romans 12 presents "an admonition concerning morals, or laws which direct the justified person," the new person.[95] It begins "a new part consisting of precepts about good works" or new obedience, "a certain beginning of fulfilling the law." Good works include inward—fear of God, faith, love, repentance, patience and invocation of God—and outward virtues. Not the coercive power of the law but God's mercy moves believers to this new obedience.[96] Throughout, Melanchthon underscored the necessity of faith in Christ as the impulse that brings good works into being.[97] "Putting on Christ" (Rom 13:14) "signifies not merely imitation" but rather "to apprehend Christ by faith and to believe that because of him the Father is kindly-disposed toward us."[98]

Melanchthon envisioned the Christian life as a life of sacrifice. He set the stage for treating new obedience by distinguishing spiritual from ceremonial sacrifices and Christ's propitiatory sacrifice, which takes away sin, from the spiritual sacrifices of believers in thanksgiving and mortifying the flesh.[99] Melanchthon's comments affirmed the godliness of all walks of life, for example, in God's ordinance of civil government.[100]

Indeed, he had earlier treated new obedience when the text suggested it. Romans 8:25 gave him grounds to discuss patience within a psychological framework: "According to the judgment of reason [patience] is a certain obedience to reason which moderates grief and forbids us when overcome by some grief, anger, or greed, to act unrighteously." Christian patience adds to this natural reasoning three other causes: God's command, the gospel's explanation that afflictions are not signs of God's wrath but of his good will, and his promise of help. Even in the midst of afflictions believers find cause to glorify God.[101]

---

[95] Melanchthon, *Annotationes*, p. K1a.
[96] Melanchthon, *Commentarii* 1540, pp. CCXXXIIa-CCXXXIIIb; *Commentary on Romans*, pp. 209-10.
[97] Melanchthon, *Commentarii* 1540, pp. CCXXXIIIb-CCXXXIIIIb; *Commentary on Romans*, pp. 210-11.
[98] Melanchthon, *Commentarii* 1540, p. CCLa-b; *Commentary on Romans*, p. 225.
[99] Melanchthon, *Commentarii* 1540, pp. CCXXXIIIIb-CCXXXVIIa; *Commentary on Romans*, pp. 211-13.
[100] Melanchthon, *Commentarii* 1540, pp. CCXLa-CCXLVa; *Commentary on Romans*, pp. 216-20.
[101] Melanchthon, *Commentarii* 1540, pp. CXCIXb-CCIIa; *Commentary on Romans*, pp. 179-81.

Romans 14 posed topics related to the life of the church as well as the individual, and these practical issues also commanded Melanchthon's attention. His deep concern for the practical problems of church life and his revulsion against superstitious practices in medieval popular piety, as well as his desire to free Christians from burdensome laws imposed by the medieval church regarding ritual practice, led him to treat liturgy and pious practices. He explained ritual or ceremonies as means of teaching and building faith in Christ, and laid out his understanding of ceremonies as *adiaphora*. That led him to discuss Christian liberty, in four degrees: freedom (1) from sin, (2) for new obedience through the Holy Spirit, (3) from ceremonies and Mosaic regulations and (4) from the necessity of keeping precise prescriptions in order to attain salvation. Offense arises from pharisaical scandal, hypocritical insistence on something not commanded by God, and wicked doctrine or action that causes the weak to stumble.[102]

Conclusion

Melanchthon's detailed hermeneutical foundations, formulated above all in his *argumentum*, fulfilled a large part of the purpose of his commentaries: to prepare his students and other readers to proclaim and teach God's Word to his people. His exegetical treatment therefore did go into significant detail in comparison with his theological discussion of the concepts he found in Paul's address of the gospel to the Romans. He believed that Paul faced the same basic human situation that he confronted fifteen hundred years later: the pious as well as those outside God's people tended to put confidence in their own efforts along with or as a substitute for trusting in God. God's intervention into a world of sin in Jesus Christ offered the solution to Jew and Gentile, to the unbaptized and baptized alike: repentance and forgiveness of sins constituted the rhythm of daily life that Paul had proposed and that Melanchthon's contemporaries needed to practice so that they would enjoy a life of new obedience. From that message, which he found set forth most clearly in Romans, Melanchthon believed the church lived. Therefore, the epistle presented a method for reading all of Scripture.

---

[102]Melanchthon, *Commentarii* 1540, pp. CCLVIa-CCLXIb; *Commentary on Romans*, pp. 230-36, cf. pp. 285-87.

4

THE TEXT *of* ROMANS *and the* THEOLOGY *of* MELANCHTHON

The Preceptor of the Germans and the Apostle to the Gentiles

Mark Seifrid

THE READING OF THE REFORMERS as interpreters of Scripture is unquestionably a salutary exercise. As in any reading of past interpreters of Scripture, it brings us the reminder that we are neither the first nor the last to engage the text. Whether we are aware of it or not, in one way or another, we have been shaped by the tradition of interpretation that we have received. In recent decades, biblical scholarship generally has become more aware of the significance of "reception history." That is a good thing. One of the common afflictions of the guild has been the imagination that we sit before the text as unbiased observers and by the power of our intellect bring forth stunning new insights, unimagined by anyone before us. It is often the case that what is insightful in our work is not original, and what is original is not insightful.[1] Ours is not the first word of interpretation, and neither will it be the last. We are called to receive that which has been

---

[1] Attributed to a discussant at a finance conference. See "Famous Economists' Most Biting Put-Downs," Economics Job Market Rumors, www.econjobrumors.com/topic/famous-economists-most-biting-put-downs/page/2.

given to us critically yet gratefully. We are likewise obligated to speak the truth of Scripture afresh in our time, with the awareness that we hand on only a partial and incomplete interpretation of the inexhaustible and unfathomable wisdom of Scripture. In that spirit, we may consider Philipp Melanchthon's interpretation of Romans.

Melanchthon's Reading and the Question of Historical Consciousness

In reading the Preceptor, one immediately becomes aware that we moderns assign an interpretive significance to historical context, background and situation that sets us apart from him. And Melanchthon is set apart from us by his intense interest in the theology or more precisely the doctrine of the text. Commonalities nevertheless exist. Melanchthon engages the text directly, frequently treating the meaning and significance of various Greek terms. While he occasionally cites church fathers, it is the text of Scripture, and not the commentaries, on which Melanchthon comments.[2] Erasmus's call *ad fontes* makes itself apparent here. Yet in contrast to modern interpretation, Melanchthon's reading of Romans is strikingly doctrinal and systematic in orientation, less oriented to the particularities of first-century Christians in Rome than to the theological debates of sixteenth-century Germany. That is not to say that Melanchthon lacks historical sensibility and interest. It was fundamental to his humanistic training. But the explanatory power that came to be attributed to history in the nineteenth century and has endured since then is alien to him. In accord with his humanistic training, he is much more interested in the fundamental ideas and basic concepts that he perceives in Romans than he is in the historical context of the letter.[3] In his reading of Romans, he is guided hermeneuti-

---

[2]See previous chapter, p. 78.
[3]See previous chapter, pp. 76-78. Melanchthon had come to regard Paul as rhetorically capable, and by 1529 had developed a detailed analysis of the disposition of his argument in Romans that informs his commentary. Rolf Schäfer has extracted Melanchthon's detailed construction of that *dispositio* and presented it in an appendix to the text of the 1532 commentary (MWA 5:374-78). While the outline is not without value, it is apparent how the *loci*, i.e., the basic concepts, dominate the analysis. Melanchthon's discussion of Paul's treatment of Jewish privilege in Rom 3:1-9 is basically on the mark, but the passage is hardly a digression as Melanchthon has it. He likewise understands Rom 4:1-25 as *confirmatio* of Paul's preceding argument concerning justification, which it certainly is. But he "sandwiches" it into the argument on justification by including Rom 5:1-11 as a confirming epilogue within the first, large movement of Paul's argument (thus missing the

cally by the aim of discovering the arguments within a text (*inventio*) and the topics (*loci*) that thereby emerge.⁴ It is in this way that antiquity offers us instruction.

Consequently, the insights that Melanchthon draws from the text almost invariably have to do with the topics of righteousness, faith, the law, works, grace and the like in their universal and abiding significance.⁵ As Robert Kolb has noted in his companion chapter to this one, the commentary on Romans serves as a companion piece to the prior *Loci communes* (first published in 1521), setting forth the same subjects "in plainer form," as Melanchthon himself indicates in the 1540 edition of the commentary.⁶ Melanchthon is a teacher, not a preacher, and not a historian in the modern sense of the term. He is especially concerned with doctrine. Above all else, Melanchthon is concerned with the doctrine of justification, which he regards as the principle and particular *locus* of Paul's theology, and indeed of all Christian theology and Scripture.⁷ In fact, he was working through his own, new understanding of justification in the period during which he produced the 1532 commentary.⁸ As we have noted, Melanchthon conceives of the historical task as retrieving universally valid truths from the ancient sources, especially from the Scriptures. His interpretation of the text is therefore bound to differ from ours, which is conditioned by a historical awareness that Melanchthon did not share.

Melanchthon may not have recognized it fully, but his commentary was just as occasional as was Paul's letter to Rome. His apologetic and

---

christological turn in Paul's argument that we will take up below). Here it is important to note that Abraham, "our father according to the flesh," can hardly be understood as a mere example (note that Melanchthon omits the significant phrase "according to the flesh"). The question of Abraham's circumcision in Rom 4:9-12 is not merely one of ceremonies and sacraments, but again the lively and controversial question of Jewish privilege. Melanchthon likewise has difficulty assimilating Paul's argument in Rom 9–11 (on which see below).

⁴See Robert Stupperich, *Melanchthon*, trans. R. H. Fischer (Philadelphia: Westminster, 1965), pp. 44-45, and previous chapter in this volume, pp. 76-78.

⁵In complete revolt against Melanchthon's *loci*, contemporary evangelical interpretation seems to have become enamored with the construction of a "story line" for the interpretation of Scripture—to its loss.

⁶Melanchthon, *Commentary on Romans*, trans. F. Kramer (St. Louis: Concordia, 1992), p. 15; MO 15:499 (*verbis planioribus*).

⁷MWA 5:33.9-14.

⁸See T. J. Wengert, *Law and Gospel: Philip Melanchthon's Debate with John Agricola of Eisleben over Poenitentia* (Grand Rapids: Baker Academic, 1997), pp. 177-85.

didactic aims were simultaneously the product of his personality, his humanistic training and the times in which he lived. He was seeking not only to establish the new, evangelical understanding of Scripture within the Reformational movement and to defend it against its adversaries, but also, rather audaciously, to preserve the unity of Christendom. The 1532 commentary is dedicated to Cardinal Albrecht of Mainz, the very authority who had commissioned the sale of indulgences that prompted the Ninety-Five Theses that Luther posted for debate in 1517. In Melanchthon's effort, we perhaps may see the confidence of the humanist theologian that, by the power of the Spirit, human beings will be moved by the arguments of Scripture, and thus by the mercy of God in Christ.[9] In retrospect, we can discern many of the ways in which Melanchthon's time is reflected in his commentary.

We are much less capable of seeing the way in which our own interpretation is shaped by the hour in which we live. Unless (or until) the times again change, however, we live in the wake of the historical consciousness that arose in the nineteenth century, a consciousness that is legitimated in a fundamental way by the Scriptures themselves. With a particularity that is especially scandalous to our time, they announce to us that our salvation has been granted by God through a specific people and culture, at particular times and places. The message of Scripture cannot be extracted from the history in which it was given without damage. The rise in interest in canonical and theological interpretation of Scripture notwithstanding, there is no going back behind the historical awareness that shapes most contemporary interpretation, nor should there be. We are aware, of course, of the dangers of historical-critical interpretation, not least of which is its tendency (in its own systematizing manner) to set up one text against another. We are likewise familiar with the dangers of atomizing interpretation, or of reconstructed backgrounds (even salvation-historical ones) that do not allow the text to speak, and of a historicism that would relegate the text to the past or relativize its voice. So long as one maintains a serious doctrine of inspiration of the Scripture, it is both necessary and proper to seek to

---

[9]Thus the conclusion of Melanchthon's introductory letter to Albrecht (MWA 5:29.19-21): "God preserve you, most illustrious Princeps, and guide your mind to the glory of Christ, which illuminates and enlarges (sc. the mind), and to the soundness of the Christian church! Amen."

hear a single voice within the Scriptures that speaks in an unequivocal way to us and to our salvation. Nevertheless, even when one takes into account the problems of contemporary interpretation, the modern concern with the historical particularities of the biblical texts is to be regarded as a benefit, not a deficit. Rightly hearing Paul's letter to the Roman Christians within its immediate context only can help us hear it as God's word to us today. At least in some measure, we thereby avoid reading ourselves and our concerns into the Scriptures. We come close to the message of the text only by allowing its distance from us and thus by hearing it as an external word. In this sense, we must stand at a distance from Melanchthon.

That is not to say that Melanchthon's reading of Romans as a *compendium doctrinae Christianae* is to be rejected.[10] It merely must be qualified by historical considerations. Paul writes to a church (or, more precisely, a circle of house churches) that he did not found and whose faith he recognizes. He does so in preparation for his long hoped-for visit there as apostle to the Gentiles, and lays out his gospel *in extenso* before them as an invitation to accept him and his message. In this sense, which is not insignificant, Romans offers a summary of Paul's apostolic teaching.

Yet Romans is undeniably an occasional letter. It reflects the transition that was taking place more broadly in earliest Christianity in the middle of the first century. As he writes the letter, Paul regards his work in the eastern part of the Mediterranean complete: "from Jerusalem as far around as Illyricum, I have fulfilled the Gospel of Christ" (Rom 15:19).[11] Faith in Jesus as the Messiah of Israel, which began with a small Jewish sect in Judea, had become a largely Gentile movement, spread across the eastern part of the Roman Empire and even to Rome itself. Paul can no longer find room in the East for the pioneering evangelism to which he is called (Rom 15:23) and therefore hopes to travel to Spain with the help of the Roman Christians (Rom 15:25). As was the case elsewhere, Christianity was becoming a largely Gentile phenomenon in Rome. Jewish believers who had planted the faith in Rome now found themselves in the minority within the circle of house churches that had sprouted up there. Judaism was the mother of the first

---

[10] On this question see Robert L. Plummer, "Melanchthon as Interpreter of the New Testament," *WTJ* 62 (2002): 257-65.

[11] Unless otherwise indicated, all Scripture quotations in this chapter are my own translation.

believers in Jesus, but for these new Gentile converts, it was their mother-in-law.[12]

The difference between a mother and a mother-in-law quickly becomes apparent in Paul's letter to Rome. He has delayed his travel to Rome on account of the uncultured "barbarians" in the provinces.[13] Now he indicates that the material need of Jewish believers in Jerusalem has pushed Rome to the periphery of his agenda. Before Paul comes to Rome, he plans to travel to Jerusalem with a gift from Macedonia and Achaia for "the poor of the saints" in Jerusalem (Rom 15:26). His delay in traveling to Rome is theologically motivated, as is his communication of his plans to the Roman Christians. The gift for Jerusalem takes priority over apostolic ministry in Rome (Rom 15:25-29). Rome might have been the center of the ancient world, but it did not stand at the center of Paul's world. If Paul's travel plans did not provide an affront to the Roman Christians, they at least must have seemed very strange. Against their expectations, he explains the propriety and indeed the necessity of the gift for Jerusalem. For Paul, no less than for John, "salvation is of the Jews." The son of God is of the seed of David, according to the flesh (Rom 1:3; see Rom 9:3-5). Jewish believers have shared their "spiritual things" with the Gentiles, who are now obligated to serve them in the lesser matter of "fleshly [i.e., material] things" (Rom 15:27). Indeed, the gospel has created an abiding link between Gentile believers in Christ and believing Israel that runs a deep root into the soil of God's goodness (Rom 11:16-24). Paul thus inserts himself provocatively into tensions within the believing community in Rome within the letter. The Gentile majority in Rome was ready to dispense with the remaining vestiges of Jewish practice in favor of a fully Gentile identity (Rom 14:1-23). For them, the conservative Jewish minority that maintained its observance of food laws and the Sabbath could be nothing other than an embarrassment. In accepting the practices of the "weak" (as he names them), Paul defends "boundary markers" of Jewish identity that in part continue to characterize the believing community, while at the same time decisively dissociating

---

[12]Jaroslav Pelikan, *The Christian Tradition: A History of the Development of Doctrine 1: The Emergence of the Catholic Tradition (100-600)* (Chicago: University of Chicago Press, 1971), p. 14.

[13]As he informs the Roman Christians, he has been prevented from visiting them until now by his obligation to proclaim the gospel to the unreached. He hints at this in the opening of the letter and makes it clear in the closing (Rom 1:13-15; 15:14-22).

them from any saving significance. He thereby calls the Gentile majority to bear the weaknesses of the powerless, following the pattern of "the Christ," who bore the reproaches directed against God (Rom 15:1-3; Ps 68:10 LXX [ET Ps 69:9]). They are thereby called to bear the scandal of the particularity of God's saving work in the world, as they glorify God "with one mouth" together with their Jewish brothers and sisters (Rom 15:5-13).

Consequently, Romans 9–11 is not to be read as an appendix to Romans 1–8, but as its necessary complement. The gospel retains its earthly roots. Paul's lament for his people and the love for them that he openly expresses to this Gentile church are intended to be much more than an example (Rom 9:1-5). The benefits granted to Israel are real and retain all their particularity, even if they have not yet come to fruition (Rom 9:1-5; 11:29). It is the sheer mercy of God that has been granted to Gentiles in Rome and elsewhere, a mercy that is received only where it is recognized as arising from the Creator, who acts in freedom (Rom 9:14-21; 11:22). Mercy and "hardening" thus lie within this absolute and unconditioned divine freedom, human responsibility notwithstanding (Rom 9:18). Blindness is overcome only by the gift of sight (Rom 9:30-33; 10:1-4; 11:8-11). Indeed, according to Paul, the work of God bears its paradoxical form within the world precisely in order to preserve the freedom of God's mercy: the Gentiles who did not seek God have met him; Israel, who zealously seeks God, has not found him (Rom 9:30-33; 11:8-10). The recipients of mercy have dramatically shifted and shall do so yet again in the course of God's unfathomable ways (Rom 11:25-27). As Paul instructs his Gentile readers, "God has consigned all to disobedience, in order that he might have mercy on all" (Rom 11:32). Against the natural course of events, Gentile believers in Rome have been given to share in the promises granted to the patriarchs of Israel. They stand by faith alone and thus are to remain within the sheer kindness of God (Rom 11:20-21). A Gentile church is not the final act on the stage of history. It is the salvation of Israel that will bring the curtain down, as God ends its disobedience in his coming (in Christ) "from Zion."[14] The story ends with a reversal just

---

[14] We need not worry here about defining the limits of "Israel." Paul does not bother to delimit precisely what he has in mind, because his concern is with the corporate realities of Israel and the nations. He obviously does not regard all Jews of all time as the recipients of salvation, otherwise he could not lament his kinspeople or speak of a remnant in the present.

as dramatic as the proclamation of the gospel to the Gentiles.[15]

Melanchthon had difficulties with the unconditioned divine freedom that appears in Romans 9-11 and ended up diluting it in favor of the contingency of human response. We shall return to this issue shortly. Our concern at the moment is to note something of the ethnic dynamic of Romans, which arises from its historical context, and which largely goes missing on Melanchthon.[16] He, as well as most other reformers, shared in the supersessionism, or more mildly put, "replacement theology," that had long been part of church doctrine.[17] Undoubtedly, the shame of the Holocaust and the history of Christian mistreatment of Jews have had their impact on us, so that we read the New Testament with different eyes. Likewise, the effects of globalization and of massive immigration into Western countries have sharpened our eyes to the ethnic dimension of Paul's argument. But before all else, it is again the need to read the material within a well-defined historical setting that distances us from Melanchthon's reading of Romans, and thus from his interpretation of Romans 9-11.

Admittedly, historical interpretation is not infallible and may sometimes lead us astray. Contemporary attempts at a "correction" of the reformers (and especially of Melanchthon's senior companion, Luther) base them-

---

[15] The οὕτως of Rom 11:26 ("And *in this way* all Israel shall be saved") should be given its full weight. The "entrance" of the Gentiles, which marks Israel's disobedience, must be completed before God "turns away godlessness from Jacob" (Rom 11:27, in remarkable alteration of Is 59:20).

[16] Admittedly Melanchthon offers a historical background to Paul's argument in Rom 9-11, claiming that he is responding to the objections of "the Jews" that the Christ could not yet have appeared because the promises (which were for all the people and the entire Jewish state) had not been fulfilled. The apostles argued that the promises had been fulfilled but that it was the few who believed who constituted the people of God. This reconstruction is not distant from the paradigm of Israel's continuing exile now proposed by N. T. Wright, *The New Testament and the People of God*, Christian Origins and the Question of God 1 (Minneapolis: Fortress, 1992), pp. 244-338. But (in both instances) it fails to find a foothold in the text of Romans itself. Moreover, Melanchthon quickly transposes the situation to his own time, in which the true church and the false church contended with each other. See *Commentary on Romans*, pp. 185-86; MO 15:677-80.

[17] Likewise chiliastic theology had long been in disrepute, and all the more in Melanchthon's time, when horrifying forms of it appeared. But the "mystery" of Israel's salvation that Paul makes known to the Gentiles in Rome does not require and in fact contradicts a premillennial reading of the text, even if it also requires a revision of most amillennial theology. In the first place, for Paul the salvation of Israel coincides with the coming of "the Redeemer from Zion" and the resurrection of the dead (Rom 11:15, 26-27), seemingly leaving no place for an earthly rule prior to the eschaton. Furthermore, the idea of a present, unqualified millennial rule of Christ through the church would seem to cut off the hope of Israel's final salvation that Paul rather clearly presents in the text (Rom 11:11-16, 25-32).

selves without exception on historical context. The "new perspective on Paul" (which itself has now grown old) trades on the argument that first-century Jews regarded themselves as objects of divine election. Salvation did not depend on "getting into" God's grace. One needed only to "stay in" the divine grace of Israel's election.[18] Where "guilt" was recognized, it was understood as *Israel's* guilt, the corporate reality of a continuing exile, manifest in the outward circumstance of Jewish subjugation to Rome.[19] What Paul attacks in Romans and elsewhere is the "sin" of exclusivity, the false imagination of first-century Jews that the promise of salvation belonged to them alone. They did not suffer from a tormented conscience or desperately search for a "gracious God," as did Luther and Melanchthon. Those concerns, it is argued, are largely a projection of the concerns of the reformers on to the text. The real problem was the refusal of first-century Jews to share the benefits of the divine covenant with Gentiles. Doesn't this problem turn out to be very much like that of comfortable Western Christians at the turn of the twenty-first century who need to be roused into sharing their abundance with the many in need within our world?

As right and true as it is that we as Western Christians need to be called afresh to our duty to share our material wealth with those who are without the basic necessities, one may question which party is more guilty of projecting their concerns on to Scripture. Historical consciousness does not in itself deliver us from anachronism. The question of adherence to the law, and the "boundary markers" within Judaism between the pious and the wicked—that is, boundaries between the heirs of salvation and those who had cut themselves off from it—have been discussed at length and need not be repeated here. It suffices to note that Jesus' table fellowship with "sinners" was a scandal to the pious and corresponds with the sort of boundary markers that are drawn in the sectarian literature of Second Temple Judaism. Paul's persecution of the earliest church was based on the same sort of "boundary marking." The advocates of Judaizing gained traction within the Pauline churches in Galatia and elsewhere only because taking on Jewish

---

[18] As is generally recognized, the starting point of this "new perspective" is found in K. Stendahl, "The Apostle Paul and the Introspective Conscience of the West," *Harvard Theological Review* 56 (1963): 199-215; and E. P. Sanders, *Paul and Palestinian Judaism: A Comparison of Patterns of Religion* (Philadelphia: Fortress, 1977).
[19] See again Wright, *New Testament and the People of God*, pp. 244-338.

identity appeared to offer saving benefits that had not been secured fully by the gospel itself. As Paul's letter to Galatia makes clear, the Jewish-Christian missionaries who have gained a reception within the churches were by no means shy about sharing the benefits of Israel's election with Gentiles. That was, in fact, the point of their mission! But those benefits were contingent on circumcision and a commitment to obedience to the law. The same may be said of the rhetorical figure of the Jew who appears in Paul's diatribe in Romans 2:17-29. The "new perspective on Paul" remains attractive in our time largely because it speaks to the felt needs of our contemporaries and because it seems (but only seems) to avoid anti-Semitism. While it may have sharpened our understanding of the biblical texts and early Jewish literature, it is not validated by them.

Indeed, the new perspective on Paul has misunderstood him in two ways. In the first place, so long as "works of the law" cannot be reduced to mere ethnic emblems, but also mark those who are truly pious and godly (and thus the heirs of salvation), Paul must be understood to be addressing the question of human goodness in his attack on the thought that such "works" contribute to salvation. Yet it is precisely the issue of "doing good and sharing" with which current forms of the new perspective have come to be concerned. It stands beyond question that Paul has a place for "the new obedience" and for doing good. But it is not the first place. That place is reserved for the unqualified love and giving of God in Christ to rebels, enemies and sinners, in whose number we are all included. Melanchthon sees this matter clearly. At least as far as I have read, advocates of the new perspective have thus far failed to make the sharp distinction between faith and works that secures God's place as the first place in the way that the apostle has done.

Second, the ethnic dimension of Paul's argument in Romans, especially as it appears in Romans 9–11, provides the same warning to the advocates of the new perspective. As we have noted, it is not the triumph of a Gentile church that Paul presents as the culmination of God's work within the world, but the salvation of (ethnic) Israel. For Paul, God has set a boundary, a limit to human striving for and doing good, not only in his work in Christ, but also in his work in the world. In all its deeds and works, our life remains one of witness to the coming kingdom. It can never become the means by which the kingdom shall be brought into the world. This understanding has gone missing on the various advocates of the new perspective, as well as on a good portion of evangelical Christianity.

Melanchthon's Reading and the Theology of Romans: Problems and Questions

What then shall we make of Melanchthon's theological interpretation of Romans? We already have noted Melanchthon's difficulty in coming to terms with the relationship between the freedom of the Creator and the responsibility of the human in Romans 9–11. The 1532 commentary on Romans may, in fact, have marked a turning point in Melanchthon's thought on this question.[20] While in the 1521 *Loci* he affirms that the mercy of God is the "true cause" of election, in the 1532 commentary he argues that "*another* cause lies in one who accepts that mercy, in so far as they do not repudiate the promise (of justification) offered to them."[21] Of course, no one can accept the promise of mercy or begin to believe apart from the Spirit moving the heart through the word to receive the gospel. Our response is one of passive reception, and even that reception is aided by the Spirit. We need only not to resist the promise given to us. On this account, for Melanchthon, the (partial) cause of salvation located within the human will does not detract from justification by faith in mercy.[22] This change in understanding marked the rest of Melanchthon's thought and appears in

---

[20]See G. B. Graybill, *Evangelical Free Will: Philipp Melanchthon's Doctrinal Journey on the Origins of Faith* (New York: Oxford University Press, 2010), pp. 199-223. The whole of this study is highly informative. Likewise, see Wengert, *Law and Gospel*, pp. 200-206.

[21]MWA 5:254.9-12. Likewise, in his discussion of predestination in the 1543 *Loci communes*, Melanchthon affirms that God is the cause of our election, but asserts that "there is some cause or reason in the one who accepts" (sc. the promise; Melanchthon, *Loci communes, 1543*, trans. J. A. O. Preus [St. Louis: Concordia, 1992], p. 173; MO 21:916). After Luther's death, Melanchthon expressed an even more fully defined affirmation of human freedom that stood in complete contrast to Luther's view: "The free will in the human being is the ability to apply oneself to grace, that is, one hears the promise and attempts to assent to it, and rejects sins against the conscience" (MWA 2.1:245.30-33 [*Loci praecipui theologici* {1559}]; Melanchthon, *The Chief Theological Topics: Loci Praecipui Theologici 1559*, trans. J. A. O. Preus [St. Louis: Concordia, 2010], p. 62). In a letter to Elector August of Saxony dated March 9, 1559, Melanchthon charges that Luther's *De servo arbitrio* is filled with Stoic and Manichean errors (MO 9:763-65 [no. 6705]; Graybill, *Evangelical Free Will*, p. 310).

[22]MWA 5:254.12-255.4. On this problematic, see O. Bayer, "Freiheit? Das Verständnis des Menschen bei Luther und Melanchthon im Vergleich," in *Zugesagte Gegenwart* (Tübingen: Mohr Siebeck, 2007), pp. 246-71.

subsequent editions of his Romans commentary, as well as those of his *Loci communes*.

It comes as no surprise that Melanchthon's comments on Romans 9-11, and especially on Romans 9, are relatively thin. In the 1532 commentary, he offers no discussion of such texts as Romans 8:29-30 and Romans 9:11.[23] His (brief) comments on Romans 9:14-18 suggest that these gaps appear because he is working out his (new) doctrine of "evangelical free will"[24]—a contradiction in terms!—within the doctrine of justification. It is this doctrine that he regards as the larger argument of Romans and the proper context for understanding predestination and election.[25] It is not unlikely that his interpretive hermeneutic of dialectical and rhetorical analysis led him to seek a rational coherence in the text, and thus to avoid the profound paradoxes that are inherent to Paul's message. As much as possible, the argument of Romans had to make sense to human reason: God is not the author of sin.[26] Melanchthon's attempt to encapsulate Paul's statements about predestination and election within his own developing understanding of justification also led him into difficulty with the text of Romans.

We need not pursue this theological issue, which was worked out within Lutheranism in the Formula of Concord (1577). Our interest rests in the underlying anthropological orientation of Melanchthon's thought that contributed to his conception of an "evangelical free will." This anthropological orientation leads Melanchthon to an anthropological construction of salvation that in other significant ways stands at odds with Paul's christocentric presentation of it in Romans.

We may note in this context that in his conception of the saving event, and particularly in his understanding of justification, Melanchthon differs not only from Paul but also from Luther. That is not to say that Melanchthon

---

[23]In the 1540 edition of the Romans commentary, Melanchthon takes up the questions of election and predestination in Rom 8:30; 9:7-11, 14-16, 18-24. Now, however, he interprets these doctrines *ecclesiologically*. It is the church that God has elected and predestined. Only those who do not resist God's grace and call in Christ belong to the church. On this topic, see R. Kolb, *Philip Melanchthon (1497-1560) and the Commentary*, ed. T. J. Wengert and M. P. Graham (Sheffield: Sheffield Academic Press, 1997), pp. 194-215.

[24]I am borrowing this apt description from Graybill, *Evangelical Free Will*, pp. 199-223, esp. pp. 220-23.

[25]This is the well-defended thesis of Graybill, *Evangelical Free Will*.

[26]See Melanchthon, *Commentary on Romans*, p. 192 (on Rom 9:18-24); MO 15:685.

makes a fatal error in this matter, even if in his time he was suspected of doing so. Luther recognized and approved Melanchthon's understanding of justification, even if he had his concerns about his younger colleague—and it was the doctrine of justification that served them both as the summary of God's saving work in Christ. Nevertheless, the two conceived of justification quite differently: "What Melanchthon sought to make clear by doctrinal definitions, Luther explained by pointing to the actuality of the believer's communion with Christ. Here lay the deepest difference between them."[27]

Wilhelm Pauck makes his point, which as far as I can discern is basically correct, by referring to Melanchthon's topical and analytical approach to theology. In a material way, the deepest difference between Melanchthon and Luther may be said to lie in the contrast between the differing anthropological and christological frameworks in which they constructed their understandings of justification. For Luther, the human being is defined, in judgment and salvation, by God's work in Christ. For Melanchthon, God's saving work in Christ must be defined in relationship to the human being, who is conceived a priori in terms of the intellect, the affections and the will.[28] It is well beyond the purpose of this chapter to engage in a detailed theological comparison of Luther and Melanchthon on the nature of justification. Nevertheless, the difference between them on this question cannot be or at least should not be overlooked.

Whether one attributes it to his anthropological orientation, to his topical approach to Romans or to both, Melanchthon misses the decisive christological shift in the argument of Romans that appears in Paul's announcement of our "peace with God through Christ Jesus our Lord" and continues through the body of the letter, all the way up to his announcement of the Redeemer who will come from Zion, bringing salvation (Rom 5:1–11:36).

---

[27]Wilhelm Pauck, "Luther and Melanchthon," in *Luther and Melanchthon in the History and Theology of the Reformation*, ed. V. Vatja (Philadelphia: Muhlenberg, 1961), p. 22. On this question, see Mark A. Seifrid, "Luther, Melanchthon and Paul on the Question of Imputation: Recommendations on a Current Debate," in *Justification: What's at Stake in the Current Debates*, ed. M. Husbands and D. J. Treier (Downers Grove, IL: InterVarsity Press, 2004), pp. 137-52; F. Nüssel, *Allein aus Glauben: Zur Entwicklung der Rechtfertigungslehre in der konkordistischen und frühen nachkonkordistischen Theologie*, Forschungen zur systematischen und ökumenischen Theologie 95 (Göttingen: Vandenhoeck & Ruprecht, 2000), pp. 31-61.

[28]Because he understands salvation christologically, divine determinism is the source of comfort for Luther (WA 18:783.17-39; *De servo arbitrio*). Because he understands salvation anthropologically, divine determinism is a source of discomfort for Melanchthon (MO 21:232; 1533 *Loci*).

This "turn to Christ" bears considerable theological significance. In the first movement of his argument, Paul presents God's saving work under the topic of "faith," which as the reception of the revelation of God's righteousness constitutes the rejection of "works of the Law" as the means of justification and yet also constitutes the fulfillment of the law (Rom 1:16–4:25). Christ—crucified and risen—appears within the argument, but primarily in its conclusion as the *locus* of the revelation of God's righteousness (Rom 3:21-26) and as the *locus* of our justification (Rom 4:24-25).[29] In both instances, Paul anticipates the shift in topic from "faith" to "Christ" that he introduces in Romans 5:1. In this second section of his argument he does not speak of faith until his concluding discussion of Israel and the nations, and there only under the topics of the proclaimed Christ (Rom 9:30-33; 10:1-21) and the failure of Israel (Rom 11:17-24).

His change in perspective from the first section to the second becomes particularly evident in his continuing description of the gospel in Romans 5:1–8:39, where (aside from the opening clause) he makes no direct mention whatsoever of faith—the fundamental topic of his preceding argument. Furthermore, he now punctuates the units of his argument with the refrain that he introduces at the outset: "through Jesus Christ, our Lord."[30] Here the title of lordship simultaneously identifies Jesus with God and expresses his saving rule, in which our sin and death have been overcome.[31] Consequently, Paul's opening statement in Romans 5:1 is to be taken not as a mere continuation of his preceding argument but as a defining announcement: "Therefore, being justified by faith, *we have peace with God through our Lord,*

---

[29]Christ appears as eschatological judge in Rom 2:16. In Rom 3:22, Christ appears already as the source of our faith. On the interpretation of "the faith of Christ," see Mark A. Seifrid, "The Faith of Christ," in *The Faith of Jesus Christ: Exegetical, Biblical, and Theological Studies*, ed. M. F. Bird and P. M. Sprinkle (Peabody, MA: Hendrickson, 2010), pp. 129-46.

[30]Rom 5:1, 11, 21; 6:23; 7:25; 8:39. It is noteworthy how the expression appears within the summary statements of each unit of Paul's argument in these chapters. The various forms of the expression correspond to the point of Paul's argument in their respective contexts. In Rom 6:23; 8:39, e.g., where he shifts to "in Christ Jesus, our Lord," he "localizes" salvation and appears to have in view the risen Christ, whom he identifies as Jesus. In the other instances he speaks first of Jesus, whom he identifies as the risen Christ. It is likely significant that Paul, in the first two uses of the expression, speaks of "our Lord, Jesus Christ" (Rom 5:1, 11), thus fronting "Lord" and making the reference to Jesus' lordship emphatic.

[31]I am employing the category of "divine identity" as it has been developed by R. Bauckham, *Jesus and the God of Israel: God Crucified and Other Studies on the New Testament's Christology of Divine Identity* (Grand Rapids: Eerdmans, 2009).

Jesus Christ." Paul is not describing the effect of justifying faith here. He is presenting the means by which justification by faith takes place: "through whom (namely, through our Lord, Jesus Christ) we have come to have the entrance into this grace in which we stand . . ."[32] *Christ himself alone works faith.* This understanding is implicit in Romans 5–8, where, without direct reference to faith, Paul presents the gift of righteousness and the new freedom from sin, law and death as effected for us "in" and "through" Christ. It comes to explicit expression again in these chapters in Romans 6:17, where Paul strikingly inverts the expected form of locution, speaking of the Roman believers as having been delivered over to the gospel, rather than the gospel being delivered over to them. This entire statement is jarring and could not express the effective nature of the gospel more pointedly: "Thanks be to God that you were slaves of sin and you obeyed from the heart the pattern of teaching to which you were delivered, and being freed from sin, you were enslaved to righteousness." Here we find an impenetrable wonder: "you were slaves of sin *and* you obeyed (the gospel)."[33] Indeed, Paul here describes a transfer of lordship from "sin" to "righteousness," which he presents as two personified powers. The gospel for Paul is a *verbum efficax*, a word that effectively calls fallen human beings out of condemnation and death into righteousness and life.[34]

The same ordering of the relationship between faith and God's saving work in Christ appears in Romans 9–11, not least in Paul's well-known defense of the apostolic proclamation: "so then, faith is from the message, and

---

[32]The dative of means τῇ πίστει that appears as a variant reading in this verse ("the entrance we have come to have *by faith*") is probably not original, even if the external evidence is rather evenly balanced. It is not at all clear that the alternative reading ἐν τῇ πίστει (a¹ A vgmss) is the result of dittography based on the inclusion of the dative (contra Bruce Metzger, *A Textual Commentary on the Greek New Testament*, 2nd ed. [Peabody, MA: Hendrickson, 2005], pp. 452-53). If this reading is not an instance of dittography, it provides evidence that scribes were inclined to add a reference to faith, extending the thought of verse 1 into verse 2. That would be natural, since Paul has insisted on "the obedience of faith" up to this point in the letter, not least in his description of Abraham's faith (Rom 4:9-25). The thematic priority of faith in Rom 1–4 likewise makes the absence of reference to it in verse 2 the *lectio difficilior*. It is also unlikely that scribes overlooked or intentionally omitted the reference to faith.

[33]Admittedly, the δὲ τῷ θεῷ ὅτι ἦτε δοῦλοι τῆς ἁμαρτίας ὑπηκούσατε δὲ ἐκ καρδίας might be rendered adversatively ("*but* you obeyed from the heart"). Yet Paul does not here use a contrastive ἀλλά.

[34]Rom 1:6-7; 4:17; 8:28-30; 9:12, 25-26.

the message is from the word of Christ" (Rom 10:17).[35] As is clear from Paul's Deuteronomic imagery in Romans 10:6-8, the "word of Christ" from which the apostolic message arises is not only the word about Christ (or from Christ), but it is the "near" word that brings Christ himself, incarnate, crucified and risen, to the human heart.[36] The word itself works faith. The effective nature of the gospel is likewise implicit to Paul's image of the ingrafting of the Gentiles (Rom 11:17).[37] The power of Christ to work faith is also implicitly, yet pointedly, present in Paul's announcement of the Redeemer who shall come from Zion to remove ungodliness from Jacob—namely, the ungodliness of unbelief (Rom 11:25-27).

As Melanchthon rightly understands, "justification" is Paul's primary topic in Romans. As both his opening announcement in Romans 1:16-17 and his transitional statement in Romans 5:1 make clear, Paul summarizes the whole of God's saving work in Christ as an act of the justification of the ungodly. Nevertheless, in light of the christological turn in Paul's thought that we have noted above, a christological correction of Melanchthon's anthropological construal of justification is necessary. As interpreters over the last fifty years or so have come to recognize, in borrowing the language of Scripture, Paul recalls the saving judgments of God, in which he works "righteousness" for his people. Thus, for example, one often finds in biblical contexts the pairing of "righteousness" and "salvation" in reference to these acts of divine judgment (or their effect), so that the two terms appear nearly synonymous: "The Lord has made known his salvation. Before the eyes of the nations, he has revealed his righteousness" (Ps 98:2).[38] As a description of God's acts of *judgment*, this "righteousness of God" is irreducibly forensic. Yet as a description of God's *acts* of judgment, it remains irreducibly effective. The Lord *works* righteousness for his people: he grants them salvation and

---

[35]In this context, ἀκοῆς signifies that which is given to be heard, i.e., "message": ἄρα ἡ πίστις ἐξ ἀκοῆς, ἡ δὲ ἀκοὴ διὰ ῥήματος Χριστοῦ.

[36]Cf. O. Hofius, "*Fides Ex Auditu*," in *Denkraum Katechismus: Festgabe für Oswald Bayer zum 70. Geburtstag* (Tübingen: Mohr Siebeck, 2009), pp. 71-86.

[37]They "stand" by faith, but the ingrafting remains entirely God's work for Paul (cf. Rom 11:20).

[38]See also, e.g., Ps 31:2; 40:11; 51:16; Is 45:8; 46:12-13; 51:6-8; 56:1; 61:10-11. It should be noted that the feminine noun צְדָקָה is a *nomen unitatis*, signifying individual instances, while the masculine noun צֶדֶק, is collective (or also abstract). See Diethelm Michel, *Grundlegung einer hebräischen Syntax: Teil 1, Genus und Numerus des Nomens*, 2nd ed. (Neukirchen: Neukirchener Verlag, 2004), pp. 65-66.

deliverance from their enemies. Paul appeals to this understanding in his opening announcement that God's righteousness has been revealed in the gospel (Rom 1:16-17).

Paul also speaks of justification as a reckoning (or, indeed, imputation) of righteousness (Rom 4:1-5). He draws this language from God's word concerning Abraham: "He believed God, and it was reckoned to him as righteousness" (Gen 15:6). Yet this pronouncement on Abraham bound up with the promise that God would not only grant him an heir but also multiply his descendants and "make him the father of many nations" (Gen 15:5; 17:1-6). It is the fulfillment of this promise that will bring about the earthly, saving effect of the pronouncement of righteousness that follows it.[39] The earthly enactment of Abraham's justification is thus separated from the pronouncement of Abraham's justification because Abraham's justifying faith is bound to the word of promise given to him.

According to Paul, the promise to Abraham finds its fulfillment in Jesus, "who was delivered up on account of our transgressions, and raised on account of our justification" (Rom 4:25). In Jesus' resurrection, the fulfillment of promise and thus the earthly enactment of Abraham's justification has entered into the present time. In Christ—and only in him—God's word and work, the divine "reckoning" and the divine "effecting," the forgiveness of our sins and the resurrection from the dead, no longer take the differing forms of faith and fulfillment but are present as an inseparable whole. Paul's understanding of justification therefore does not deviate from the biblical conception of it as an effective judgment that brings deliverance. In the promise to Abraham he sees all the biblical announcements of that saving righteousness as awaiting their eschatological fulfillment in Jesus.

We must also take account of a further dimension of Paul's description of Abraham's justifying faith. Paul presents Abraham's faith as a heroic confidence in the word of promise (Rom 4:18-22). Yet this dramatic description of Abraham's faith—in which Paul pointedly glosses over the doubts and failures that appear within the Genesis narrative—is prefaced by Paul's identification

---

[39]In his appeal to Ps 32:1-2, Paul interprets the "reckoning of righteousness" as the "forgiveness of sins" and describes that forgiveness as "blessing" and "happiness" (Rom 4:6-8). This earthly effect of forgiveness in blessing should not be overlooked. Yet this new reality of blessing awaits the fulfillment of promise.

of God as the Creator, "who gives life to the dead and calls into existence that which is not."[40] Abraham's faith itself, the means by which Abraham is justified and by which the promise is effected, is contained within the prior call of the Creator, which is nothing other than a word of promise. The promise, although it awaits its fulfillment in Jesus, is immediately effective within the world. In this way, the effective dimension of God's righteousness enters the world even prior to Abraham's faith, creating the faith by which Abraham is justified. The matter is no different with the righteousness of God revealed in the gospel: it too springs forth from the promise that has now been fulfilled in Jesus (Rom 3:21-26).

With this understanding of justification as arising from an effective word of promise that has its fulfillment in the risen Jesus, Paul introduces the christocentric section of the letter that we already have considered: "Therefore, having been justified by faith, we have peace with God through our Lord, Jesus Christ" (Rom 5:1). It is not without significance that not only in the opening words of this section but throughout his opening argument (Rom 5:1-21) he presents salvation in terms of God's justifying work in Christ. Furthermore, as his transitional statement in Romans 6:1 ("What shall we say, then . . .") makes clear, Romans 6–8 presents the entailments of what he has said already in Romans 5:1-21. Again, in this second lengthy section of the letter, then, Paul presents salvation as consisting in the justification that is present in the risen Christ and given to faith.[41] Paul presents justification as christologically conceived in such a way that the justifying word and work of God are inseparably joined in Christ. Thus, still in the introduction to the second section, Paul speaks of righteousness both as arising from the *grace* of God and Christ, and also as the *gift* of God and Christ (Rom 5:12-21). The relationship is ordered. The grace of God is not contingent on a gift of righteousness already received. The inverse holds. The gift of righteousness arises from the grace of God—and that of Christ—in response to transgressions (Rom 5:15-16). "Grace" exercises its saving rule through (the gift of) right-

---

[40]Or better for the last part of Rom 4:17, "calls (for his purposes) the things which do not exist, as if they existed."

[41]In Rom 9:1–11:36, while the christological thematic continues, Paul moves to the question of God's dealings with Israel and the nations. Nevertheless, when he presents the apostolic message of salvation, he does so again in terms of the revelation of God's righteousness in Christ and the gift of faith (Rom 9:30–10:21).

eousness, so that this gift abidingly remains the vehicle of God's saving favor and not the cause of it. "Righteousness" never becomes a possession of the human being but unendingly remains a gift given in unconditioned grace. Nevertheless, Paul presents God's justifying grace as inseparable from his justifying gift in Christ. There is no saving grace outside that saving gift. Indeed, the language of "gift," which is represented here by a rich variety of terms, introduces Paul's argument and dominates his presentation.

This rich language for "the gift" finds its counterpart in the rich and remarkably concrete language of "righteousness" by which Paul names and defines the gift. Not only the concrete terminology for "righteousness" but also the context itself suggests that he has in view not merely a forensic status but also the salvation to which that status is bound. Just as judgment resulted in condemnation, so the gift of God and Christ resulted in (undeserved) "vindication," that is, effected righteousness (Rom 5:16; δικαίωμα). Those who receive the abundance of grace and "the gift of righteousness" rule through Christ (Rom 5:17; δωρεᾶς τῆς δικαιοσύνης). Through the righteous act of Christ (δικαίωμα, again, "effected righteousness") the "justification that is life" (δικαίωσιν ζωῆς) comes to all human beings (Rom 5:18). In all of these statements, Paul presents "justification" as a reality that is simultaneously irreducibly forensic (and thus an expression of "grace") and irreducibly effective and concrete within the world (and thus a "gift").[42]

As we have noted, Melanchthon conceives of the event of justification in anthropological terms. Justification takes place when a person hears the promise of mercy and forgiveness in the gospel, is moved in his or her affections by the Holy Spirit, and does not resist the offer of grace but instead accepts it. Even if this response is merely passive, a mere receiving of the offer of mercy in which one does not resist the impulses of the Spirit, it nevertheless remains an act of the human being on which salvation is now contingent. This contingency, after all, is Melanchthon's point: God is thereby relieved of the charge of doing evil, and the human being is held responsible. Consequently, in contrast with the ambiguity that appears in the 1530 Augsburg Confession (Article IV), Melanchthon *must* now con-

---

[42]The same may be said of Paul's subsequent use of righteousness language in Rom 6:7; 8:4, 30.

strue justification as the mere imputation of righteousness out of sheer mercy.⁴³ Because he has invested the human being with a choice in being justified or not, he cannot allow that justification has anything to do with a change in the human being.⁴⁴ Within the framework of his thought, he was right in doing so, since he thereby preserved an essential element of Paul's gospel: the justification of the ungodly. But he therewith misses the christological nature of Paul's argument, in which justification entails *not* a change *in* the human being *but* the change *of* the human being, from the fallen creation present in Adam to the new creation present in the crucified and risen Christ.

Consequently, a couple of nagging questions remain.⁴⁵ If justification is in some way contingent on the human response of faith, how is it that faith is not counted as a work? In fact, Melanchthon is prepared to concede that faith is a work, like the other virtues of love, patience and chastity.⁴⁶ But it is not *counted* as a work. It is only an instrument and the mere means by which we receive the mercy of God. But *why* should faith be regarded as a mere instrument? Is it simply because it is an act of receiving God's mercy, and a weak one at that? As Melanchthon himself points out, the human being is more than a stone or block of wood. Passive, receptive and weak though it may be, faith remains a human action and in that sense a "work." One must therefore press the question with Melanchthon as to why faith should not be regarded as an act of obedience to God—an act on which salvation itself is contingent.⁴⁷

---

⁴³Melanchthon's difficulty in coming to terms with Paul's statements concerning the sovereignty of God in Romans appears to bear a significant relationship to his construal of justification as a bare forensic judgment or declaration. Both dimensions of Melanchthon's thought, the freedom of the will to apply itself to grace and the understanding of justification as mere imputation, developed within the same period of his life. Both take their orientation from the conception of the human being as endowed with the faculties of intellect, affections and will that had been inherited from antiquity and transmitted to Melanchthon through his humanistic training.

⁴⁴It is not clear, however, that Melanchthon's attempt to redefine faith as a relation (and not a quality in the human being) is successful (see Nüssel, *Allein aus Glauben*, pp. 39-40), since, according to his understanding, faith arises in *the human act* of accepting grace.

⁴⁵On the questions that we take up here, see Nüssel, *Allein aus Glauben*, pp. 31-61.

⁴⁶*Commentary on Romans*, p. 57; MO 15:544-45. Admittedly, this conception of a "work" is different from that of Paul, for whom a "work" is an outwardly observable act.

⁴⁷See, e.g., Luther's preface to Romans: "Faith, however, is a divine work in us which changes us and makes us to be born anew of God, John 1. It kills the old Adam and makes us altogether different men, in heart and spirit and mind and powers; and it brings with it the Holy Spirit. O it is a living, busy, active, mighty thing, this faith" (LW 35:370; WADB 7:11).

This issue is all the more urgent in that, according to Paul, "faith" is the one true act of obedience that God requires of human beings. His dramatic presentation of Abraham's faith underscores this truth (Rom 4:13-25). Paul's apostolic task is to establish the "obedience of faith" (i.e., "the obedience which is faith") among the nations.[48] Indeed, he speaks without hesitation of our being justified "by faith" (ἐκ πίστεως), and not merely "through faith" (διὰ πίστεως). The distinction *propter Christum, per fidem* ("because of Christ, through faith") is foreign to Paul, even if it preserves an essential element of his thought within an anthropological framework. He understands faith itself as the *creation* of God by the gospel. As his description of conversion in Romans 6:17 makes clear, to believe is to be transferred from one lordship to another, from the lordship of sin to the lordship of the gospel and of righteousness. According to Paul, faith is the newness of eschatological life beyond sin, death and judgment (Rom 6:4). It is the presence of the eschaton that God has brought into the world in Christ. Within God's saving work in Christ, human beings are not merely dealt with in their intellect, affections and will. They are put to death and raised to life (Rom 6:1-11). The anthropological framework that Melanchthon employs to analyze justification thus stands in tension with Paul's christological framework in Romans. While Melanchthon is able to present a critical and essential element of Paul's understanding of justification, he fails to capture the whole of what Paul is saying. He rightly affirms that Paul conceives of justification in "the Hebrew manner" as forensic judgment or imputation, and not as an approval of a moral quality within the human being.[49] Yet he does not see that within the Hebrew usage of the Scripture, the pronouncement of judgment and the effecting of judgment are joined, and that this understanding of righteousness and justification lies behind Paul's christological definition of it.

As a result, a certain inconsistency regarding the significance of faith inheres within his thought. On the one hand, faith is not counted within justification. On the other hand, it is not at all clear why this should be so,

---

[48]His very mission is that of bringing about "the obedience of faith" among the nations (Rom 1:5; 16:26). Abraham's faith provides footsteps that even those "of the circumcision" must follow (Rom 4:12). The conversion of the Roman Christians is nothing other than their obedience to the pattern of teaching that is the gospel (Rom 6:17). Not everyone obeys the gospel (Rom 10:16).

[49]MWA 5:33-36 (1532); *Commentary on Romans*, pp. 25-26; MO 15:510-11.

especially given Melanchthon's understanding that the human will plays a role in the acceptance of mercy. If we speak of justification as "effective" for Melanchthon, it is only in the sense that the promise of mercy and the influence of the Holy Spirit move the human being to accept the comfort offered in the gospel. Afterward, the Spirit brings new impulses to the human heart to desire and to seek to obey God. The human being remains intact. "Renewal" for Melanchthon is not an immediate, unqualified new creation but the incremental reordering of the affections.[50] That is a very different sense of "effective justification" from that which one finds with Paul (and with Luther), which might more properly be described as "creational justification."[51]

Correspondingly, there is distance between Paul's presentation of "the new obedience" of the Christian in Romans and the conception of it that we find with Melanchthon. Once again, even if we should describe Melanchthon's understanding of justification as "effective," it is in a much different sense from what we find with Paul. While Melanchthon understands salvation as a unity, he nevertheless construes it as containing two distinct steps. As we have noted, there is first the offer of mercy that the Holy Spirit moves the heart to receive. Once the heart has received mercy, the Spirit then gives it new impulses, by which the flesh "begins" to be mortified and the believer "begins" to be vivified. In this way, under the terms of Melanchthon's anthropological approach, justification is kept from being contingent on any moral change within the believer.[52] But faith

---

[50]*Pace* Kolb, in the previous chapter in this volume, pp. 84-86, 89. It is not without significance that in his 1529 *Dispositio* Melanchthon ignores baptism and concentrates on the reason that faith produces good works, and that likewise in the 1532 and 1540 commentaries his discussion is oriented to the *beginning of* the mortification of sinful desires and of vivification (previous chapter, p. 92).

[51]In a misguided way, Andreas Osiander attempted to capture this element of Paul's thought by insisting that our justification is based on the indwelling divine nature of Christ. He thus (1) separates the divine nature of Christ from the human nature, so that he no longer has in view the death and resurrection of Christ; (2) implicitly understands union with Christ in what must be described as an ontology of substance that implies the merging of persons, while Paul's understanding of the communicative union between the sinner and the crucified and risen Lord must be regarded in terms of an ontology of relation in which the distinction between persons remains; and (3) is likewise based on an anthropological framework of soteriology, so that the grace of God becomes contingent on the gift of God. On Melanchthon's debate (as well as that of others) with Osiander, see T. J. Wengert, *Defending Faith: Lutheran Responses to Andreas Osiander's Doctrine of Justification, 1551–1559*, Spätmittelalter, Humanismus, Reformation 65 (Tübingen: Mohr Siebeck, 2012).

[52]From the very start of his new understanding of justification, Melanchthon separated the vivifying effect of faith from justification. See Nüssel, *Allein aus Glauben*, p. 43.

and obedience now come to be two distinct acts. Even if the Holy Spirit is at work in both faith and obedience, the Spirit performs two different operations, first moving the heart toward mercy, and then moving it toward obedience. Even if one should insist that salvation remains indivisible in Melanchthon's thought, in practice it comes in two parts. The connection between faith and ethics starts to become unclear, in spite of Melanchthon's clear affirmation that they belong to each other.[53] Beyond Melanchthon's proper insistence that the Spirit is at work in both believing and behaving, the question remains as to what, if any, other connection exists between justification and justice. In other words: what is the material relation between justification and sanctification?

Matters are quite different with Paul, since for him faith itself is nothing other than the new creation and therewith true obedience. Just as God's work in Christ effects faith within the human being, so faith "reckons" with the whole of God's work in Christ, namely, the death to sin and new life for God that are present "in Christ Jesus" (Rom 6:11). Protestant theology, which largely has been the heir of Melanchthon's anthropological construal of salvation, has alternatively struggled with these issues or ignored them.

MELANCHTHON'S READING: WHERE HE GOT IT RIGHT

These questions concerning Melanchthon's reading of Romans do not, however, detract from his fundamental concern to present the gospel as God's comfort in Christ to terrified consciences. In this interpretation of Paul, he was not alone in his time and remains a much better reader of Paul than many of our contemporaries, especially the advocates of the "new perspective." Even if Melanchthon's analysis of Romans 1–2 does not fully explore the historical connections of the text, he obviously has a firm grasp on what Paul is doing in the passage in exposing human guilt, particularly the guilt of those who imagine themselves to be guiltless. In other words, Melanchthon by no means imagines that all human beings are plagued by

---

[53]This difficulty comes to expression in Melanchthon's shift from the early (and correct) affirmation *lex semper accusat* (in "Apology to the Augsburg Confession IV") to his later (problematic) development of the idea of a *tertius usus legis* ("third use of the law"), in which the law no longer condemns the believer but only provides instruction in living. This shift is likely due to Melanchthon's introduction of human freedom into salvation. This idea stands in conflict with the distinction between law and gospel, as Bayer, "Freiheit?," p. 257, observes.

guilty consciences. While there is a natural law that instructs every human being that God punishes evil and rewards the good, the human heart is carried away by various impulses and doubts, so that this knowledge is obscured and becomes ineffective. For this reason, teaching about the law is necessary within the church.[54] The law must trouble the comfortable before the gospel can comfort the troubled. That our contemporaries no longer feel the need "to find a gracious God" is not a mark of progress but of decline.[55] This poverty is largely the result of our prosperity, which has brought with it the loss of the horizon of final judgment. Yet Melanchthon is surely correct in supposing that while the inward voice of the conscience can be suppressed, it cannot be silenced. No matter that our contemporaries may for a time ignore the inward voice that calls them to account; they cannot finally rid themselves of the burden of an anguished conscience. As Alan Jones, former dean of Grace Cathedral, has observed, we live in an age in which *everything* is permitted and *nothing* is forgiven.[56] In this respect, it is high time that we gave heed to the Preceptor and his interpretation of the apostle to the Gentiles.

---

[54]Melanchthon, *Commentary on Romans*, pp. 73-98; MO 15:568-86.
[55]Karl Barth, *CD* IV/1, p. 531.
[56]Cited by G. O. Forde, *On Being a Theologian of the Cross: Reflections on Luther's Heidelberg Disputation, 1518* (Grand Rapids: Eerdmans, 1997), p. x.

Ephesians *and* Martin Bucer

5

Martin Bucer's Reading *of* Ephesians

Brian Lugioyo

*Remember the reading and preaching of God's
prophet and true preacher Martin Bucer.*

John Bradford, 1555

Remembering Martin Bucer

Today's Protestant churches are plagued with hermeneutical dementia. This, no doubt, is the result of a misunderstood slogan, *sola Scriptura*, a slogan only precariously associated with the first generation of reformers.[1] The idea that the reformers rejected the interpretation of a millennia and a half is unfathomable. In fact in many instances they were fighting for the right to interpret the church fathers as evangelicals. In other words, the Magisterial Reformation was also a battle for who could claim Augustine or interpret him rightly.[2]

---

[1] The Protestant Reformers never used the slogan *sola Scriptura* in their writings. See Anthony N. S. Lane, "Sola Scriptura? Making Sense of a Post Reformation Slogan," in *A Pathway into Holy Scripture*, ed. Philip E. Satterthwaite and David F. Wright (Grand Rapids: Eerdmans, 1994), pp. 297-327.

[2] See Arnold S. Q. Visser, *Reading Augustine in the Reformation: The Flexibility of Intellectual Authority in Europe, 1500-1620* (New York: Oxford University Press, 2011).

For good or bad, the Protestant Reformation heritage has bequeathed to us a sense of interpretational autonomy, which has led to the idea that the *sola* individual is capable of being an authority on Scripture without recourse to how the church has read these texts across generations.[3] But this is never how the reformers read the text. The reformers always read their biblical texts with ancient friends. This volume reminds us of the need to rekindle some of these friendships, lest our dementia become crippling. It is within this context, then, that I echo John Bradford's appeal to "remember the reading and preaching of God's prophet and true preacher Martin Bucer."[4]

The Strasbourg reformer is an apt hermeneutical mentor for our age on two accounts. First, in an era where the theological curriculum has been partitioned into separate disciplines, Bucer reminds us that biblical studies and systematic theology are not independent of each other; theology and exegesis go hand in hand. Theology both flows out of exegesis and informs it—as we will see. Second, in an age when theological study is predominantly focused on serving the academic guild, Bucer reminds us that the work of exegesis and theology is for the edification of God's people.

Martin Bucer's commentaries were notorious for their theological depth and ecclesial focus.[5] Theological discussion arose from the en-

---

[3]For an interpretation of the effects of the *sola Scriptura* principle in the American context, see Stanley Hauerwas, *Unleashing Scripture: Freeing the Bible from Captivity to America* (Nashville: Abingdon, 1993).

[4]John Bradford, "Farewell Letter to Cambridge," 1555, in John Bradford, *Writings of Rev. John Bradford* (Philadelphia: Presbyterian Board of Publication, 1842), p. 14.

[5]Unfortunately, the writings of Martin Bucer have predominantly remained in sixteenth-century printings. Hence his corpus, which has only limitedly been translated, is not familiar to those outside the academy. Bucer's early lectures on Ephesians while in Strasbourg were published as a commentary titled *Epistola D. Pauli ad Ephesios . . .* (Straßburg: Johann Herwagen, 1527), available at http://archive.org/details/epistoladpauliado0buce. The lectures from Cambridge were published posthumously by Immanuel Tremellius as Martin Bucer, *Praelectiones Doctiss. in Epistolam D. P. ad Ephesios . . .* (Basel: Petrus Perna, 1562), available at http://books.google.com/books/about/Praelectiones_doctiss_in_epistolam_D_P_a.html?id=B7xk9zEXq18C. Other sections of these latter lectures were published posthumously as well. Based on Bucer's work while in England, Conrad Hubert, Bucer's secretary, edited various works of Bucer with the help of Edmund Grindal. A portion of Bucer's lectures on Ephesians is published in this collection: Martin Bucer, *Scripta Anglicana fere Omnia a Conr.*, Huberto collecta (Basle, 1577), available at www.e-rara.ch/bau_1/content/titleinfo/2587324. Also, there is in manuscript form notations of Bucer's lectures from John Banck, a pupil who attended the lectures. See Constantin Hopf, *Martin Bucer and the English Reformation* (Oxford: Basil Blackwell, 1946), pp. 19-21, on these developments. Portions of his lectures have been translated in Martin Bucer, *Common Places of Martin Bucer*, trans. and ed. by

gagement with the Word of God; thus his biblical commentaries were his theological treatises, and on account of his fecund mind this made them on multiple accounts long and for many tedious.[6] That being said, they were tedious due to his commitment that exegesis was a theological enterprise. It is my hope that this investigation into Martin Bucer's reading of Ephesians inspires fresh readings in the same way that he inspired a renewal of biblical exegesis in England during the sixteenth century.[7]

Prior to arriving on the English shore, Bucer spent the majority of his efforts advocating for and administering the reformation in Strasbourg. There he worked tirelessly for twenty-five years until having to flee after the Augsburg Interim of 1548. Thomas Cranmer saw the implementation of the Interim on the Continent as an opportunity to shift the theological leadership of the Reformation to England. Hence he invited various exiled theologians, the most prominent being Peter Martyr Vermigli and Martin Bucer, to aid him in the English Reformation. Cranmer's guests did just that. At the University of Cambridge, Bucer inspired the English Reformation through his challenging lectures, primarily on Ephesians.[8] These lectures were given during his final years as Regius Professor of Divinity from 1550 to 1551 and were published posthumously in 1562.[9] Immediately preceding Bucer's ar-

---

David F. Wright (Appleford: Sutton Courtnay Press, 1972). Wright's translation will be cited from here on as *CP*. There is a desperate need for a critical edition.

[6]In his preface to his *Commentary on Romans*, John Calvin states that Bucer is too verbose and intellectual to be read quickly. Hence Calvin developed his writing project in distinction from his Strasbourg mentor. Calvin wanted to provide clear and lucid commentaries, and the *Institutes of the Christian Religion* would be the location for more lengthy theological comments—in effect distancing rigorous theological analysis from biblical commentary. See Calvin's dedicatory letter to Simon Grynaeus of Basel prefacing his *Romans Commentary* (October 18, 1539); CO 10, no. 191, p. 404; ET in LCC 23:75. See also See Wulfert de Greef, "Calvin's Writings," in *The Cambridge Companion to John Calvin*, ed. Donald K. McKim (Cambridge: Cambridge University Press, 2004), p. 44.

[7]David F. Wright states that "his lectures on Ephesians stimulated a renewal of biblical exegesis in England." In "Martin Bucer," in *Historical Handbook of Major Biblical Interpreters*, ed. Donald K. McKim (Downers Grove, IL: InterVarsity Press, 1998), p. 158.

[8]My analysis of this commentary has benefited greatly from N. Scott Amos's insightful dissertation, "The Exegete as Theologian: Martin Bucer's 1550 Cambridge Lectures on Ephesians and Biblical Humanist Method in Theology and Exegesis" (PhD diss., University of St. Andrews, 2003).

[9]Bucer's time in England profoundly influenced the English Reformation. See Hopf, *Martin Bucer and the English Reformation*; Martin Greschat, *Martin Bucer: A Reformer and His Times*, trans. Stephen E. Buckwalter (Louisville: Westminster John Knox, 2004), pp. 227-49; and Basil Hall, "Martin Bucer in England," in *Martin Bucer: Reforming Church and Community*, ed. David F. Wright (Cambridge: Cambridge University Press, 1994), pp. 144-60.

rival in England, the young King Edward VI established new injunctions on the teaching of theology, one of which required that the apostle Paul's epistles be taught in the curriculum.[10] In accordance with this injunction and due to the epistle's theological depth, Bucer decided to lecture on Ephesians. He viewed this epistle as a compendium of Pauline theology: "[Paul], while in chains in Rome and also daily anticipating the end, wrote the most perfect commentary on the entire doctrine of Christ, which contains everything he had ever taught whether to the Ephesians or to others."[11] In this regard, the epistle to the Ephesians offered a great opportunity to lecture on theology.

This essay will proceed, first, by looking at Bucer's exegetical method and how he placed his theological discussions within the interpretation of Scripture. Then, second, we will look closely at Bucer's exegesis in regard to one portion of his lectures on Ephesians (Eph 1:3-6)—a section that highlights his methodology and his theological perspective on the doctrine of election.

Bucer the Exegete

Martin Bucer's exegesis emerged from the lecture hall.[12] Later on these lectures were consolidated and published as commentaries for the purpose of training preachers in the true meaning of Scripture.[13] The methodology he applied in his Cambridge lecture hall was preserved in the preface to his Ephesians commentary. Summarizing his method, he stated:

---

[10]See Amos, "Exegete as Theologian," pp. 81-90, 107.
[11]Bucer, *Praelectiones*, p. 5B.
[12]The most important studies on Martin Bucer's exegesis have been by Bernard Roussel and Gerald Hobbs, who have articulated a Rhenish school of exegesis, which Bucer belonged to. See Bernard Roussel, "Martin Bucer Exégète," in *Strasbourg Au Cœur Religieux Du XVIe Siecle: Hommage a Lucien Febvre: Actes Du Colloque International De Strasbourg (25-29 Mai 1975)*, ed. George Livet and Francis Rapp (Strasbourg: Librairie Istra, 1977), pp. 153-66; Roussel, "Strasbourg et l'école rhénane d'exégèse (1525-1540): Une école et son programme," *Bulletin Société De L'Histoire Du Protestantisme Français* 135 (1989): 36-41; R. Gerald Hobbes, "How Firm a Foundation: Martin Bucer's Historical Exegesis of the Psalms," *Church History* 53 (1984): 477-91; Hobbes, "Strasbourg et l'école rhénane d'exégèse (1525-1540): L'hébreu, le Jusdaïsme et la Théologie," *Bulletin Société De L'Histoire Du Protestantisme Français* 135 (1989): 42-53. For a more extensive list of works dealing with Bucer as an exegete, see Brian Lugioyo, "Martin Bucer," in *Oxford Bibliographies in Renaissance and Reformation*, ed. Margaret King (New York: Oxford University Press, 2014).
[13]For instance, these commentaries originated from his lectures: the Synoptic Gospels (1527), Ephesians (1527), the Gospel of John (1528), Zephaniah (1528), Psalms (1529), Romans (1536), Judges (1544) and Ephesians (posthumously) while in Cambridge (1562).

Also for whom it is the office to study more accurately one book at a time let them in each book both diligently take careful note of its *common topics* [*locos communes*], and continually *be mindful of them in considering other topics*;[14] also let them meticulously *attend to the syntax* of each author, and *to the proper meaning of sacred language*—which must be studiously learned. Regardless of what they will seem to have learned in this manner (repeatedly adding their prayers), let them as fervently as possible bring together the aim of the Holy Scriptures and the idioms of sacred language *together with the principle doctrines of our religion*, until the *Holy Spirit*, who alone leads into all truth, seals its meaning and makes certain its doctrine on his mind.[15]

This summary highlights five key elements in his hermeneutical method. First is the use of a *loci communes* methodology within the context of scriptural exegesis.[16] As we mentioned, exegesis and theology go hand in hand. Accordingly, the principal theological topics for him needed to be discussed in the course of exegeting Scripture—this in part is in contrast to Philipp Melanchthon's *loci communes* method of a collection of topics apart from scriptural commentary.[17] Bucer's keenness to mine theological topics in Scripture disposed his decision to lecture on Ephesians, since it lent itself to the theological *loci* of election and the church—two *loci* foundational for the Protestant Reformation over against the views of the established Roman Church.[18]

Second, Bucer relies on other scriptural places and doctrines to help him interpret the present text. For him the whole of Scripture was united on account of the agency of the Spirit.[19] Bucer's deep familiarity with Scripture tuned his ear to hear the rich resonances between various biblical books. On each page of the epistle of Ephesians, he heard echoes from the Old Testament and particularly from Paul's epistle to the Romans. The third aspect of his approach is tied to grammar and philology. Bucer urges interpreters to pay attention to the turns of phrase and the grammar of the text; this

---

[14]Here we have Bucer's principle of having Scripture interpret Scripture.
[15]Bucer, *Praelectiones*, p. 14D (my translation, emphasis added).
[16]Amos, "Exegete as Theologian," pp. 222-43.
[17]Philipp Melanchthon, *Loci communes theologici* . . . (Strasbourg: Johann Albrecht, 1536).
[18]Peter Stephens, "The Church in Bucer's Commentaries on the Epistle to the Ephesians," in *Martin Bucer: Reforming Church and Community*, ed. David F. Wright (Cambridge: Cambridge University Press, 1994), pp. 45-60, esp. pp. 53-57.
[19]See Amos, "Exegete as Theologian," pp. 151-52.

means that students must learn Hebrew and Greek. The use of these sacred languages unearths lexicological riches that edify the reader and the church. Thus throughout his commentary Bucer singles out small clauses and words to better interpret them. His analysis constantly tells of his skill as a Hebraist, as he often seeks to interpret the original Greek by means of a familiar Hebrew cognate.[20] A fourth aspect of his methodology is reading with the aid of the church fathers and the creeds. The ancient creeds of the church provide the "fundamental axioms of our knowledge of the Scriptures."[21] They function as an initial map that guides the interpreter's reading. On this account, we are obliged to interpret the Scriptures within the historic tradition. Bucer does not read Scripture alone. Repeatedly throughout the commentary Bucer appeals to the fathers, especially Augustine.[22] Last, but most important, the interpreter must rely completely on the work of the Holy Spirit to make effective one's diligent exegetical work. Bucer accepts that true exegesis occurs only when the exegete's mind is transformed and fortified by the Holy Spirit. In an earlier memo, he stated, "No one will skillfully explain the nature of faith and love—although it is beautifully and brilliantly described everywhere in Scripture—who has not, to some degree, had personal experience of it."[23] In line with his emphasis on the Holy Spirit, a disciplined and pious life was mandatory for the task of interpreting Scripture.[24] Exegesis is a churchly endeavor, for "a true understanding and interpretation of Scriptures is gained only in the genuine churches of Christ."[25] The life and context of an exegete affect the interpretation.

Bucer began each of his lectures praying the following:

> Eternal God, most kindly Father, it is thy will that we should unite in thy name and hold godly assemblies and that also academies [*scholas*] should exist

---

[20]See Hobbes, "Strasbourg et l'école rhénane d'exégèse (1525–1540)," pp. 42-53.
[21]Bucer, *Praelectiones*, p. 12 (my translation).
[22]On Bucer's use of the fathers see Marijn de Kroon, "Bucerus Interpres Augustini," *Archive for Reformation History* 74 (1983): 75-93; and Irena Backus, "Ulrich Zwingli, Martin Bucer and the Church Fathers," in *The Reception of the Church Fathers in the West: From the Carolingians to the Maurists*, ed. Irena Backus (Leiden: Brill, 1997), 2:627-60.
[23]In 1531 Martin Bucer wrote a short treatise titled "Quomodo S. Literae pro Concionibus tractandae sint Instructio." This work was published by Pierre Scherding and François Wendel, eds., "Un Traité d'exégèse pratique de Bucer," *Revue d'Histoire et de Philosophie Religieuses* 26 (1946): 32-75, 62.
[24]Bucer, *Praelectiones*, p. 9B.
[25]Ibid., p. 12 (my translation).

among thine own by which should be preserved and set forth thy law and doctrine; to those of us assembled here in thy name grant thine aid so that whatever we say or do will serve to show forth thy glory and renew thy church, through thy Son, our Lord Jesus Christ who lives and reigns in the unity of the Holy Spirit, for ever. Amen.[26]

BUCER'S EXEGESIS OF EPHESIANS 1:3-6

With attention to his method throughout we will look at Bucer's exegesis of Ephesians 1:3-6. Bucer regards the beginning of the epistle (*initium epistolae*) as starting in verse 3, after Paul's salutation.[27] He introduces his exegesis of the following four verses by highlighting the theological *locus* of this pericope, stating that "the first theological locus [*primus locus Theologiae*], which Paul handles in this Epistle, is concerning our election to an eternal inheritance."[28] The role of this doctrine for Bucer and other reformers should not be understated.

The place of election in Reformation theology. The doctrine of election holds a key place in the theology of Paul for Bucer on account that election is both the efficient cause of salvation (which means that God alone is responsible for salvation) and the final cause of salvation (which is our holiness of life and the glory of God).[29] Hence Paul's aim "is the increase of godliness, not only in knowledge, but also in practice, for both the Ephesians and us, . . . so that an encouraged faith may unfold abundantly in every good work."[30] Paul emphasizes the doctrine of election, since knowledge of God's election "encourages faith and fully incites a pursuit for integrity."[31]

In this light, the doctrine of election for Martin Bucer is categorically a

---

[26]Translated in Hall, "Bucer in England," p. 149; from J. V. Pollet, ed., *Martin Bucer études sur la correspondence* (Paris: Presses Universitaires de France, 1958–1962), 1:257-58.

[27]Bucer, *Praelectiones*, p. 19C.

[28]Bucer, *Praelectiones*, p. 19C (my translation). For further analysis on Bucer's exegesis of this important pericope, see Amos, "Exegete as Theologian," pp. 246-99.

[29]*CP*, p. 109; *Praelectiones*, pp. 19C-20D. On election being the foundation of Martin Bucer's theology see Peter Stephens, *The Holy Spirit in the Theology of Martin Bucer* (Cambridge: Cambridge University Press, 1970), pp. 23-41; Brian Lugioyo, *Martin Bucer's Doctrine of Justification: Reformation Theology and Early Modern Irenicism* (New York: Oxford University Press, 2010), pp. 43-79; and Augustus Lang, *Der Evangelienkommentar Butzers und die Grundzüge seiner Theologie* (Aalen, Germany: Scientia Verlag, 1972), p. 104.

[30]*Praelectiones*, p. 20D (my translation). This conforms to how Bucer describes the genre of this epistle as admonitory, doctrinal and exhortatory; see *Praelectiones*, p. 18E.

[31]*Praelectiones*, p. 20D (my translation).

positive and joyous doctrine. It is the expression of God's gratuitous love toward the believer and on that account is the foundation for thanksgiving and praise. Unfortunately, within the context of sixteenth-century polemic, this doctrine was rejected or misunderstood, and thus often presented in an apologetic key rather than a celebratory one.

In Bucer's long career, this doctrine became a point of issue frequently with Anabaptists. For example, in Strasbourg, in an early debate with the Anabaptist Conrad Treger, Bucer emphasized this doctrine in contrast to Treger's understanding of the church.[32] In his *Romans Commentary* of 1536 he addressed the position of *apokatastasis* that was promoted in Münster.[33] When he arrived in England in the late 1540s, he was apparently aware of the group called the "Freewillers," who were mounting a similar attack on the reformed teaching of election.[34] John Bradford, one of Bucer's friends while in England, wrote a treatise against the "Freewillers" in 1554 based on the first chapter of Ephesians titled *In Defence of Election*, which had incorporated some of Bucer's exegetical observations.[35]

The doctrine of election was important for the Protestant reformers and Bucer because of how it illumined the gospel of grace within a theological context where uncertainty of one's salvation was encouraged—a view based on the Vulgate's translation of Ecclesiastes 9:1, "Man knows not whether he is worthy of love or of hatred." From this verse the medievalists developed a pastoral theology that could soothe the uncertain conscience by encouraging a faith that emphasized works.[36] Bucer saw that this pastoral theology resulted for some in a vain trust in one's own righteousness, and in others despair, because no one can win God's gift of reconciliation.[37] This works-focused theology, it seemed to Bucer, stemmed from the obvious mistranslation of the Hebrew of Ecclesiastes 9:1, which had nothing to do with un-

---

[32] Bucer's early debate with Conrad Treger concerned whether the church was defined by baptism or by election and faith. See Stephens, "Bucer's Commentaries on Ephesians," p. 48.
[33] *CP*, p. 98; Bucer, *Metaphrasis et enarratio in Epistolam d. apostoli Pauli ad Romanos* . . . (Basel: Peter Perna, 1562), p. 410. See George H. Williams, *The Radical Reformation*, 3rd ed. (Kirksville, MO: Truman State University Press, 2000), pp. 553-88.
[34] Williams, *Radical Reformation*, p. 1198.
[35] Bradford, *Writings of Rev. John Bradford*, pp. 331-40.
[36] See Heiko Oberman, *The Harvest of Medieval Theology: Gabriel Biel and Late Medieval Nominalism*, 3rd ed. (Grand Rapids: Baker Academic, 2002), p. 230.
[37] See *CP*, p. 182; *Metaphrasis* (1562), pp. 17-18.

certainty but rather with a certainty that whatever your lot God was in control.[38] Bad and good things in the life of a sinner or saint are not a sign of God's hatred or love, since both good and bad happen to both. Hence it was pure foolishness to discourage God's love (election) toward the believer—especially based on this poor translation. A Christian must be certain of God's love for them. So it is from a firm assurance of our election, Bucer maintained, that we can cry out to God, "Abba, Father."[39] Bucer asked, If you doubt that God is your Father and your Savior, what is the basis of your love for God? If you doubt your salvation, what do you have to be thankful about, since you believe that God can just as easily forsake you?[40] Accordingly, if the doctrine of election is not loudly preached, what is left of God's gospel of love?

Ephesians 1:3: "Blessed be the God and Father of our Lord Jesus Christ, who has blessed us with every spiritual blessing in the heavenly places, in Christ . . ."[41] Keeping the context in mind, we begin by looking at Bucer's exegesis of verse 3. He primarily focuses on three phrases: "Blessed be God" (*Benedictus Deus*), "who has blessed us with every spiritual blessing" (*qui benedixit nos omni benedictione spirituali*), and "in the heavenly places, in Christ" (*in caelestibus, Christo*).

What does it mean to "bless" God? What is the idiomatic background of this idea of blessing God? To answer this, Bucer applies his knowledge of Hebrew philology. The term for blessing in the Hebrew is *brk* (ברך), and it "sometimes means to bestow a benefit and sometimes to praise. When it is used of God, it denotes his showering us with benefits, but when it is predicated of ourselves, then it means to praise and give thanks."[42] Hence Bucer views this statement as one of deep thanksgiving.[43] In this way, he shows

---

[38]See *CP*, p. 180; *Metaphrasis* (1562), p. 17. On the significance of this verse, see also John Calvin, *Institutes of the Christian Religion*, III.2.38.
[39]*CP*, p. 181; *Metaphrasis* (1562), p. 17.
[40]*CP*, pp. 181-82; *Metaphrasis* (1562), p. 17.
[41]It needs to be noted that Bucer himself does not divide his commentary verse by verse. He proceeds in a linear fashion through the text; however, on account of his theological exegesis he is often expanding his comments to include the general argument of the entire pericope. Nevertheless, I find it heuristically helpful for our purposes to artificially divide his discussion verse by verse. The biblical citations used throughout are my translations of Bucer's Latin translation in *Praelectiones*, p. 17.
[42]*CP*, p. 110; *Praelectiones*, p. 20D.
[43]It may be that he sees a parallel here with Deut 33:11, where Moses blesses the Lord.

the importance of knowledge of "sacred languages," since to bless the most blessed would make no theological sense. "Blessed be God" is a doxological statement; Paul blesses God on account of the gratitude that comes from knowing his election.

The following subordinate clause, "who has blessed us with every spiritual blessing," Bucer primarily explains by refuting the opinion of John Chrysostom, who views the spiritual blessings referred to here as diametrically opposed to the blessings of Israel, which were temporal.[44] Appealing to Deuteronomy, Bucer highlights the fact that God promised spiritual blessings to the Israelites, not just temporal ones.[45] Yet, in regard to temporal blessings, he states, "We too, like them [Israelites], need good things of this life, and ask for them in prayer, and receive them; hence we pray, 'Give us today our daily bread.'"[46] Thus Bucer addresses the highly problematic dichotomy between the Old Testament (material) and the New Testament (spiritual).

On this account, the phrase "in the heavenly places" is not meant to place spiritual blessings in a future or otherworldly location. Bucer acknowledges that this phrase sometimes denotes the "abodes of evil spirits" or in Ephesians 6:12 can mean the location where wicked powers are active; however, Bucer interprets this phrase in association with the phrase "in Christ" (*Christo*). The association of the heavenly places with Christ leads Bucer to profoundly state that the living saints "already . . . live the life of heaven."[47] Receiving spiritual blessing is part of what it means to live the heavenly life today, in Christ. He continues to explain this, saying that "Christ dwells in our hearts and will not desert us even until the consummation of the world; he comes to the man who loves the Father, and abides with him."[48]

In light of Christ dwelling in the elect, the question arises for Bucer about how it is that the elect can have Christ in their hearts but yet sin. To resolve this question he appeals to an anthropological distinction in regard to a "higher nature" (*potiorum partem*): "Therefore, although the saints fall into

---

[44]*CP*, p. 110; *Praelectiones*, p. 20D. See Chrysostom, *Homilies on Ephesians* 1.1; PG 62, p. 11; NPNF 13, pp. 50-51.
[45]Perhaps referencing Deut 30:15-20.
[46]*CP*, p. 110; *Praelectiones*, p. 20D-E.
[47]*CP*, p. 110; *Praelectiones*, p. 20E; *quorum iam conversatio in caelis est*.
[48]Ibid.

sin every day, nevertheless by their higher nature they are heavenly. Our faith and our sanctification are heavenly, and are bestowed by Christ who is in heaven, and we keep company with him through faith and ardent desire."[49] In the end, the heavenly or spiritual blessings we receive are faith and sanctification. And he adds that Paul inserts here "in Christ" (*Christo*) to highlight that these blessings bestowed on the elect are on account of his righteousness and merit.[50] Ultimately, the spiritual blessings in the heavenly places that we receive are christologically conceived, in that for Bucer we enter heaven (and heavenly life) through Christ's merit, not our own.

Ephesians 1:4a: *"Just as he elected us in him before the foundations of the world were established . . ."* Bucer's exegesis of the first part of verse 4 zeroes in on the theological locus of election.[51] He proceeds by explaining five points: (1) the security of election, (2) the need for this doctrine to be preached, (3) the two uses of *electio*, (4) the mystery of the divine counsel that chooses and (5) the supreme encouragement this doctrine provides.

For Bucer, the heart of Paul's argument is that "you ought to be grateful to him who has freely given you all things—election, adoption, calling, faith, etc."[52] These gifts, highlighting election, are unshakably firm, since they originate from God. God's choice is secure, and thus those he chooses are secure. Nevertheless, security does not warrant pastoral idleness. Bucer exhorts that we must be "zealous that for our part . . . they may become ever more firmly established."[53] The work of firmly establishing this doctrine in the minds of congregants means that people more fully understand and accept their election: "The man who reflects deeply on his election by God before he was born is set on fire with an amazing longing and desire to cleave to the benefits of God, and to acknowledge his Benefactor in every part of life."[54] Thus understanding God's divine and therefore secure choice is a primary responsibility. Ministers of the gospel must encourage those in the congregation to understand Paul's teaching here.

On that account, Bucer prescribes that this doctrine be preached boldly

---

[49]Ibid.
[50]Ibid.
[51]*CP*, p. 110; *Praelectiones*, p. 20E-F.
[52]*CP*, p. 110; *Praelectiones*, p. 20E.
[53]*CP*, p. 110; *Praelectiones*, p. 20F.
[54]*CP*, pp. 110-11; *Praelectiones*, p. 20F.

to congregations, particularly because the preaching of election was being regulated. Late in 1551, for example, the popular public debates between Jérôme-Hermès Bolsec and John Calvin led the magistrates in Bern to enact a policy banning the preaching of predestination. The policy was instituted to restore peace since the doctrine had caused quite a tumult—tumult caused in part by Bolsec's declaration, in Geneva, that to hold Calvin's position on predestination was to make God the author of evil.[55] Such was the case in Geneva and Bern, because there the controversy centered on Calvin's more scrupulous doctrine of double predestination. Bucer acknowledges that the doctrine of election and predestination implies exclusion; however, he—following the medieval theologians—refuses to place reprobation within the doctrine of predestination, allocating reprobation its own theological place in relation to but different from the doctrine of election.[56] As we mentioned before, for Bucer the doctrine of election is a positive doctrine tied to God's love. Thus Bucer sees a ban on preaching this doctrine as foolishness; since we are to "magnify among men the benefits of God, surely we cannot pass over in silence what is the greatest of them all. Following Paul's example we must celebrate God's election, for the consideration of election must lead to the strengthening of faith among men, and it is pointless to fear that mention of it might induce laxity of life and religion as a whole."[57]

That understood, Bucer acknowledges that the term *elect* (*electio*) can be understood in different ways, and for him there are primarily two ways. The first is in regard to being chosen to an office. His example here is Jesus' choosing of the twelve disciples. He goes on to state that Judas was chosen to the position of disciple but "he was not elected to the inheritance of eternal life."[58] The other way the term can be used is to designate the "elect" as those who "by the pure grace of God, of some out of the general mass of lost mankind, attain to the knowledge of the will of God and finally to

---

[55]MO 7:237-42. See Bruce Gordon, *Calvin* (New Haven, CT: Yale University Press, 2009), pp. 205-9.
[56]This comes through in his *Romans* commentary, when, after describing how the doctrine of predestination is God separating the elect from those who are not, he states that "the theologians, however, refuse to call this 'predestination,' preferring 'reprobation' instead." See *CP*, p. 97; *Metaphrasis* (1562), p. 410.
[57]*CP*, p. 111; *Praelectiones*, p. 20F.
[58]*CP*, p. 111; *Praelectiones*, pp. 20F-21A.

eternal life."[59] It is this latter use that Bucer sees Paul using here and that must be taught to the congregations on account of the strength it gives to believers. He states:

> If we lack this certainty of faith, if we are not convinced of it, we cannot look forward to eternal life nor acknowledge God as our Father or Christ as our redeemer—in short, no element of true religion or genuine love of God can reside in us. We must therefore overthrow the view that we should silence every mention of election in the assembly of the faithful.[60]

The preaching of election is celebratory!

Election reminds the believer that "in our election God had regard only to himself and his Son, and not ourselves."[61] There is no recourse to oneself for receiving the love of God. It is gratuitous. For support Bucer invokes Augustine's position over against the Pelagian view. Even the view that God's election is on account of his foreknowledge is refuted, since that would be to base election on the believer's merit and not Christ (a view medieval nominalists were known to hold). These attempts to disambiguate election, for Bucer, are based on the desire to understand the unknowable divine counsel. Referring to 1 Corinthians 2:14, Chrysostom and Jerome, he asserts that the appeal to make election understandable apart from the merit of Christ is an appeal to elevate nature over grace; in other terms, "It is the mark of antichrist to exalt nature over against grace so that he may reign in the stead of Christ."[62] For him, one must understand that human choice is fundamentally different from God's choice. These two types of choice rest on different fundamental principles, which he sees echoed in the work of Augustine. This then leads him to remind his hearers that it is dangerous to form a theology based on human opinions (in this case in regard to election) and not from Scripture itself. This is the cause of many controversies and disputes.[63]

In his exposition of this verse, Bucer notes that the most fitting context for understanding the teaching of election is found in Paul's epistle to the Romans.[64] Invoking Romans 8, Bucer demonstrates the encouragement

---

[59]*CP*, p. 111; *Praelectiones*, p. 21A.
[60]Ibid.
[61]*CP*, p. 111; *Praelectiones*, p. 21B.
[62]*CP*, p. 112; *Praelectiones*, p. 21B.
[63]Ibid.
[64]Ibid.

this doctrine provides in the context of trials and misfortunes, which left alone can lead to the diminishing of faith. About its inspiring ability he states:

> Nothing can debar them from their inheritance which is in Christ Jesus. Our mediator is eternal, and we are eternally united with Him; our union with Christ is unbreakable and cannot be other than everlasting. Now both a blessing as great as this and its revelation through faith are not within our own power but are entirely the merciful gifts of Christ alone. For as we have said already, of ourselves we cannot even conceive thoughts of this nature, but he himself is the sole author of our every spiritual blessing, our faith, our possession of the Spirit, and, to sum up everything in one word, our complete regeneration.[65]

Whatever the cause for doubt, the realization that God chooses us to be his own without recourse to our works or situation is the greatest inspiration of faith possible.

Bucer's theological *locus* concludes with an appeal to the Holy Spirit's illumination of this doctrine. The Spirit is superior to the church fathers and more clearly demonstrates to believers the love of God for them than any human opinion can. Yet Bucer affirms that even this clear and eloquent work of the Spirit demands that believers zealously grow in the love of God "according to the measure of the grace of God in us."[66] In this way, the exegesis of the first part of Ephesians 1:4, "as he elected us in him before the foundations of the world were established," is explained by means of a theological discussion, which then leads into Paul's goal of the doctrine, our regeneration.

Ephesians 1:4b: "that we might be holy and blameless before him, in love . . ." Concluding the *locus*, Bucer picks up on the clause "that we might be holy and blameless before him." In this section he examines what Paul is trying to indicate by the term *blameless* (ἀμώμος). Employing his Hebraic philological skills, he views the word *blameless* (*irreprehensibiles*) as better defined by the term *whole* (*integros*), on account of the Hebrew term תמימים. The appeal to the Hebrew is, it seems, tied to Leviticus 14:10 and Ezekiel 43:25,

---

[65]Ibid.
[66]*CP*, p. 112; *Praelectiones*, p. 21C.

which associate the term with unblemished animals being offered for a sin offering. In Hebrew, the term means "complete," "sound," "whole," "entire," "wholesome," "healthful," "innocent," "having integrity." And this is how elect believers ought to live, "far removed . . . from earthly desires."[67]

But such holiness of life is impossible, and often claims to it are hypocritical. Thus Bucer comments on how Paul adds the phrase "before him" (*Coram ipso*) to discredit hypocritical holiness, for many seem holy before others, but not "before him." Referencing Psalm 143:2, Bucer affirms that through our own effort it is impossible to claim this blamelessness before God.[68] Nevertheless, we are elect for the purpose of being holy and blameless, and thus Bucer interprets this phrase as an imputed benefit of Christ's, that is, solely on account of "his mercy for the sake of his Son he reckons [*imputat*] the perfection of the Son's will to be in the elect."[69] In this way, Bucer states, we ought to read both Romans 8:33, "Who shall bring any accusation against God's elect?" and Luke 1:6, in regard to Elizabeth and Zechariah being seen as righteous before God.[70] Thus the holiness and blamelessness of the Son becomes that of the elect.

While our holiness before God is imputed, it does result in real holiness of life, which becomes its own confirmation of election. Consequently discipline and holiness ought to be encouraged.[71] Referring to 1 John, "The man who keeps the commandments knows that he is of God" (a reference to 1 Jn 2:3; 3:21; 5:2), Bucer views these fruits from the work of the Holy Spirit as confirming our conscience.[72] He states:

> Those who lack the confirmation of this favourable testimony of conscience cannot be assured of their election nor of the hopes in store for the elect. But yet all believe, let all repent, let all hear the words of the gospel and God's counsel of election, also let their faith in this infallible election be steadfast, let the elect finally be holy and blameless.[73]

Here we see how Bucer views Paul's teaching on election as not primarily a

---

[67]Ibid.
[68]Ibid.
[69]*CP*, p. 113; *Praelectiones*, pp. 21C-22D.
[70]*CP*, p. 113; *Praelectiones*, p. 22D.
[71]Ibid.
[72]Ibid.
[73]Ibid.

choice for exclusivity but for the edification of the people of God. And therefore it must be preached and everyone must be encouraged to believe that they are elect, that the fruit of holiness would increase and become the true confirmation of election. Rather than using this doctrine to speak of reprobation, Bucer sees that this note of election is a positive doctrine of God's grace over against our fallen human nature.

All of this, Bucer notes, is confirmed when Paul adds "in love" (*per charitatem*). For though this phrase can be understood in two senses—one being the love between neighbors—Paul means here to emphasize "the love of us in an objective sense, the love wherewith God has loved us."[74] This sense is the way in which Bucer takes this clause, since it demonstrates a further cause of our election through "God's loving embrace of us in the Son."[75]

Ephesians 1:5: "who predestined us that he might adopt us as sons through Jesus Christ, according to the good pleasure of his will . . ." Bucer continues his exegesis and theological analysis in the next verse, accentuating Paul's emphasis on Christ and his righteousness. Commenting on the clause "who predestined us that he might adopt us as sons through Jesus Christ," he states that here "Paul stresses Christ, because in him is found assurance of faith when we have him as our reconciler and the giver of perfect righteousness."[76] Relying on our imperfect righteousness and thanking God adequately for his kindness must be abandoned.[77] Our attention, as Paul's, must be on the free gift received in Christ.

The glorifying of the Son and the kindness of God are the ultimate and final cause of our election.[78] Thus Bucer exhorts us to loudly praise God abroad for God's wonderful and secure decision to choose the elect in Jesus, not that God needs our praise, but that through the church's praise "others are brought to salvation and to the blessedness he offers to all, as happened when the gospel was preached among the Gentiles."[79] This is why Paul stresses Christ in this passage, according to Bucer: to show that this election in Christ is pure mercy, pure gratuity, the whole gospel of God's love toward us.

---

[74]*CP*, p. 113; *Praelectiones*, p. 22E.
[75]Ibid.
[76]*CP*, p. 114; *Praelectiones*, p. 22E.
[77]Ibid.
[78]Ibid.
[79]*CP*, p. 114; *Praelectiones*, p. 22E-F.

Hence Bucer holds that Paul elucidates the doctrine of election here as a basis for encouraging the Ephesians in praise and thanksgiving. This is the doxological nature of the text for Bucer. The doctrine of election is corrupted when it is removed from the foundation of God's love and when philosophy intervenes. Bucer believes that philosophy often became the basis of theology, confusing divine election with human choice. This error—which has at times allowed a misconstrued doctrine of election to view God as capricious—grew from Platonic philosophy that penetrated the fathers from the beginning of the church's history.[80] On this account, he admonishes his hearers again to look to the authority of Scripture as more authoritative than even the fathers.

At this point, Bucer offers the following summary statement of Paul's argument of the passage up to this point:

> To sum up: election is the pure gift of God; therefore it is grace, not reward. . . . Election, therefore, is the purpose and sure mercy of God from eternity before the creation of the world, whereby he separates those whom he will have mercy upon from the whole race of lost mankind, and assigns them to eternal life out of his patently gratuitous mercy, before they could do either good or evil. Election is certain, I say, and immutable, through Jesus Christ the only-begotten Son of God, our mediator, from eternity the destined head of the Church and our reconciler according to God's own eternal and immutable counsel.[81]

To further illustrate what Paul is saying, Bucer thinks it necessary to illustrate the view of God's free choice in regard to Romans 9 and Exodus 33. Bucer sees Paul in Romans 9 as extending God's choice of Jacob over Esau "to the whole posterity of each family, and therefore to all the righteous and all the unrighteous."[82] In the same way, he sees the Exodus passage "I will be gracious to whom I will show grace, and I will have mercy on whom I am pleased to have mercy" as applying "generally to all men."[83] These two passages are relevant "to this one in Ephesians because each speaks of God's

---

[80]See *CP*, p. 114; *Praelectiones*, p. 22F.
[81]*CP*, pp. 114-15; *Praelectiones*, pp. 22F-23A.
[82]*CP*, p. 115; *Praelectiones*, p. 23A.
[83]Ibid.

election, and teaches the completely free will of God."[84]

Nevertheless, though God's free choice radically differs from humanity's, it does not demolish human free choice. Bucer states that "we freely assent to God's word through God's Spirit dwelling in us; for his Spirit sets our enslaved will free. When God draws us to himself, we are not passive like wood or stone, but he grants us to will and to accomplish the very thing he works in us."[85] This leads him to the next clause, "according to the good pleasure of his will." Here he combats the idea of antinomianism that could be seen as arising from the doctrine of election, which was an attitude that was being actively promoted by English radicals.[86] For him, election is continuous with good works, because "the person who firmly believes that election proceeds solely from the will, love, and mercy of God, will be more warmly enthused for good works, while those who do not so believe seize every occasion for liberty in sinning."[87] He also here combats the idea that God is capricious in his decision to elect some and not others. But Bucer relies on the fact that God's ways are not ours, referring to Romans 9. We should not set ourselves as judges over God but subject ourselves to the Word of God.

Ephesians 1:6: "so that the glory of his grace be praised, whereby he had rendered us dear [charos] in the Beloved [dilecto]." Bucer moves to the last verse of this pericope to briefly summarize Paul's discussion. Looking at the latter clause of this verse, he highlights the fact that we were born not beloved but children of wrath, again highlighting that Paul's articulation of the gospel revolves around grace and not works. Thus to be called beloved, Bucer shows, is Paul's employment of a rhetorical trope, *antonomasia* (or periphrasis), which is "the substitution of an epithet, etc., or the name of an office or dignity, for a person's proper name."[88] Christ is the sole "Beloved" by which we too are deemed beloved. It is thus in Christ and not of ourselves that God has chosen to make us his loved ones.

---

[84]Ibid.
[85]*CP*, p. 115; *Praelectiones*, p. 23B.
[86]See Williams, *Radical Reformation*, p. 1196. One English radical, the Libertine John Champneis, stated that "a man after he is regenerate in Christe, cannot synne." These libertine (antinomians) views, mingled with other problematic beliefs, were being actively suppressed by Thomas Cranmer. Bucer was aware of this.
[87]*CP*, p. 115; *Praelectiones*, p. 23B.
[88]*CP*, p. 118 n. 28.

Conclusion

This passage of Scripture was extremely important for articulating the Protestant understanding of the gospel in the sixteenth century. Bucer's analysis of this passage, and the entire epistle, is thoroughly theological. Repeatedly he refers to various church fathers, especially Augustine. Repeatedly he reads this text with the help of multiple other texts, especially Romans. Repeatedly he reminds his hearers that Scripture and the work of the Holy Spirit are the best means to understand the heart of God over against philosophers and even the fathers. And repeatedly he relies on his knowledge of the "sacred languages" to understand more clearly the Word of God.

Bucer remained true to his task as a theologian and pastor. During this time, the church had used Paul and his words about election and predestination as basis for division. Bucer seeks to demonstrate how the epistle of Ephesians, especially the first chapter, when read properly, unfurls not only Paul's intent but the heart of God for the church. Reading with this sixteenth-century theologian and exegete, we can come to a deeper understanding of the rich and gratuitous love of God for us. Reading with this committed pastor, the most loving of all decisions captures us and makes our hearts leap with praise and thanksgiving!

Remember the reading and preaching of God's prophet and true preacher Martin Bucer.

6

The Text of Ephesians and the Theology of Bucer

Wesley Hill

One of the most discussed questions in contemporary study of the Christian Bible is what constitutes "theological interpretation" of Scripture. There are many new calls to think about "Scripture" and "theology" together, rather than separately, but questions remain about how to achieve an integration. Does such interpretation depend on practicing certain sorts of historical criticism, or do the conclusions reached in theological interpretation *not* depend at all for their legitimacy on what we may say about a text's historical origins and earliest reception?[1] Does theological interpretation rest on the interpreter's adhering to a certain creedal or confessional framework, or is it able to hold loosely to any one tradition and adopt a kind of hermeneutical pluralism?[2] Insofar as these remain

---

[1] Karl Barth argues for the former in the preface to his *Epistle to the Romans*, 6th ed., trans. Edwyn C. Hoskyns (London: Oxford University Press, 1933 [orig. 1916–1921]). The latter is the position of Dale B. Martin, *Pedagogy of the Bible: Analysis and Proposal* (Louisville: Westminster John Knox, 2008); compare also the similar viewpoint of Stephen E. Fowl, *Engaging Scripture: A Model for Theological Interpretation* (Oxford: Blackwell, 1998).

[2] See Markus Bockmuehl's queries for Francis Watson's approach to theological interpretation in his *Seeing the Word: Refocusing New Testament Study*, Studies in Theological Interpretation (Grand Rapids: Baker Academic, 2006), p. 58: "[Watson] never quite proceeds to an account of the church in which [the] ecclesial hermeneutic [he advocates] actually resides, offering no concrete reference to baptism or Eucharist, to local or global mission, to lay groups reading Scripture, or to bishops or priests."

open questions, another set of questions is also left open—namely, how is one to *evaluate* any given "theological interpretation" of a portion of the Christian Bible? If no consensus exists about what *counts as* theological interpretation, then no consensus exists about how to *measure* efforts to practice it. Coming across a piece of "theological interpretation" of Scripture, then, how are we to go about rendering a judgment about it?

In light of these questions, one could imagine several ways of trying to assign some value to Martin Bucer's exegesis of Ephesians 1:3-6. On the one hand, it would be easy enough to evaluate Bucer on the basis of the criterion of internal consistency. Has he been faithful within the context of his own stated aims and norms (philological accuracy when drawing on the Hebrew text, fidelity to Reformational theology and preaching, etc.)? Or, taking a slightly different tack, one could ask how Bucer's exegesis fares when considered against the backdrop of the widely agreed-upon exegetical canons of his day. Here the question would not be so much whether Bucer in fact achieved what he said he wanted to, but rather whether he counts as a good exegete given the way his peers would have evaluated him. Mention could be made of commentaries written at the same time as his, and a comparative study could be attempted.

Another approach altogether would be to ask whether Bucer's exegesis has stood the test of time and is still usable today. Here the question is less one of historical curiosity (what was Bucer up to in his own day?) and more one of contemporary relevance: Does Bucer's exegesis exhibit such depth and insight that it remains worthwhile and beneficial to those who wish to hear Paul afresh in the church today? This is the approach I want to pursue in this chapter, but in order to do so, I need to sharpen the question.

Previously I attempted a similar evaluation of a portion of Karl Barth's exegesis of Romans 9. In that study I compared two places where Barth engages with Romans 9:1-5, and I noted the differences between Barth's two treatments. Near the end of the study, however, I went beyond the merely descriptive and asked whether Barth's readings were *good* ones. Here were my criteria for evaluation:

> [I will] attend . . . to Barth's exegetical practice as opposed to his hermeneutical method—that is, the way in which Barth moves from a given biblical text to specific comments on that text, thus focusing on what might be called

Barth's *acts* of interpretation. Rather than attempting an assessment of the theological proposals that are the fruit of Barth's exegesis, and without necessarily trying to buttress either a critical or appreciative approach to Barth's exegetical practice or conclusions, my aim is to concentrate on the mechanics of that exegesis itself. My approach will thus be to ask some questions like these: What is there in the text that causes Barth to start off in such-and-such a direction? What does Barth see *here* that causes him to say *this*? Is what he says there simply a "ruminative overlay"[3]—a comment affixed to the words of a text (Paul's) to which they bear little or no relation? Is this or that comment of Barth's an actualization of some of the text's own semantic potential[4] or is it better described as a theological "performance" of a text which says nothing about what Barth goes on to say by means of it? Above all, how is Barth's exegesis explicable as a *reading* of a *text*?[5]

These questions still seem to me to be useful, and I think they are applicable to Bucer as well as Barth. But one further methodological qualification is needed before I proceed to look at Bucer's exegesis in detail.

In what follows, I want (among other things) to put Bucer's exegesis into conversation with current Pauline scholarship, using contemporary discussions of Paul to shed light on the Pauline text and thereby enable a deeper grappling with Bucer's handling of the same text. But I do not want to imply that evaluating Bucer's exegesis is as simple or straightforward as asking whether he *anticipates* current conclusions (and thus may be said to be a *good* reader of Paul) or *disagrees* with current conclusions (and thus may be said to be a *bad* reader of Paul). Rather, I hope to demonstrate that reading Bucer is not just a matter of seeing how one interpreter has learned or failed to learn from a text (thus moving in my evaluation from more distant past [Paul] to more recent past [Bucer]). Reading Bucer is also, or should be, a way of seeing how a commentary *may lead one back into the text* from which it originated (thus I want to move, in this essay, from past commentator [Bucer] *back* to more distant past author [Paul]).[6] In other words, I hope

---

[3]The phrase is Ephraim Radner's, as quoted in Stanley Hauerwas, *Matthew*, Brazos Theological Commentary on the Bible (Grand Rapids: Brazos, 2006), p. 18.
[4]I borrow this phrase from Francis Watson.
[5]Wesley A. Hill, "The Church as Israel and Israel as the Church: An Examination of Karl Barth's Exegesis of Romans 9.1-5 in the *Römerbrief* and *Church Dogmatics* II/2," *Journal of Theological Interpretation* 6, no. 1 (2012): 139-60, at pp. 139-40.
[6]On this, see David Yeago, "The New Testament and the Nicene Dogma: A Contribution to the

that in following Bucer's exegesis we may be led to reflect on the way that a commentary generated by the Pauline text (the forward movement) may cast light retrospectively, as it were, illuminating features of the Pauline text that elicited the commentary in the first place (the backwards movement). Paying attention to Bucer's exegetical moves—which we may disagree with either in part or wholesale—will remind us that *all* interpretation depends on such a to-and-fro, past-and-present spiral. Nicholas Lash has made the point well:

> If the questions to which ancient authors sought to respond in terms available to them within their cultural horizons are to be "heard" today with something like their original force and urgency, they have first to be "heard" as questions that challenge us with comparable seriousness. And if they are to be thus heard, they must first be articulated in terms available to us within *our* cultural horizons. There is thus a sense in which the articulation of what the text might "mean" today, is a necessary condition of hearing what that text "originally meant." . . . I am . . . concerned to insist, as a matter of general hermeneutical principle, that understanding what an ancient text "originally meant," in the circumstances in which it was originally produced, and understanding what that text might mean today, are mutually interdependent and not merely successive enterprises.[7]

The upshot of this is that we should expect a reading of Bucer on Ephesians will not simply tell us things about Bucer but will also prepare us to better probe the depths of Paul's Ephesian letter itself in our current task of hearing and proclaiming Paul's gospel in our world.

Paul's Benediction

Bucer's treatment of Paul's letter to the Ephesians, after discussing introductory material (Eph 1:1-2), begins by teasing out what it means to call God "blessed" (εὐλογητός) in Ephesians 1:3.[8] Drawing on the Hebraic background

---

Recovery of Theological Exegesis," *Pro Ecclesia* 3, no. 2 (1994): 152-64; R. W. L. Moberly, *The Bible, Theology and Faith: A Study of Abraham and Jesus*, Cambridge Studies in Christian Doctrine (Cambridge: Cambridge University Press, 2000), p. 6. The crucial point is that later, textually derived conceptualities may serve as enduring prompts to engage the text afresh.

[7]Nicholas Lash, "What Might Martyrdom Mean?," in *Theology on the Way to Emmaus* (London: SCM Press, 1986), pp. 75-92, at p. 81.

[8]As Francis Watson has pointed out (*Agape, Eros, Gender: Towards a Pauline Sexual Ethic* [Cambridge: Cambridge University Press, 2000], p. 223 n. 3), the question of whether Paul actually wrote

of this liturgical word, Bucer argues that it must be a reference to believers' praise of God. This is in keeping with how the LXX regularly employs εὐλογητός to translate the Hebrew root בָּרוּךְ. In making this observation, Bucer is firmly rooted on terrain shared with current scholarship that emphasizes the Jewish, traditional character of the benediction here.[9]

However, Paul Christianizes this benediction, a point that Bucer does not linger over. Yet this is a point that many recent Pauline interpreters have considered central to Pauline theology. Paul specifies that the God to be praised or blessed is the "God and Father of our Lord Jesus Christ" (cf. 2 Cor 1:3-4). This amounts to a definitive statement of God's eschatological self-revelation, a sort of "christologizing" of monotheism.[10] This does not mean that the Jewish understanding of God has been jettisoned altogether, after the fashion of Marcion. Paul's benediction here does not assume that God was never known in the past, which would cut against the grain of the account of God giving his name to Moses (Ex 3:14). But the "christological" focus of God's newly revealed identity as "Father of our Lord Jesus" does mean that Paul has rethought and reconfigured his understanding of the character and purposes of Israel's God—God's narratable identity—around the orientating point of the Christ event (as opposed to an exclusive focus on, for instance, the exodus). Jesus Christ has been *included* in the identity of Israel's God in such a way that now, whenever "God the Father" is named, "Jesus Christ" requires "dramatically coordinating mention."[11] The Christ event cannot anymore be conceived of as an afterthought, a late addition to an already complete divine identity. Instead the Christ event belongs to the

---

this letter is not an idle one, since if it is an authentic letter, it bears the marks of a crowning summary (so J. A. Robinson, *St Paul's Epistle to the Ephesians* [London: Macmillan, 1928], p. vii), but if it is an inauthentic letter, it may easily be relegated to a "catholicizing" trend in which the original, apocalyptic Pauline gospel becomes blunted and softened (see Ernst Käsemann, "Ephesians and Acts," in Leander E. Keck and J. Louis Martyn, eds., *Studies in Luke-Acts* [Nashville: Abingdon, 1966], pp. 288-97, at p. 296). For a recent careful defense of Pauline authorship, see the introduction in Harold W. Hoehner, *Ephesians: An Exegetical Commentary* (Grand Rapids: Baker Academic, 2002).

[9]See, e.g., Andrew T. Lincoln, *Ephesians*, Word Biblical Commentary 42 (Nashville: Nelson, 1990), pp. 10-11.

[10]See N. T. Wright, "Poetry and Theology in Colossians 1.15-20," in *The Climax of the Covenant: Christ and the Law in Pauline Theology* (London: T&T Clark, 1991), pp. 99-119, at p. 99; Richard J. Bauckham, *God Crucified: Monotheism and Christology in the New Testament* (Grand Rapids: Eerdmans, 1998).

[11]Robert W. Jenson, *Systematic Theology* (Oxford: Oxford University Press, 1997), 1:92.

self-definition of God, and this is organically related to Paul's incipiently "trinitarian" recognition that God *has always been* Father and Son (and, as Paul's discourse elsewhere indicates [Rom 8:9-11; Gal 4:4-6], also Spirit).[12] This important recent achievement of Pauline interpretation will become significant when we come to discuss Paul's treatment of election, and Bucer's interpretation of it, below.

In explicating the next clause, "who has blessed us with every spiritual blessing in the heavenly places in Christ" (Eph 1:3b), Bucer worries over an untenable separation of spiritual and material blessings.[13] His comment on this text tries to establish that "spiritual" is not meant to be played off against "material," as if believers couldn't ask for daily physical sustenance (cf. Mt 6:11). He places his reading in contrast to John Chrysostom's, which set the spiritual blessings of the church over against the material, temporal blessings Israel enjoyed in the Old Testament. Bucer finds this contrast dubious, and he stresses that Christian believers may ask for temporal blessings just as Israel did. Bucer also tries to demonstrate that insofar as the salvation of believers depends on Christ's achievement on their behalf, that salvation is not subject to the vicissitudes of even the regenerate human heart—it is "spiritual" insofar as it is located where Christ is, in heaven (cf. Col 3:1).

Here, however, it appears that Bucer does not understand πνευματικός with reference to its context in the remainder of Ephesians, where it derives its meaning not from any contrast with the earthly, bodily or material but rather from God's Spirit. The nearest place where the word appears again is Ephesians 5:19. There it modifies the songs that believers are to sing to one another, and the point is not that addressing one another ᾠδαῖς πνευματικαῖς is an immaterial activity that could improperly, as Bucer fears, be set over against God's material blessings. Rather, such songs are inspired ἐν πνεύματι, as believers are filled with the Spirit, which is why they can be designated "spiritual." Therefore, it seems best to take "spiritual" in Ephesians 1:3 to mean "characterized by the Spirit" or "given through the Spirit's agency" and dis-

---

[12]See especially C. Kavin Rowe, "Biblical Pressure and Trinitarian Hermeneutics," *Pro Ecclesia* 11 (2002): 295-312; Francis B. Watson, "The Triune Divine Identity: Reflections on Pauline God-language, in Disagreement with J. D. G. Dunn," *Journal for the Study of the New Testament* 80 (2000): 99-124. For further discussion and bibliography, see my *Paul and the Trinity: Persons, Relations, and the Pauline Letters* (Grand Rapids: Eerdmans, 2015).

[13]Unless otherwise noted, Scripture quotations are my own translation.

pense with Bucer's complicated response to Chrysostom altogether.[14]

Bucer's reading of the next clause, "in the heavenly places, in Christ" (Eph 1:3c), nicely dovetails with reading πνευματικός as a reference to the activity of the Spirit, even if Bucer himself does not make that connection. Bucer's concern is to locate believers' blessings in Christ himself, not in some ethereal realm or unknown future. Insofar as believers find their identity in Christ, their blessedness is identical with Christ's. If Christ is seated in the heavenly places, as Ephesians 1:20 indicates, then believers are in turn the recipients of all the privileges that attend Christ's exalted state. And Paul explicitly says as much in Ephesians 2:6: "[God] raised [us] up with him and seated us in the heavenly places in Christ Jesus." If *heavenly* is to be understood as "where Christ is," then *spiritual* can easily be understood as "of or by the Spirit," and Bucer's concern to guard believers' utter dependence on the work of God accomplished outside themselves can be preserved.

ELECTION IN CHRIST

From there, following Paul's lead, Bucer moves on to further explicate the meaning of the final prepositional phrase in the last part of Ephesians 1:3. That phrase is unpacked in Ephesians 1:4, which offers a causal explanation (καθώς) for how believers become the recipients of the Spirit's blessings in Ephesians 1:3.[15] The reason, Paul says, that believers have been given every spiritual blessing in the heavenly places in Christ is that they have been chosen in him before the foundation of the world: "Blessed be the God and Father of our Lord Jesus Christ, who has blessed us with every spiritual blessing in the heavenly places in Christ, just as he chose us in him before the foundation of the world."

Here we arrive at one of the most discussed texts in the history of Pauline exegesis. For his part, Bucer advocates a "Calvinist" place in the tradition because he stands at the head of the stream later occupied by Calvin and his

---

[14]For this reading of πνευματικός, see Gordon D. Fee, *God's Empowering Presence: The Holy Spirit in the Letters of Paul* (Peabody, MA: Hendrickson, 1994), pp. 666-67, contra, e.g., G. B. Caird, *Paul's Letters from Prison* (Oxford: Oxford University Press, 1976), p. 33. However, Fee does show some awareness of the importance of Bucer's problem: "It is extremely doubtful whether Paul would have thought of the blessings associated with the Spirit as being over against . . . 'material blessings'" (p. 667 n. 28).

[15]So Peter T. O'Brien, *The Letter to the Ephesians*, Pillar New Testament Commentary (Grand Rapids: Eerdmans, 1999), p. 98.

heirs (historically, Calvin is *Bucer's* heir, despite the former's greater fame).[16] The "choosing," or election (ἐκλέγομαι), in view here, according to Bucer, is the eternal decree whereby the triune God chooses some who will become the recipients of salvation in redemptive history, while passing over others, leaving them in their sin, without regard to foreseen merit or demerit.[17]

Several features of Paul's text could be appealed to in support of this view. First, Paul specifies the object of the verb as "us" (ἡμᾶς), thus indicating that, whatever else the divine choice may have in view, it concerns believers. Second, the temporal indicator "before the foundation of the world" (πρὸ καταβολῆς κόσμου) would seem to rule out this choice being made in view of some determining *human* action or lack of action, since believers or unbelievers were not yet created.[18] Third, the result of this choice is said to be the holiness of believers (εἶναι ἡμᾶς ἁγίους καὶ ἀμώμους κατενώπιον αὐτοῦ). This would suggest that holiness is *effected by* the divine election, rather than forming part of its rationale.[19] Using the categories that I introduced above for evaluating theological exegesis, then, it would seem that Bucer's reading has a firm basis to regard itself a realization of some of the Pauline text's own "semantic potential." It can appeal to certain obvious features of the text in order to defend its character as a genuine reading of Paul.

This reading does have rivals, however. In the twentieth century, the stream of interpretation Bucer represents was subjected to searching criticism, most famously in the second volume of Karl Barth's *Church Dogmatics*.[20] Barth's objection to the Bucerian/Calvinist (and Augustinian) reading of Ephesians 1:4 was stated by way of a fresh question: Who is the acting subject, and who is the object, of the election described in Ephesians 1:4? Famously,

---

[16]Max Scheibe, *Calvins Prädestinationslehre: Ein Beitrag zur Würdigung der Eigenart seiner Theologie und Religiosität* (Halle: M. Niemeyer, 1897), pp. 17-19, 69-71.

[17]For Calvin's own treatment, see John Calvin, "John Calvin to the Reader," in *Institutes of the Christian Religion*, ed. John T. McNeill, trans. Ford Lewis Battles, Library of Christian Classics 20 (Philadelphia: Westminster, 1960), III.21.1-III.24.17. For a recent situating of Calvin on this point in wider historical and theological perspective, with up-to-date bibliography, see Matthew Levering, *Predestination: Biblical and Theological Paths* (Oxford: Oxford University Press, 2011).

[18]O'Brien, *Ephesians*, p. 100: "To say that election took place before creation indicates that God's choice was due to his own free decision and love, which were not dependent on temporal circumstances or human merit."

[19]So Calvin, *Institutes*, III.22.3, p. 935: "Say: 'Since he foresaw that we would be holy, he chose us,' and you will invert Paul's order. Therefore you can safely infer the following: if he chose us that we should be holy, he did not choose us because he foresaw that we would be so."

[20]*CD* II/2.

Barth's answer to this question depended, first, on his rejection of what he saw as the Calvinist answer. The classical Reformed doctrine of predestination was wrong, Barth maintained, when it argued that a subset of humanity is chosen and a mass of humanity left unchosen. On the contrary, according to Barth, Ephesians 1:4, by highlighting the prepositional phrase ἐν αὐτῷ, stresses a hitherto downplayed *christological* focus of the divine election. The decree of election takes Christ as its object: *he* is the elect one, and he is also the reprobate. Insofar as he takes humanity's judgment on himself, he is the rejected one, standing in the place of Judas; and insofar as he is loved and raised by the Father, he is the elect one who opens the way for humanity to hear only the word of grace from the Father:

> As elected man He does not stand alongside the rest of the elect, but before and above them as the One who is originally and properly the Elect. From the very beginning (from eternity itself), there are no other elect together with or apart from Him, but, as Eph. 1:4 tells us, only "in" Him.... "In Him" means in His person, in His will, in His own divine choice, in the basic decision of God which He fulfills over against every man.[21]

What this means for Barth (and others who follow him)[22] is that Ephesians 1:4 is primarily a christological text and secondarily a soteriological one. In order to read in such a way, Barth thought he had to correct the Calvinist emphasis on *humanity* as the object of God's election and replace it with an emphasis on an inclusive Christ, whose election secured blessing and salvation for all those "in" Christ.

But we can say more about Barth's reading than this. For Barth, what is wrong with a reading of Ephesians 1:4 like Bucer's is that it separates the election that is displayed in time—that is, Christ's being for humanity in his historical life and death—from a supposed "eternal" decree whose content is not given in time. According to Barth, the Calvinist reading of Ephesians 1:4 posits "a decree of election different from the decree of salvation."[23] Barth continues:

---

[21] *CD* II/2, pp. 116-17.
[22] The commentary of his son, Markus Barth, adopts a very similar line of interpretation: *Ephesians 1-4*, Anchor Bible 34 (Garden City, NY: Doubleday, 1974), pp. 107-9; Carey C. Newman, "Election and Predestination in Ephesians 1:4-6a: An Exegetical-Theological Study of the Historical, Christological Realization of God's Purpose," *Review and Expositor* 93 (1996): 237-47.
[23] *CD* II/2, p. 69.

On the one hand, then, the decree of salvation was emptied of meaning, for quite unintentionally it was rendered inevitable that the true divine decision should be sought elsewhere than in the Saviour, Jesus Christ. And, on the other hand, the decree of election was also emptied of meaning, for it was removed to the divine sphere above and behind Christ where it could not in fact be known as Christian truth. And that meant that there could be no sure knowledge of it at all, and that it was set in the light of a purely speculative axiom.[24]

In this way, Barth explains, by way of negation, what he finds wrong with the kind of interpretation represented by Bucer and Calvin: it does not take the man Jesus Christ as the *author* and *content* of the decree of election. Or, putting the point exegetically, it does not deal adequately with the ἐν αὐτῷ of Ephesians 1:4.

Recent study of John Calvin's doctrine of election, however, carried out in Barth's wake, has carefully queried and qualified Barth's criticism of Calvin.[25] Certainly Barth's and Calvin's doctrines remain visibly distinct, but Barth now appears, in light of more fine-grained studies of Calvin, to have overlooked some of the means the classical Reformed tradition already possessed within itself to address a few of the questions Barth's revisionist treatment raised. In his own exegetical and dogmatic work, Calvin was equally concerned with establishing the christological basis of election, although he did not take the extra step Barth took in making the historical life of Jesus Christ determinative for election's *content*.[26] In his *Institutes of the Christian Religion*, Calvin offers the following account of how Ephesians 1:4 should play a role in elucidating the doctrine of election:

> Accordingly, those whom God has adopted as his sons are said to have been chosen not in themselves but in his Christ [Eph 1:4; *sed in Christo suo*]; for unless he could love them in him, he could not honour them with the inheritance of his kingdom if they had not previously become partakers of him.

---

[24]Ibid.
[25]See Richard A. Muller, *Christ and the Decree: Christology and Predestination in Reformed Theology from Calvin to Perkins* (Durham, NC: Labyrinth, 1986; repr., Grand Rapids: Baker Academic, 1988), and now David Gibson, *Reading the Decree: Exegesis, Election and Christology in Calvin and Barth*, T&T Clark Studies in Systematic Theology (London: Continuum, 2009).
[26]For recent discussion of Barth at this point, see the essays collected in Michael T. Dempsey, ed., *Trinity and Election in Contemporary Theology* (Grand Rapids: Eerdmans, 2011).

> But if we have been chosen in him, we shall not find assurance of our election in ourselves; and not even in God the Father, if we conceive him as severed from his Son. Christ, then, is the mirror wherein we must, and without self-deception may, contemplate our own election. For since it is into his body the Father has destined those to be engrafted whom he has willed from eternity to be his own, that he may hold as sons all whom he acknowledges to be among his members, we have a sufficiently clear and firm testimony that we have been inscribed in the book of life if we are in communion with Christ.[27]

This conclusion is one of Calvin's attempts to specify in what sense Christ is key to the doctrine of election. Although Calvin has a doctrine of Christ's role in the pretemporal eternal divine decree, this is not where his emphasis falls (as Barth's does). For Calvin, Christ is central to election insofar as he is the focal point who binds together the eternal divine decision and its temporal outworking in the history of redemption, thereby making possible human *assurance* of election. This is what Calvin means by calling Christ the "mirror" of election. It is only by looking to him that believers are permitted to maintain any confidence in their election. Such confidence certainly cannot come from their own works, or from attempting to peer into the hidden divine counsels that, Calvin thinks, are not revealed for humans to know (cf. Deut 29:29). Calvin's emphasis does not fall on Christ as the acting *subject* of election, or as election's *object*, but as the *means* by which election is realized in redemption and experienced by the believer as consoling.

Given that Calvin was initially led to consider the doctrine of predestination under Bucer's influence, it is not surprising to see these themes and questions adumbrated—though not worked out in any detail—in Bucer's exegesis of Ephesians 1:3-6. In his electing choice "God had regard only to himself and his Son," Bucer says. And Bucer's objection to viewing election as based on foreseen human faith is that, if that were true, election would no longer have a christocentric basis. Bucer attributes the assurance election affords, along with its other benefits, to "the merciful gifts of Christ alone." "This is why Paul stresses Christ in this passage, according to Bucer," writes Lugioyo, "to show that this election in Christ is pure mercy, pure gratuity, the whole gospel of God's love toward us."[28] Insofar as these themes are

---

[27]Calvin, *Institutes*, III.24.5, p. 970.
[28]See chapter five in this volume, p. 138.

sounded in Bucer's treatment, however undeveloped they may seem when compared to the (differing) treatments in Calvin and Barth, they put Bucer in the christological stream initiated by Paul's own repeated prepositional phrases ("in Christ," "in him"). Whether those phrases *require* to be read as Bucer reads them, and whether, consequently, Barth's reading is ruled out, is another matter.

THE QUESTION OF ROMANS 9–11

Bucer senses the need for his reading to have further support, and so he turns to what he takes to be a parallel passage, Romans 9–11, in which Paul also discusses election but at greater length. In Bucer's reading, Romans 9–11 is to be read as making the same claim that Ephesians 1:3-6 makes, which is that salvation comes to individuals as the result of God's unconstrained, impartial choice to elect some to be recipients of it. He focuses on Romans 9:15, which contains a quotation from Exodus 33:19, where God says to Moses, "I will have mercy on whom I have mercy, and I will have compassion on whom I have compassion." Bucer takes this to be an announcement of a timeless principle or mode of divine operation. It applies, Bucer says, "generally to all men."

Perhaps more than any other exegetical move Bucer makes, this one has been most questioned in recent Pauline scholarship. Few Pauline exegetes today would agree that Romans 9–11 is the kind of widely applicable text Bucer construes it to be. In light of newer studies of the New Testament's formation in the context of Second Temple Jewish literature, beginning in earnest in the twentieth century with the work of E. P. Sanders and others, the tendency in current exegesis is to see Romans 9–11 as the opposite of a timeless or "general" discussion of predestination.[29] On the contrary, the text is now most often read as an argument that although the community of first-century Jews was, for the most part, rejecting Paul's claim that Jesus was

---

[29]For a classic twentieth-century statement that Rom 9–11 is not about the predestination of individuals throughout history to either salvation or damnation but about the specific first-century communal situation of Jews and Gentiles, see Krister Stendahl, *Paul Among Jews and Gentiles and Other Essays* (London: SCM Press, 1977); for Sanders's work, see his *Paul and Palestinian Judaism* (London: SCM Press, 1977). Speaking of the need to reject a position like Bucer's, Francis Watson says, "This is one point where the familiar plea for a historically informed exegesis, unfettered by the constraints of church dogma, seems not unreasonable" (*Paul, Judaism, and the Gentiles: Beyond the New Perspective*, rev. ed. [Grand Rapids: Eerdmans, 2007], p. 314 n. 24).

Messiah, nonetheless God would act climactically to remove their hardness of heart in the soon-to-come parousia of Jesus and reinstate them as recipients of mercy, in and through faith in Jesus. What is in view in Romans 9–11, according to newer scholarship, is a *collective* predestination to a *temporary* unbelief, not an *individual* election to an *eternal* salvation (or else an individual passing-over leading to an eternal judgment). Israel is indeed predestined to remain hardhearted toward Christ—but only until the fullness of the Gentiles has come in, at which point Israel's hardheartedness will be softened and the broken-off branches of their olive tree will be grafted back in (as Rom 11 unfolds as the sequel to Rom 9–10).[30] In light of this recent work, how does Bucer's conclusion fare?

Three responses (among others) may be made. In the first place, accepting for the sake of argument the cogency of the more recent readings of Romans 9–11, one could respond by saying that Bucer's mistaken belief that Romans 9–11 teaches the predestination of individuals to eternal life does not necessarily invalidate his conclusions about the meaning of Ephesians 1:3-6. This could be an instance of Bucer finding the right doctrine in the wrong text—thinking that Ephesians 1 and Romans 9–11 parallel each other in one significant way, whereas in fact they do not. So, one could agree with Bucer that Ephesians 1 envisions the election and predestination of individuals to eternal life but think that Romans 9–11 addresses a different matter. Bucer brings in the latter as a support for his interpretation of the former, but one could simply reply to him that he needs to find better, more relevant support.[31]

Or, second, one might decide that Bucer's reading is largely correct in what it affirms but needs to be contextualized within a wider frame of reference, in light of some of the insights of more recent biblical interpretation. The indisputable gain of newer biblical studies is to highlight the immediate cultural context of the Pauline texts, especially their attention to the relationship between Jews and Gentiles. This is certainly true, as indicated above,

---

[30] See Florian Wilk and J. Ross Wagner, eds., *Between Gospel and Election: Explorations in the Interpretation of Romans 9-11*, WUNT 257 (Tübingen: Mohr Siebeck, 2010); and J. Ross Wagner, *Heralds of the Good News: Isaiah and Paul "in Concert" in the Letter to the Romans*, NovTSup (Leiden: Brill, 2002), for recent discussion of Rom 9–11.

[31] As an interesting parallel, one might consider Barth: Barth rejected the sort of reading Bucer gave of Rom 9–11, but he maintained that the New Testament taught that faith is a gift (cf. Eph 2:8). So Bucer might have interpreted Rom 9–11 differently and still ended by affirming his conclusions on the basis of Eph 1:3-6 and other texts.

with respect to Romans 9–11, but it also pertains to the interpretation of Ephesians 1:3-6. As Stephen Fowl notes with respect to the Ephesians text, "It appears that Paul is telling or reminding the Ephesians that through Christ they have become participants in God's election of Israel, when God chose Abraham from among all people and graciously made a covenant with him."[32] Taking one's cues from this insight, one could recognize that Bucer's affirmations are true as far as they go—that by God's sovereign plan, Paul's addressees have been ushered into an unmerited salvation—but that they do not go far enough in explaining how that salvation is essentially a matter of being made part of God's covenant people, Israel (as Eph 2:11-22 makes plain). Bucer's treatment of election does not emphasize that election is, first and foremost, a doctrine already in play in Israel's Scriptures (see, e.g., Deut 7:6-8), and thus his treatment could be refocused and sharpened with the aid of more contemporary scholarship.

But, third, one could equally decide—and not as an alternative to the second option—to take Bucer as a critical dialogue partner when assessing contemporary scholarship. The more recent readings of Romans 9–11 and Ephesians 1 emphasize that Paul has collectives in mind—the people of Israel considered as a whole and the Gentiles considered as a distinct corporate whole. Thus, it is alleged, Paul is not speaking of the eternal destinies of *individuals* when he speaks of "hardening" and "mercy" in Romans 9–11; he is thinking, rather, of the large-scale rejection of Christ and the mass conversion of pagans to faith in Christ, respectively. And yet, at the time of writing Romans 9–11, Paul views Israel as bifurcated between a minority of Jews who have believed in Jesus as Messiah and a "hardened" majority who do not. Eventually, Paul thinks, this split will be healed, and *all* Israel will be saved (Rom 11:26), but in the meantime the divide remains. Grappling with this reality, Paul goes back to reread Israel's foundational stories in such a way as to expose a similar divide within its *past* history as a people (Rom 9:6-13), and it is here that Bucer's question—about who believes and who does not, on an individual level—does indeed seem to be raised by the Pauline text. Among other things, Paul's main point in retelling Israel's past stories of hardening and merciful acceptance seems to be that Israel has

---

[32]Stephen E. Fowl, *Ephesians: A Commentary*, New Testament Library (Louisville: Westminster John Knox, 2012), p. 39.

always been constituted by divine grace and thus, simultaneously, is never assured of its own favored status simply on the basis of ethnicity.[33] Thus, even in a reading that takes seriously the particularities of Paul's first-century missionary situation, Paul may be shown to be concerned with individuals as well as communities.[34]

In this way, we may decide that Bucer is both inadequate and usefully provocative in his handling of Romans 9-11. On the one hand, Bucer pays scant attention to the concrete situation that prompted the writing of these chapters, and insofar as he neglects the question of "Jew and Gentile," his reading is in need of supplementation. But on the other hand, Bucer's *questions* about the ultimate fate of specific persons in election may not be foreign to Romans 9-11 in the way that many contemporary scholars claim.[35] Those questions must be situated in a different context than Bucer placed them, but that does not mean they are irrelevant to the interpretation of Romans 9-11, or Ephesians 1:3-6.

BUCER ON THE CHRISTIAN'S RIGHTEOUSNESS

Finally, we may ask about Bucer's understanding of the purpose clause of Ephesians 1:4, in which Paul says that God's decree of election was executed in order that we might be "holy and blameless before him in love." Bucer takes the final reference to love to modify the verb "chose," specifying the manner of the divine choosing. He speaks of "God's loving embrace of us in the Son." This *could* be the text's original import, though it is striking that in the remainder of the letter "love" most often refers to human love (see, e.g., Eph 1:15; 4:2, 15, 16; 5:2), and elsewhere in Paul election is not typically associated with the word or its cognates. In any case, Bucer wishes to stress that the blamelessness and holiness of believers is an *objective* holiness, theirs only insofar as they are united to Christ. He cites Psalm 143:2 to stress

---

[33]Cf. J. Louis Martyn, "Romans as One of the Earliest Interpretations of Galatians," in *Theological Issues in the Letters of Paul* (London: T&T Clark, 1997), pp. 37-46, at p. 45.

[34]On this whole question, see Ben C. Dunson, *Individual and Community in Paul's Letter to the Romans*, WUNT 2/332 (Tübingen: Mohr Siebeck, 2012).

[35]For an argument conversant with contemporary biblical scholarship as well as Karl Barth that suggests Paul is still thinking of the destiny of individuals, see David Gibson, "The Day of God's Mercy: Romans 9-11 in Barth's Doctrine of Election," in David Gibson and Daniel Strange, eds., *Engaging with Barth: Contemporary Evangelical Critiques* (Nottingham, UK: Apollos, 2008), pp. 136-67.

that, left to their own devices, believers would not be able to attain the requisite blamelessness "before God." (Paul alludes to the LXX version of this text in Romans 3:20 via the catchwords πᾶσα σὰρξ ἐνώπιον αὐτοῦ; compare Ps 142:2 LXX: ἐνώπιόν σου πᾶς ζῶν.) What is needed, then, is an imputed righteousness not subject to the ups and downs of believers' sometimes-visible, sometimes-faltering holiness: "[God] reckons [*imputat*] the perfection of the Son's will to be in the elect."

In line with Calvin and the rest of the Reformed tradition, Bucer also stresses that there is an experiential holiness that is the fruit of receiving the imputed holiness of Christ. Bucer attributes the former to the work of the Spirit and also grants it a confirmatory role in relation to election. As believers actively discipline themselves in the practice of holiness, their consciences are "confirmed" (a theme that is hinted at in other portions of the New Testament and developed more fully in later Reformed theology; see 2 Pet 1:10).

Yet again, this is a way of construing Pauline theology that has fallen out of favor with many contemporary Pauline exegetes. N. T. Wright has famously dismissed the idea of imputed righteousness as a category confusion: "Righteousness is not an object, a substance or a gas which can be passed across the courtroom" of divine justice.[36] Less stridently than Wright, though no less insistently, most scholars would now want to stress that the language Bucer here fixates on—that believers will be "holy and blameless"—is Israel-centered vocabulary that has been expanded and applied to Gentile believers. By the same token, it is *eschatological* terminology. The pairing of ἅγιος language (and cognates) and ἄμωμος vocabulary is found in Exodus 29:37-38, where the altar and sacrifice are to be set apart. Each of the terms also appears elsewhere in the Old Testament, in ethical contexts (see, e.g., Ps 14:2 LXX for ἄμωμος and Ex 19–20 for ἅγιος).[37] For Ephesians, many contemporary exegetes suggest, these associations remain definitive for the meaning of the terms in Ephesians 1:4: the new Jew-and-Gentile community is to partake, via divine election and the eschatological achievement of the

---

[36] N. T. Wright, *What Saint Paul Really Said* (Grand Rapids: Eerdmans, 1997), p. 98.

[37] On the link between liturgical or cultic holiness and moral holiness in Exodus, see Stephen C. Barton, "'Mercy and Not Sacrifice'? Biblical Perspectives on Liturgy and Ethics," *Studies in Christian Ethics* (2002): 25-39.

Christ event, in the holy conduct and the holy status (cf. the address of believers in Eph 1:1, τοῖς ἁγίοις) that Israel was expecting to enjoy on the day of judgment.[38] This eschatological cast is confirmed for many interpreters by the recurrence of the two terms in Ephesians 5:27, where they are apparently "best taken as referring to the spiritual and ethical perfection *on the last day.*"[39] And it is for that reason that treatments like Bucer's, which are less obviously focused on the Jewish and eschatological import of these phrases, have fallen by the wayside in much contemporary exegesis.

So is Bucer's exegesis simply unrecoverable at this point? It is hard to answer with a definitive no. Although, as we saw with his treatment of election, Bucer ignores the Old Testament background of the holiness terminology, there is still wide overlap between Bucer's reading and more recent treatments insofar as both highlight the status-oriented or forensic dimension of the language *and* the lived, ethical dimension of Paul's language. As Markus Bockmuehl has put it, "Paul's theological toolbox has no concept of new holy being that does not issue forth in the pursuit of holy and morally pure doing."[40]

As for the dismissal of any doctrine of "imputed righteousness" altogether, after the fashion of Wright, caution is needed. Certainly Paul does not *say* that it is the holiness and blamelessness of Christ that is credited to the church—which is what contemporary exegetes have been so concerned to point out. But, as D. A. Carson and others have noted, it is also important to keep in mind the limits of such a claim.[41] The realms of exegesis and

---

[38]Sanders points out that elsewhere in the Pauline corpus conversion terminology often centers on the "justification" word group, whereas "community maintenance" within the church uses other words, "many drawn from the purity language of the Bible, such as 'blameless'" (E. P. Sanders, *Paul, the Law, and the Jewish People* [Philadelphia: Fortress, 1983], p. 45). But this needs to be qualified with the recognition that "holiness" language can refer to both status and conduct, as it does here in the opening of Ephesians: "If ἅγιος in 1:1 denoted primarily status, here in 1:4 it indicates the moral condition that belongs to such a status" (Lincoln, *Ephesians*, p. 24).

[39]O'Brien, *Ephesians*, p. 425, emphasis added. Compare on this Col 1:22, where the same pairing occurs and where the reference is clearly eschatological: "he has now reconciled [you] in his body of flesh by his death, in order to present you holy and blameless [ἁγίους καὶ ἀμώμους] and above reproach before him, if indeed you continue in the faith, stable and steadfast."

[40]Markus Bockmuehl, "'Keeping It Holy': Old Testament Commandment and New Testament Faith," in Carl E. Braaten and Christopher R. Seitz, eds., *I Am the Lord Your God: Christian Reflections on the Ten Commandments* (Grand Rapids: Eerdmans, 2005), pp. 95-124, at p. 111.

[41]D. A. Carson, "The Vindication of Imputation: On Fields of Discourse and Semantic Fields," in Mark Husbands and Daniel J. Treier, eds., *Justification: What's at Stake in the Current Debates* (Downers Grove, IL: InterVarsity Press, 2004), pp. 46-78; R. Michael Allen and Daniel J. Treier,

dogmatic theology are distinguishable, and therefore to show that Paul does not explicitly *articulate* a doctrine is not the same thing as to prove that such a doctrine has no Pauline *basis*.[42] If we ask whether Paul *says* that there is an imputation of Christ's holiness to believers who lack it, then we must agree that the conceptual register of the language in Ephesians 1:4 does not point in this direction. But at the same time, there are contextual indications that all blessings, whether of status ("adoption," "forgiveness") or of moral character ("holy"), are given to believers through their union with Christ. The blessings of Ephesians 1:3 come to the Ephesians "in Christ," the grace they enjoy as a result of predestination is theirs "in the Beloved" (Eph 1:6), and redemption and forgiveness are granted "in him" (Eph 1:8). When this is coupled with the later emphasis in Ephesians on the preconversion "deadness" of believers (Eph 2:5), the exclusion of their works as efficacious for salvation and the concomitant exclusion of boasting (Eph 2:8-9), and the character of their faith as a gift (Eph 2:8), then it becomes easier to see the deep Pauline roots for Bucer's main point: that before the ethical dimension of holiness can be stressed, there must first be a gracious "seating" of believers with Christ, in his place of honor (Eph 2:6), on the basis of which believers may *then* begin to perform "good works, which God prepared beforehand, that we should walk in them" (Eph 2:10). In stressing this point—that imputation grounds and makes possible holy living—Bucer would seem to be on firm Pauline territory.

Conclusion

So is Martin Bucer a good reader of Ephesians 1:3-6? In order to answer that question, we need to return to our criteria outlined at the beginning. Certainly Bucer exhibits admirable consistency, taking his stand squarely in the developing Reformation tradition of reading Paul and also in line with that tradition's best aims, returning to the sources of the original languages and making use of the tools of literary analysis available to him. As we saw, he was at pains to demonstrate the Hebrew roots of Paul's language in Ephe-

---

"Dogmatic Theology and Biblical Perspectives on Justification: A Reply to Leithart," *WTJ* 70 (2008): 105-10.

[42]This way of putting the matter owes something to David Yeago's distinction between "concepts" and "judgments" in his "The New Testament and Nicene Dogma: A Contribution to the Recovery of Theological Exegesis," *Pro Ecclesia* 3, no. 2 (1994): 152-64.

sians 1:3 and to cross-reference other portions of Scripture where they might prove illuminating.

However, more can be said. Not only is Bucer a faithful exemplar of his own tradition, but he is also a good reader of Paul if "good" connotes canons of interpretation by which interpreters of today still abide. Bucer's comments are tethered firmly and tightly to "the way the words go" in Ephesians 1:3-6. He hews closely to their order, taking up theological themes for comment only as they are indicated by the text. Even where he makes a possible misstep—for instance, in naming Romans 9–11 as primarily a discussion of individual predestination—his readings have heuristic value and may serve to point out some of the lacunae in allegedly more historically sensitive readings from our contemporary contexts.

Finally, Bucer's comments point to the need for a *renewal* of the kind of exegesis he practiced. We do not need simple *repetition* of his work, since, as we have seen, Bucer's exegesis appears historically impoverished in certain ways—when it neglects the Old Testament or Jewish roots of some of Paul's terminology, for instance, or when it downplays the theme of the fulfillment of Israel's eschatological hopes (such as in his discussion of "spiritual"). For these reasons, we cannot follow Bucer in every particular. But neither do we need to *reject* his work. Carving out a path in between repetition and rejection, we need to learn from his approach and practice our own form of theological exegesis that, in a real sense, takes up where Bucer left off and reinvigorates his way of proceeding. We need to practice a renewed theological interpretation that is alert to the canonical context of Pauline texts, their grammatical forms, their use and proclamation in our traditions. And above all, we must attempt interpretations that treat the Pauline texts first and foremost as witnesses to Christ and his unsurpassable work. Bucer offers this kind of reading of Ephesians 1:3-6, and in this respect he remains a pioneer and a model.

1 & 2 Corinthians and John Calvin

7

John Calvin's Reading *of the* Corinthian Epistles

Michael Allen

Calvin's Geneva may be viewed now as a reformational hub, and it did receive praise in its time as paradise, but Calvin's own testimony shows the multipronged challenges faced there. Comparison to Corinth in the time of Paul can be fertile for reflecting on ways in which the Reformed movement was generated by Paul's own reforming efforts. Corinth required discipline in several ways—theological, moral, liturgical, economic, and ecumenical or ecclesial polity. Calvin's study of these reforms illumines his own commitments and therefore warrants our attention.

This chapter investigates John Calvin's practice of reading Paul as a Reformational theologian-pastor.[1] In so doing, I will consider three things. First, I will survey Calvin's corpus and show the place of his reading of Paul's epistles. Second, I will describe the shape of his commentaries on 1 and 2 Corinthians, noting his view of their themes as well as key features of his interpretation. Third, I will focus on a central theme—the theology of the cross—that flows from Calvin's exegesis of the Corinthian writings and shapes much of his theological and pastoral reflection in those commentaries and elsewhere.

---

[1] I employ the term *Reformational* with respect to the sixteenth-century context rather than any twentieth-century link to the work of Herman Dooyeweerd (as it is sometimes used).

Calvin as Reader of Paul

To this day, John Calvin is perhaps the most respected Reformation-era interpreter of the Bible. While Luther's 1535 *Lectures on Galatians* are surely the most famous biblical interpretation of this period, Calvin's exegetical writings still garner a wider and more straightforward respect than those of his forerunner from Wittenberg or any other Reformational figure. Yet respect is not the same thing as recognition. Calvin's writings are viewed highly, but they are rarely located in their intended rhetorical and pastoral place and thus are somewhat frequently misunderstood. So, a few words concerning the nature of Calvin's literary works serve as a wise introduction to any study of a particular part of that wider output.

Calvin's calling was twofold. Though technically never ordained, Calvin trained laypeople and pastors for decades in Geneva. His work in the church and in the academy involved biblical interpretation in the form of both sermons and commentaries.[2] Yet Calvin remains most famous for his *Institutes of the Christian Religion*, which in its various editions (from 1536 to 1559) rivals Luther's *Lectures on Galatians* as perhaps the most noted book to arise from the Protestant Reformation. Most accounts of Calvin's thought or studies of his theology fix on this specific text alone (and typically the final 1559 edition) as the full summary of what he believed.[3]

Calvin had a different perspective, however, and viewed his *Institutes* as but one aspect of a two-pronged theological program. He intended that text to serve as a guide to prepare pastors for the reading and preaching of the Bible. As he famously states in his "Letter to the Reader": "Moreover, it has been my purpose in this labor to prepare and instruct candidates in sacred theology for the reading of the divine Word, in order that they may be able both to have easy access to it and to advance in it without stumbling."[4] But he then expected those same pastors to make use of his many biblical commentaries for specific guidance in interpreting scriptural passages.

---

[2]Calvin wrote in Latin for the educated class, but he regularly translated his writings into French for the laity. On his diverse reading audiences, see Serene Jones, *Calvin and the Rhetoric of Piety*, Columbia Series in Reformed Theology (Louisville: Westminster John Knox, 1995), chap. 2.

[3]See, e.g., Alister McGrath, *A Life of John Calvin: A Study in the Shaping of Western Culture* (Oxford: Blackwell, 1993).

[4]John Calvin, "John Calvin to the Reader," in *Institutes of the Christian Religion*, ed. John T. McNeill, trans. Ford Lewis Battles, Library of Christian Classics 20 (Philadelphia: Westminster, 1960), p. 4.

Calvin's commentarial approach is marked by what has become a well-known phrase in biblical hermeneutics: "lucid brevity." In the dedicatory letter to Simon Gryneé, found in his first commentary (on Romans), he stated: "Both of us felt that lucid brevity constituted the particular virtue of an interpreter. Since it is almost his only task to unfold the mind of the writer whom he has undertaken to expound, he misses his mark, or at least strays outside his limits, by the extent to which he leads his readers away from the meaning of the author."[5] He believed that the writings of his good friend Philipp Melanchthon lacked lucidity inasmuch as Melanchthon's selective expositions did not address or clarify every verse of the Bible. Yet the more prolix writings of Martin Bucer, which certainly dealt with every verse, were so profuse as to overwhelm the reader. Calvin aimed for—and to a remarkable extent succeeded in attaining—"lucid brevity," by addressing the specifics of any given verse without being compelled to unpack all its theological implications and doctrinal connections in its every occurrence. He intended the *Institutes* to serve as that gathering of common places (*loci communes*) wherein each doctrine would be addressed in a full, orderly manner.

So the wise reader is instructed to move backwards and forward. When Calvin notes a biblical passage in the *Institutes*, he is typically intending his reader to search out greater exegetical reflections on that portion of Scripture in his commentary on that text.[6] And when a specific paragraph or verse of Scripture seems to imply a particular doctrinal claim, Calvin will only briefly mention it in the commentary but will unfold the topic on a grander scale in the *Institutes*. As he said of his 1539 *Institutes*,

> If, after this road has, as it were, been paved, I shall publish any interpretations of Scripture, I shall always condense them, because I shall have no need to

---

[5] Calvin, "Dedicatory Epistle," *Iohannis Calvini Commentarius in Epistolam Pauli ad Romanos*, ed. T. H. L. Parker, Calvin's New Testament Commentaries 8 (Leiden: Brill, 1981), p. 1.

[6] For contextually reasoned approaches to the genre of the *Institutes*, see Richard A. Muller, "To Elaborate on the Topics: The Context and Method of Calvin's *Institutes*," in *The Unaccommodated Calvin: Studies in the Foundation of a Theological Tradition*, Oxford Studies in Historical Theology (New York: Oxford University Press, 2000), pp. 112-17; Elsie A. McKee, "Exegesis, Theology, and Development in Calvin's *Institutio*: A Methodological Suggestion," in *Probing the Reformed Tradition: Historical Studies in Honor of Edward A. Dowey, Jr.*, ed. Brian G. Armstrong and Elsie A. McKee (Louisville: Westminster John Knox, 1989), pp. 154-72. For Calvin's use of proof texts, see Michael Allen and Scott Swain, "In Defense of Proof-Texting," *Journal of the Evangelical Theological Society* 54, no. 3 (2011): 600-603.

undertake long doctrinal discussions, and to digress into commonplaces. In this way the godly reader will be spared great annoyance and boredom, provided he approach Scripture armed with a knowledge of the present work, as a necessary tool.[7]

In light of this rhetorical and pastoral strategy, how do we inquire about Calvin's reading of Paul? We must address both the *Institutes* and the commentaries. Furthermore, we must consider their interplay and the way in which they point to each other.

Calvin comments on and preaches through the whole Pauline corpus. Not only does he cover the whole terrain, but he also begins his commentary work with this material. It holds a position of obvious prestige in his career. T. H. L. Parker has argued that the historical primacy of the Pauline epistles in Calvin's work mirrors that of the epistles within the New Testament itself, and that Calvin viewed this literary history of the biblical writings as pivotal for his own ministry.[8] By the end of the 1540s, Calvin had commented on the entirety of the Pauline epistles.[9] The prestige of Paul is not mere historical happenstance, though, for Calvin also shapes his theological structure according to a specifically Pauline architecture. Richard Muller has observed that the early shaping of the *Institutes* was generated by engagement with Paul's theology. In particular, Calvin's budding friendship with Philipp Melanchthon convinced him that this remarkable Lutheran theologian was right to structure his own theological text, the *Loci communes*, around the order of Paul's epistle to the Romans.[10] Calvin believed that this epistle was

---

[7]Calvin, "John Calvin to the Reader," pp. 4-5.
[8]*Calvin's New Testament Commentaries*, 2nd ed. (Edinburgh: T&T Clark, 1993), pp. 31-32.
[9]R. Ward Holder has claimed that "the sixteenth century was a Pauline age," noting that at least twenty-eight commentaries were written on 1 and 2 Corinthians in German libraries alone during this time period ("Introduction—Paul in the Sixteenth Century: Invitation and a Challenge," in *A Companion to Paul in the Reformation*, Companions to the Christian Tradition [Leiden: Brill, 2009], pp. 1, 2).
[10]Richard A. Muller, "Establishing the *Ordo docendi*: The Organization of Calvin's *Institutes*, 1536-1559," in *Unaccommodated Calvin*, pp. 127-30; cf. Randall C. Zachman, *John Calvin as Teacher, Pastor, and Theologian: The Shape of His Writings and Thought* (Grand Rapids: Baker Academic, 2006), pp. 29-53. Stephen Edmondson thinks Muller's analysis of Calvin's order of teaching (*ordo docendi*) does not take this last reorganization (1559) seriously and thus privileges the Melanchthonian/Pauline emphasis too much (*Calvin's Christology* [Cambridge: Cambridge University Press, 2004], p. 44 [cf. p. 87]). Edmondson may have a point about a particular section of the *Institutes* (the specifically christological material); even so, Muller's account surely seems a fair portrayal of the wider scope.

an entry point to the whole Bible; as he said, "If we have gained a true understanding of this epistle, we have an open door to all the most profound treasures of scripture."[11] Beginning in 1539, Calvin adopts this pathway: the basic order of the *Institutes* follows the doctrinal sequence of Romans. Paul's influence is clearly crucial.

Calvin, however, was not exclusively dependent on Romans as a template, and this is true in at least two respects. First, he moves toward a more explicitly creedal structure in the 1559 *Institutes*, where the four books follow the four parts of the creed (Father, Son, Spirit, church). The order still follows much the same course as Romans (doctrine of revelation, God, humanity, sin, Christ, salvation, Spirit, church, etc.), yet it is framed in a slightly different style. Second, he adds other elements that are not features of Romans into the *Institutes*. Such a maneuver cannot be avoided, of course, but it does show that Calvin's dependence on Paul and Romans is surely not a restrictive or exclusive focus. Even so, a survey of Calvin's works shows the remarkable place of Paul in his theology, in terms of both scope and sequence.

CALVIN AS READER OF THE CORINTHIAN EPISTLES

Calvin devotes serious attention not only to Paul in general but to the Corinthian epistles in particular. After commenting on Romans and writing a short treatise on Jude, Calvin next turned to 1–2 Corinthians. These commentaries appeared six years after the famed volume on Romans, a delay likely due to the stresses and demands of his pastoral vocation. We will consider the shape of his commentaries, each in turn, before pointing to some key features and notable facets of his interpretive work present here.

In his typical fashion, Calvin begins his work on 1 Corinthians by charting the "theme of the epistle."[12] He notes the nature of Corinth, indeed, that there are particular dangers of living in "rich, commercial cities."[13] The attentive reader, of course, will wonder in what ways Calvin presents Corinth

---

[11]John Calvin, *The Epistles of Paul the Apostle to the Romans and to the Thessalonians*, ed. David Torrance and Thomas F. Torrance, trans. Ross Mackenzie (Grand Rapids: Eerdmans, 1960), p. 5.

[12]John Calvin, *The First Epistle of Paul the Apostle to the Corinthians*, ed. David W. Torrance and Thomas F. Torrance, trans. John W. Fraser, Calvin's Commentaries (Grand Rapids: Eerdmans, 1960), pp. 7-14.

[13]Ibid., p. 9.

as an ancient analogue for his Geneva. He describes the false apostles who have settled there: devaluing Paul's rhetoric, dividing the church and seeking to enhance their own reputations.[14] Their error appeared pastoral and not overtly doctrinal: "They did not detract from the substance of the Gospel in any respect; but since they were burning with a misguided and passionate desire for prominence, I think that they had devised a new method of teaching, that was not consistent with the simplicity of Christ; and they hoped that it would make them the objects of people's admiration."[15] The congregation in Corinth apparently suffered from this infusion of false teaching, earning the title "babes in Christ" from Calvin: "Although they were not entirely without grace, yet they had more of the flesh than of the Spirit in their lives."[16]

Calvin then traces the order of Paul's argument, as is his standard practice in beginning a commentary.[17] Paul begins with words of congratulation but quickly turns to exhortations that the Corinthians flee pride and return to a posture of humility (1 Cor 1). He then reflects on the way that preaching is seemingly foolish, when viewed against the backdrop of worldly wisdom (1 Cor 2); "he points out that the distaste for the Word, which was so strong in them, did not come from any defect in the Word itself, but from their ignorance" (1 Cor 3).[18] He must address the nature of the apostolic office, says Calvin, arguing that his sufferings demonstrate the genuine calling he has been given by the risen Lord (1 Cor 4).

Paul then turns to other exhortations, according to Calvin. Paul strongly berates the Corinthians for tolerating incestuous relations between a man and his stepmother (1 Cor 5). He rebukes their willingness to run to court to settle internal matters as well as their overindulgent sexual behaviors (1 Cor 6). Because sex has proven a debilitating stumbling block, Paul then reflects at some length on virginity, marriage and celibacy (1 Cor 7). He also must address the practice of joining in idol worship, a practice that the Corinthians seem to have accepted, provided they did not intend to offer genuine worship to idols in their hearts; again, Paul emphasizes that bodily

---

[14]Ibid., p. 7.
[15]Ibid., p. 8.
[16]Ibid., p. 65 (1 Cor 3:1).
[17]Ibid., pp. 9-14.
[18]Ibid., p. 10.

and social actions matter, for they are God's temple (1 Cor 8).

Motivation proves important, believes Calvin, so he says that Paul offers two key arguments for obeying his commands. First, Paul describes his own willingness to use his Christian freedom for the sake of others (1 Cor 9). Second, he points backwards to the example of the faltering Israelites in the wilderness, suggesting that they are a negative example of a people who believed for a time yet fell away due to unbelief (1 Cor 10). He then turns to ways that they ought to receive grace and power for perseverance: worship, sacraments, community and spiritual gifts. Paul suggests that, unfortunately, the Corinthians' embodiment of each of these callings has taken a turn to the disorderly. So Paul describes what proper sacramental practice looks like (1 Cor 11), what Christian unity involves (1 Cor 12), the nature of living together in love (1 Cor 13) and, finally, the purpose of spiritual gifts and their place in the Christian life (1 Cor 14). Last, Paul summarizes the gospel of the Christ's resurrection (1 Cor 15) and exhorts the Corinthians to participate in the offering for the church in Jerusalem and offers them warm greetings (1 Cor 16).

When he turns to 2 Corinthians, Calvin again begins by reflecting on the themes of the epistle in sequential order.[19] He relates the two epistles in this manner: "From the connexion between the two epistles we may infer that the first had some good effect among the Corinthians, although not as much as it should, and, further, that some wicked men were still refusing to acknowledge Paul's authority and persisting in their obstinancy."[20] According to Calvin, Paul reconsiders some old issues and presses onward to others.

Paul praises the Corinthians and also tells them that his recent sufferings work for their good. Yet he immediately points to their problems as precluding his peaceful visit (2 Cor 1). He turns to discuss the glory of his apostolic work (2 Cor 2–3) as well as the perseverance he shows in ministering in the face of persecution and pain (2 Cor 4). The hope of new creation and the promise of reconciliation sustain this kind of self-sacrificial service (2 Cor 5); in light of this glorious future, Paul presses them to flee

---

[19]John Calvin, *The Second Epistle of Paul the Apostle to the Corinthians and the Epistles to Timothy, Titus, and Philemon*, ed. David W. Torrance and Thomas F. Torrance, trans. T. A. Smail, Calvin's Commentaries (Grand Rapids: Eerdmans, 1964), pp. 3-6.

[20]Ibid., p. 3.

idolatry (2 Cor 6). "But in order to avoid discouraging or alienating their tender minds by too sharp a rebuke, he once again assures them of his own goodwill towards them and returns to his explanation of his past severity with them, which he broke off abruptly before, and continues with it though now in a different way" (2 Cor 7).[21]

Calvin then observes a shift in Paul's argument: "From the beginning of chapter 8 to the end of chapter 9 he goes on to deal with cheerfulness in the giving of money, a subject he had already raised in the last chapter of the first epistle" (2 Cor 8–9).[22] Paul then defends himself from accusations: he possesses the powers of an apostle, he has exercised his pastoral concern in a measured and loving way (rather than out of defensiveness), and he will return to Corinth to minister among them (2 Cor 10). "In the eleventh chapter he recalls the Corinthians from the misguided enthusiasms which have been corrupting them and warns them that there is nothing more dangerous than to be led astray from the straightforward integrity [*simplicitas*] of the Gospel" (2 Cor 11).[23] He returns to his own credentials, refusing to boast and yet boasting in a godly way, all the while admitting that this is another instance of him willingly being made a fool on their behalf (2 Cor 12). He concludes by warning them and calling them to honor his ministry: "It is dangerous for them to despise a man whom they know by experience to be the undoubted and faithful ambassador of the Lord."[24]

What are some characteristic features of Calvin's interpretative work in these commentaries?

One is that Calvin's interpretive practice places marked importance on the role of paraphrase. Ward Holder has suggested that this is one of Calvin's key exegetical practices, and these volumes bear his claim out.[25] Paraphrase can be specific, marked by the explicit statement "that is to say" or "in this sense," or it may operate at a more implicit level. The chief task of commentary is restatement of the text for the sake of elucidation;

---

[21] Ibid., p. 5.
[22] Ibid.
[23] Ibid., p. 6.
[24] Ibid.
[25] R. Ward Holder, *John Calvin and the Grounding of Interpretation: Calvin's First Commentaries*, Studies in the History of Christian Thought (Leiden: Brill, 2005), pp. 91–97.

John Calvin's Reading of the Corinthian Epistles

thus, Calvin's initial outlines of each epistle as he addresses its themes (implicit paraphrase) and numerous explicit occurrences of close textual restatement (explicit paraphrase) are a constant fixture in his commentaries and crucial to using them.[26] The large-scale thematic paraphrase and the occasional short paraphrases serve the same function: to elucidate the particular shape of the text.

Furthermore, Calvin's exegetical approach evidences four nuances that might seem surprising to those who perceive him according to his common caricature as a self-assured, imposing tyrant, who brought his legal training to bear on the pastoral-theological tasks before him by reducing reflection on the mysteries of the gospel to the thorough application of logic. First, Calvin may have been a lawyer by training, but he showed a poet's awareness of metaphor and imagery. He employs some recurring metaphors in his writings, and he insistently fixes on the metaphorical language employed throughout these epistles by Paul.[27] Second, Calvin demonstrates a willingness to observe exegetical options. In many instances, he notes alternative interpretations, presents each of them, points to his favored choice, and yet insists that (at least some) others are feasible and fruitful.[28] For example, he realizes that 2 Corinthians 4:6 lends itself to four possible interpretations of the statement that God said, "Light shall shine," and he relays them all. While he prefers John Chrysostom's interpretation, the idea that this is an allusion to God's action in the original creation, he also notes that Ambrose's approach is suitable, focusing strictly on the gospel and God's new creation. "Everyone may use his own judgment."[29] Calvin surely cannot be perceived as a theologian unaware of the hermeneutical

---

[26]Holder refers to two types of paraphrase as the "doctrinal" and the "textual" (ibid., pp. 94-97). I suggest that the more apt distinction is between explicit and implicit, inasmuch as Calvin offers paraphrase en masse without noting that he is doing so (thus implicitly), while he also makes a point within the commentary of giving very specific paraphrase (thus explicitly). Both occurrences can address doctrinal or textual points—that is not the key distinction.

[27]For examples, see Calvin, *First Epistle*, p. 186 (1 Cor 9:5-7), pp. 198-99 (1 Cor 9:26-27), p. 263 (1 Cor 12:12), p. 353 (1 Cor 16:9); as well as Calvin, *Second Epistle*, p. 39 (2 Cor 2–3), p. 68 (2 Cor 5:4), p. 11 (2 Cor 1:8), p. 107 (2 Cor 8:2).

[28]Because examples would be so numerous, I limit myself to 2 Corinthians alone; see Calvin, *Second Epistle*, p. 9 (2 Cor 1:6), p. 18 (2 Cor 1:15), p. 31 (2 Cor 2:10), p. 55 (2 Cor 4:4), p. 56 (2 Cor 4:5), p. 57 (2 Cor 4:6), p. 60 (2 Cor 4:10), p. 64 (2 Cor 4:17), p. 67 (2 Cor 5:1), p. 86 (2 Cor 6:5), p. 101 (2 Cor 7:11), p. 103 (2 Cor 7:12), p. 125 (2 Cor 9:11), pp. 131-32 (2 Cor 10:7), pp. 148-49 (2 Cor 11:20), p. 163 (2 Cor 12:11), p. 174 (2 Cor 13:9).

[29]Calvin, *Second Epistle*, p. 57 (2 Cor 4:6).

and doctrinal judgments that must be made or of the possibility of acceptable diversity in expression.[30]

Third, Calvin is a canonical reader. Of course, he reads the Corinthian epistles as coherent texts on their own terms; this leads him, for example, to ask how 2 Corinthians 1:12 (a claim of boasting in one's clean conscience) can fit with 2 Corinthians 10:17 (the imperative to boast in the Lord).[31] In various ways, he goes still further and illumines Corinthians by reading it alongside other texts. In some cases, this involves the pursuit of harmony, when Corinthians seems to conflict with other biblical teachings regarding history (as in his comparison of 1 Cor 10 with the original account of the Israelites' wilderness wanderings in Numbers).[32] In other occurrences, seeming theological divergences are occasions for Calvin to probe toward greater exegetical specificity. For example, 1 Corinthians 11:3 seems so clearly to conflict with Galatians 3:28 regarding the equality of men and women in Christ Jesus. Reading these texts together leads Calvin to reflect on how 1 Corinthians 11 addresses the civic order (where men may excel women in "preeminence") while Galatians 3 addresses the heavenly order (both men and women are equally "innocent").[33]

Fourth, one notable feature of Calvin's work on 1 Corinthians would not be noticed unless one had first read his earlier *Commentary on Romans*. That previous work, released in 1540 and written during his banishment from Geneva, showed very little specifically pastoral advice. Yet Ward Holder has tallied more than seventy such instances of pastoral reflection in the commentary on 1 Corinthians, written just six years later.[34] Two factors can likely

---

[30]Indeed, Calvin's ecumenical career bears out this exegetical principle in confessional form, for Calvin shows a willingness to express what he believes is catholic and evangelical doctrine (inclusive of the Reformational distinctives reclaimed at such great cost to him and others) in a variety of forms, whether written by Lutherans or various Reformed churches. Furthermore, his theological flexibility extends to issues of polity: "We know that each church is free to set up the form of polity that suits its circumstances, and is to its advantage, because the Lord has not given any specific directions about this" (*First Epistle*, p. 228 [1 Cor 11:2]).

[31]Calvin, *Second Epistle*, p. 15 (2 Cor 1:12). Calvin offers a remarkably cogent three-pronged defense of noncompetitive divine and human action; therefore, boasting in human success need not imply stealing glory from God, for "it is God's gifts of which he is boasting so that he is glorifying God as their sole author."

[32]Calvin, *First Epistle*, pp. 208-9 (1 Cor 10:8).

[33]Ibid., p. 229 (1 Cor 11:3).

[34]R. Ward Holder, "Calvin as Commentator on the Pauline Epistles," in *Calvin and the Bible*, ed. Donald K. McKim (Cambridge: Cambridge University Press, 2006), p. 236.

account for this shift. Subjectively, Calvin is a vindicated man, recalled to Geneva, and a man on a mission, trying to reform the pastoral practice of those ordained to serve in his city. He can and must engage pastoral issues. Objectively, there is surely more direct reflection on pastoral practice in 1 Corinthians than in Romans, so the text itself cries for such analysis. Some specific examples will be seen later as we turn to the practical implications of Calvin's focus on the theology of the cross.

While many observations could be made and numerous exegetical decisions might be noted, we have seen the basic shape of Calvin's exposition of the Corinthian epistles via his study of their themes and have noted four major features of his interpretive work: his regular use of paraphrase, his sensitivity to metaphor and to ambiguity of meaning, his canonical breadth and his pastoral bent.

CALVIN AND THE CROSS: REVELATION, THEOLOGY, SPECULATION

We turn now to one central aspect of the Corinthian epistles—the theology of the cross (*theologia crucis*)—which also operated as a major fixture of Reformational theology. I will seek to show the exegetical roots and systematic import of this feature in Calvin's theology, looking backwards to its setting in the Corinthian epistles and straining forward to appreciate its widespread influence across Calvin's exegesis of those epistles and his whole pastoral theology. In so doing, we will consider the way in which Calvin views theology as a practice undertaken between revelation and speculation.

Revelation. Martin Luther sets the gold standard, of course, for defining the theology of the cross. His Heidelberg Disputation of 1518 most famously addresses the topic, although the concept continues to shape Luther's thinking throughout his ministry (as is evident in his last lecture cycle on Genesis).[35] The theology of the cross is a subtle, easily misunderstood doctrine, precisely because it involves the application of the atonement to Christian epistemology and spirituality. As Luther says, "That person does

---

[35] Martin Luther, "Heidelberg Disputation, 1518," in *Career of the Reformer 1* (LW 31), ed. Harold J. Grimm (Philadephia: Fortress, 1957), pp. 35-70; cf. *Lectures on Genesis 1-5* (LW 1), ed. Jaroslav Pelikan (St. Louis: Concordia, 1958), pp. 11, 13, 14 (on Gen 1:2), p. 45 (on Gen 6:5-6), p. 72 (on Gen 6:18). For helpful reflection on the theology of the cross in Luther, see Gerhard Forde, *On Being a Theologian of the Cross: Reflections on Luther's Heidelberg Disputation, 1518* (Grand Rapids: Eerdmans, 1997).

not deserve to be called a theologian who looks upon the invisible things of God as though they were clearly perceptible in those things which have actually happened [Rom. 1:20]. He deserves to be called a theologian, however, who comprehends the visible and manifest things of God seen through suffering and the cross."[36] The issue is one of epistemological access and assurance—where one looks to see God and how one believes one knows him. Luther thinks different approaches lead to radically different results: "A theologian of glory calls evil good and good evil. A theologian of the cross calls the thing what it actually is."[37]

The doctrine flows from exegetical roots and deep pastoral motivation. Both are evident in Calvin's commentaries on 1 and 2 Corinthians. As Calvin puts it, "Paul's fear was not that the Corinthians would make an immediate, open, and complete break with Christ, but that they would turn aside little by little from the simplicity and purity they had learnt to profane and alien inventions and would at length fall away."[38] The diagnosis involves an unchecked confidence in human reasoning—a belief that we are in glory already—that makes one a theologian of glory, that is, someone who believes they can trust their own intuition and impulse because they have already arrived in the spiritual and epistemological promised land. The remedy comes in the form of God's life-giving Word putting one's natural self to death and giving birth to a spiritual self. Nothing short of the cross is capable of giving life to those stuck in darkness and death. The cross reminds us we are those still journeying in the wilderness, ever in need of deliverance, promised grace in Christ that is given ever anew in his revelation through his prophets and apostles.

We begin with the nature of revelation, according to John Calvin. "Put briefly, the entire authority [*maiestas*] of the Gospel collapses unless we know that the living Christ speaks to us from the heavens."[39] For Calvin, revelation is an activity of the risen Christ by his Spirit. Jesus speaks. His Spirit illumines. While we have no independent wisdom worthy of

---

[36]Luther, "Heidelberg Disputation," p. 40 (theses 19-20).
[37]Ibid., p. 40 (thesis 21). For warnings against the attempt to ponder glory apart from the cross, see John Calvin, *Genesis* (Edinburgh: Banner of Truth Trust, 1965), 1:58-59.
[38]Calvin, *Second Epistle*, p. 141 (2 Cor 11:3).
[39]John Calvin, *The Acts of the Apostles, Chapters 1-13*, trans. W. I. G. MacDonald, Calvin's Commentaries (Grand Rapids: Eerdmans, 1989), p. 24 (on Acts 1:3).

knowing or judging God on our own, we are given understanding in Christ. "'For who has understood the mind of the Lord so as to instruct him?' But we have the mind of Christ" (1 Cor 2:16).[40] Revelation is not so much a principle, then, or an epistemological source, as it is an ongoing activity of the ascended Lord. Now, in so revealing himself, the speaking Son does give birth to theological sources and even, at a further remove, to doctrinal principles.

Calvin is not alone in the Reformed world in his affirmation of the importance of sticking closely, exclusively, to God's revelation when and where it is given. The Ten Theses of Berne (1528), for example, begin by stating that "the holy, Christian Church, whose only Head is Christ, is born of the Word of God, abides in the same, and does not listen to the voice of a stranger."[41] The Westminster Confession similarly begins with discussion of the Word of God (chap. 1). While the phrase "theology of the cross" is not regularly employed in the Reformed tradition, as in the Lutheran world, the focus on God's Word and the function of its sanctifying power are continually affirmed.[42] These reflections on revelation flow from consideration of Paul's declaration: "I decided to know nothing among you except Jesus Christ and him crucified . . . that your faith might not rest in the wisdom of men but in the power of God" (1 Cor 2:2, 5).

Character of theology. Second Corinthians 5 reminds us that the mind must be reconciled to God, and this requires a light that cannot be lit by those who find themselves to be utter darkness (2 Cor 5:3-4; cf. 1 Cor 2:14). Like John the Evangelist, Paul affirms that God has given us such light in the message of the cross of Christ. Calvin says, "This is an important passage from which we may learn that God is not to be sought after in this inscrutable majesty (for he dwells in light inaccessible) but is to be known in so far as He reveals Himself in Christ. Thus the attempts of men to know God apart from Christ are ephemeral for they wander from the right way."[43] The object

---

[40]Unless otherwise indicated, all Scripture quotations are from the ESV.
[41]"Ten Theses of Berne (1528)," in *Reformed Confessions of the Sixteenth Century*, ed. Arthur Cochrane (Louisville: Westminster John Knox, 2003), p. 49.
[42]See the analysis in Michael Allen, *Reformed Theology*, Doing Theology (London: T&T Clark, 2010), chap. 1.
[43]Calvin, *Second Epistle*, pp. 57-58 (2 Cor 4:6); cf. Calvin, *Acts of the Apostles*, p. 190 (on Acts 7:30): "Let us therefore establish in the first place that right from the beginning God made no communication with men except by Christ. For there is no relationship between God and us unless the

of knowledge shapes the order of knowledge. Thus the nature of revelation determines the theological approach of John Calvin. A gracious God gives revelation and in so doing shapes the scope and parameters of its occurrence.

The theology of the cross does not negate all human learning, or even the validity of general revelation. Indeed, "by these words the apostle does not ask us to make a total surrender of the wisdom which is either innate or acquired by long experience. He only asks that we subjugate it to God, so that all our wisdom might be derived from His Word."[44] Calvin suggests that there are two limits to natural wisdom. First, it fails to reach to heaven—it is natural and not supernatural. Second, it is spoiled even in what it does know by sin. We might say that Calvin here posits both a nature-grace and a sin-grace distinction.[45] Natural theology can attain a limited knowledge (coming short of heaven and the gospel), but it also is inhibited by sin's distortions. Death and resurrection are needed to make good use of the world's wisdom: "If the earth and its fullness belong to the Lord, there is nothing in the world which is not sacred and pure."[46] Thus fit eyes are needed to understand the sacred and fathom the pure. Only the Spirit of God can fashion eyes capable of such vision through the application of the "spectacles" of Holy Scripture.[47]

Luther had identified the spiritual importance of the theology of the cross: "That is the reason why our theology is trustworthy: because it tears us away from ourselves and places us outside of ourselves—in such a way that we do not rely on our own powers, our conscience, our senses, our person, our works, but it supports us instead on that which is outside of ourselves [*extra nos*], namely, on the promise and truth of God, which cannot deceive."[48] Calvin provides a similar take on the implications of the theology of the cross—namely, the surety of Christian assurance. When addressing Paul's teaching that the spiritual person is to be judged by no one (1 Cor 2:15), Calvin says, "Paul lifts our faith above the world" and gives us

---

Mediator be present to procure His favour for us."
[44]Calvin, *First Epistle*, p. 80 (1 Cor 3:18); cf. Luther, "Heidelberg Disputation," pp. 40-41 (thesis 22).
[45]Calvin, *First Epistle*, pp. 38-39 (1 Cor 1:20). On the notions of nature and grace in Calvin, see Calvin, *First Epistle*, p. 61 (1 Cor 2:14-15), p. 164 (1 Cor 7:35).
[46]Calvin, *First Epistle*, p. 222 (1 Cor 10:26).
[47]Calvin, *Institutes*, I.11.1.
[48]Martin Luther, *Lectures on Galatians 1-4, 1535*, ed. Jaroslav Pelikan LW 26 (St. Louis: Concordia, 1963), p. 387 (Gal 4:6).

genuine assurance.⁴⁹ He will go so far as to define faith as inclusive of assurance. "Now we shall possess a right definition of faith if we call it a firm and certain knowledge of God's benevolence toward us, founded upon the truth of the freely given promise in Christ, both revealed to our minds and sealed upon our hearts through the Holy Spirit."⁵⁰ He summarizes later that he defines "faith as knowledge of divine benevolence toward us and a sure persuasion of its truth."⁵¹

Calvin emphasizes the surety of God's revelation; hence his definition sounds close to Luther's statement on the trustworthiness of theology. Elsewhere Calvin (and Luther as well) will address the question of waxing and waning subjective assurance.⁵² Calvin refuses to define faith, though, by its faltering occurrence in not-yet-perfected believers; instead, he defines it based on its objective source in God's sure Word. Doubts and weaknesses do remain in believers, and assurance does flag at times, but these events are moments of unbelief rather than aspects of belief itself.⁵³ Calvin locates this unbelief outside the believer's heart, yet internal to the believer's self.⁵⁴ Calvin grounds this assurance primarily in the Word of God as it promises eternal life and only secondarily in one's manifest evidences of renewal.

Speculation. The movement from revelation to theological confession always runs the risk of lapsing into speculation. The shift from listening to speaking always possesses the possibility of a misstatement or mangled transmission; 1 Corinthians 1 makes plain that "the word of the cross is folly" to many (1 Cor 1:18). Calvin most frequently identifies such errors with two

---

⁴⁹Calvin, *First Epistle*, p. 59 (1 Cor 2:15).
⁵⁰Calvin, *Insitutes*, III.2.7. Calvin never abandons this definition, according to Barbara Pitkin, *What Pure Eyes Could See: Calvin's Doctrine of Faith in Its Exegetical Context*, Oxford Studies in Historical Theology (Oxford: Oxford University Press, 1999), p. 29. For reflections on Calvin's doctrine of faith, see Michael Allen, *The Christ's Faith: A Dogmatic Account*, T&T Clark Studies in Systematic Theology (London: T&T Clark, 2009), pp. 83-88.
⁵¹Calvin, *Institutes*, III.2.12.
⁵²See, e.g., John Calvin, *Sermons on 2 Samuel*, trans. Douglas Kelly (Edinburgh: Banner of Truth Trust, 1992), pp. 199-201. Lively debate about Calvin's doctrine of assurance has ensued in recent years (since the controversial study of R. T. Kendall in the 1980s); the most important figures have been Randall Zachman, *The Assurance of Faith: Conscience in the Theology of Martin Luther and John Calvin* (Louisville: Westminster John Knox, 1993), p. 246, in criticism of Calvin's view as inherently unstable; and Paul Helm, *John Calvin's Ideas* (Oxford: Oxford University Press, 2004), p. 416, defending Calvin's view as coherent.
⁵³Calvin, *Institutes*, III.2.18; cf. Victor A. Shepherd, *The Nature and Function of Faith in the Theology of John Calvin* (Macon, GA: Mercer University Press, 1983), pp. 24-28.
⁵⁴Calvin, *Institutes*, III.2.21.

terms: *idolatry* and *speculation*.[55] He defines idolatry quite clearly in his comments on the Acts of the Apostles: "The basic difference between proper worship and idolatry is that the godly undertake nothing except what is in conformity with the Word of God; but others think that they are entitled to do anything that suits themselves, and so they have their own will in place of a law, when the fact is that God approves only what He Himself has prescribed."[56] Elsewhere he notes the prevalence of idolatry: "Man's nature, so to speak, is a perpetual factory of idols.... Man's mind, full as it is of pride and boldness, dares to imagine a god according to its own capacity; as it sluggishly plods, indeed is overwhelmed with the crassest ignorance, it conceives an unreality and an empty appearance as God."[57]

An example might be instructive. Paul recounts his visionary experience in 2 Corinthians 12. Calvin reminds us:

> From this passage we should allow ourselves to be reminded of the bounds we must set to our knowledge. We are naturally given to curiosity, so that we tend to pass over carelessly, or, at least, taste only slightly teaching that tends to edification while we become involved in frivolous questions. To this curiosity we add boldness and rashness, so that we are ready without hesitation to pronounce on things about which we know nothing and which are hidden from us. From these two sources there has sprung up a great deal of scholastic theology and everything that that trifler Dionysius has had the audacity to invent about the hierarchy of heaven. It is all the more incumbent upon us to seek to know nothing but what the Lord has been willing to reveal to His Church. Let that be the limit of our knowledge.[58]

One facet of Calvin's approach that has roots in the Corinthian epistles and widespread import is his focus on human sinfulness, rather than demonic or Satanic influence, as the primary force behind idolatry.[59] The

---

[55]See, e.g., Calvin, *Acts of the Apostles*, p. 202 (Acts 7:41).
[56]Ibid., p. 207 (Acts 7:44).
[57]Calvin, *Institutes*, I.11.8.
[58]Calvin, *Second Epistle*, p. 157 (2 Cor 12:4).
[59]See Carlos M. N. Eire, "John Calvin, Accidental Anthropologist," in *John Calvin and Roman Catholicism: Critique and Engagement, Then and Now*, ed. Randall C. Zachman (Grand Rapids: Baker Academic, 2008), pp. 145-64 (especially pp. 158-60). Eire suggests that Calvin's dismissal of the demonic as a nonnecessary factor in idolatry eventually prepared the way for religious studies as a fully anthropological, intellectual endeavor. One need not agree with this wider judgment to see the validity of his claims regarding Calvin's focus on human sinfulness as the chief instigator of idolatry.

text of 1 Corinthians fixes on human problems. Powers and principalities are not the fixtures here that they are in Ephesians 6 or Romans 8. The text addresses the natural person, the sinful person, the unillumined person. The epistle promises the outpouring of the Spirit, the mortification and vivification of the mind, the shedding abroad of God's light. The focus is firmly on human sin—intellectual and theological—and the divine remedy given in the gospel.

Like Luther, Calvin argues that theology is bound to the Word: "We must desire to learn as much as our heavenly Master will teach us: but let no one presume to grasp after what He wishes to keep hidden from us, so that we may be wise, but with sobriety."[60] He will even organize his *Institutes* according to the two forms of God's revelation in Christ: the knowledge of God the Creator (book one) and the knowledge of God the Redeemer (books two through four). It is crucial to see that while Calvin does affirm the place of natural theology (contra Barth), he does so precisely because the writings of the prophets and apostles affirm its givenness.

Implications for Theology

We will consider three areas in which the theology of the cross has implications: the Christian life, the Christian ministry and the means of grace.

1. The Christian life as a cross-shaped existence. Calvin finds the theology of the cross to present us with a sober yet hopeful view of the Christian's persona: "In short, when the Christian looks at himself he can only have grounds for anxiety, indeed despair, but because he is called into fellowship with Christ, he can think of himself, in so far as assurance of salvation is concerned, in no other way than as a member of Christ, thus making all the blessings of Christ his own."[61]

The boast of a Christian, then, involves not merely a recital of successes but recognition of struggle as the nature of the cross-shaped life. Paul's movement between refusal to boast and willingness to boast in the latter part of 2 Corinthians demonstrates this counterintuitive calling, leading Calvin to say:

---

[60]Calvin, *Acts of the Apostles*, p. 30 (Acts 1:7).
[61]Calvin, *First Epistle*, p. 24 (1 Cor 1:9).

This is the conclusion of all that has gone before, that Paul would rather boast of all those things that are concerned with his *weakness*, that is, things that might bring him contempt rather than glory in the world's eyes, like hunger, thirst, imprisonment, stonings, stripes, and so on—things of which indeed we are usually ashamed as through them we incur great disgrace.[62]

2. The Christian ministry as a cross-bearing endeavor. Naming the problem is always the first step: "Paul does that in order to turn them away from a misplaced confidence in their own understanding, which gives wrong assessments of everything."[63] But Paul sees not only a congregation with sinful proclivities in need of mortification, but also a people with daily need of vivification.[64] The theology of the cross speaks to such a situation.

The pastor should expect particular struggle. But the pastor cannot exert efforts to guard his reputation, for such affairs will never cease and are—in most cases—beside the ministry of the gospel: "It is indeed a sound rule that is here laid down, that a pastor should have no regard for himself, but should be devoted exclusively to the building up of the Church. Let him be concerned for his own reputation in so far as he sees that it affects the public advantage, but let him also be ready to neglect it, whenever he can do so without public disadvantage."[65]

Yet Calvin does not believe the failings of the minister, the Christian and the church preclude involvement in the Christian community. Far from it, for "it is a dangerous temptation to think there is no Church where perfect purity is lacking."[66] Failure does not negate holiness. As he will say in the *Institutes*, "The church is holy, then, in the sense that it is daily advancing and is not yet perfect: it makes progress from day to day, but has not yet reached its goal of holiness."[67] God promises lasting forgiveness for the church—indeed, this is why the creed moves from confession of the "holy,

---

[62]Calvin, *Second Epistle*, p. 153 (2 Cor 11:30).
[63]Calvin, *First Epistle*, p. 10.
[64]On the order of mortification and vivification, see Calvin, *Second Epistle*, pp. 12-13 (2 Cor 1:9).
[65]Ibid., p. 174 (2 Cor 13:7); earlier he claimed that "once again it is a fault in the servants of Christ to be too anxious about their reputations" (p. 166 [2 Cor 12:19]); similar comments arise in Calvin, *Acts of the Apostles*, pp. 167-68 (Acts 6:14).
[66]Calvin, *First Epistle*, p. 17 (on 1 Cor 1:2); cf. *Institutes*, IV.1.12 (2:1025-26); IV.1.13 (2:1027-28); IV.1.14 (2:1028-29).
[67]Calvin, *Institutes*, IV.1.17 (2:1031); cf. *Acts of the Apostles*, pp. 157-58 (on Acts 6:1).

catholic church" and "communion of saints" to "forgiveness of sins."[68]

Again, this means that the church must be engaged, even if it is a merely human conduit of God's miraculous grace. Ministers, as well, are vessels of grace, even though they are mere treasures of clay. Calvin speaks in two ways of such pastors.[69] They are productive, and thus they do genuinely give grace. But they are also mere instruments or vessels of God's mercy. They do not have authority or efficacy of their own making. All their doings are derivative to God's agency. As Calvin says of Pentecost:

> Surely the fact that the Church is diminishing rather than increasing is to be ascribed to our slothfulness, or indeed our sinfulness. But although they all strove earnestly to increase the Kingdom of Christ, yet Luke claims this honour for God alone, that it was He who brought those outside into the Church. And surely this is His own special work.[70]

The ministry's failures owe to human frailty, while the successes stem from divine sustenance and generosity. Pastors are called to faithfulness—telling the truth even when it may not seem the best path to win friends and influence people—not to effectiveness.

In many ways, Calvin serves as a living image of such ministry. After he had been excused from his pastoral role in Geneva and spent a profitable time in Strasbourg, he was called back by his former congregation. He did not warm immediately to the idea. He told them:

> If you desire to have me for your pastor, correct the disorder of your lives. If you have with sincerity recalled me from my exile, banish the crimes and debaucheries which prevail among you. I cannot behold without the most painful displeasure ... discipline trodden under foot and crimes committed with impunity. I cannot possibly live in a place so grossly immoral. ... I consider the principal enemies of the Gospel to be, not the pontiff of Rome, nor heretics, nor seducers, nor tyrants, but bad Christians. ... I dread abundantly more those carnal covetousnesses, those debaucheries of the tavern, of the brothel, and of gaming. ... Of what use is a dead faith without good works? Of what importance is even truth itself, where a wicked life belies it and actions make words blush? Either command me to abandon a second

---

[68]Calvin, *Institutes*, IV.1.21 (cf. IV.1.23-27).
[69]Calvin, *First Epistle*, p. 70 (1 Cor 3:6-7).
[70]Calvin, *Acts of the Apostles*, p. 90 (Acts 2:47).

time your town and let me go and soften the bitterness of my afflictions in a new exile, or let the severity of the laws reign in the church. Reestablish there pure discipline.[71]

But he did come. For Calvin, it was essential to do two things: first, to identify good and evil as they really are; second, to really love God and the people of God. In so doing, he sought to embody the Pauline teaching about the cross-shaped life and ministry.[72]

3. The means of grace as God's particular gifts for the people of God. The concern about idolatry and the awareness of indwelling sin leads Calvin—like Luther—to focus on the particular and concrete ways that God meets us: "Indeed Paul is teaching here not only what sort of men the disciples of Christ ought to be, and the proper way by which they ought to learn, but also what the method of teaching should be in the school of Christ. 'The cross of Christ would have been rendered useless,' he says, 'if my preaching had been tricked out with eloquence and brilliance.'"[73] What is Calvin's pastoral advice, then, for those tempted to "trick out" their preaching? They ought not to lay another foundation (other than Christ), but they also must not raise a superstructure "out of keeping with this foundation."[74]

Pastors, then, are to employ their authority only inasmuch as it is mandated by God's Word. They are not to call for uniformity along the lines of their own personal preferences or even individual spiritual gifting. Calvin notes that Paul felt called to be celibate—and he argues this was a *good*

---

[71]Theodore Beza, *Life of Calvin* (Darlington, UK: Evangelical Press, 1997), pp. 25-26 n. 1.

[72]The suggestion that Calvin's life bears a cross-shaped form may seem remarkably counterintuitive to those encumbered by the typical understanding of the execution of Michael Servetus. However, it is very clear that the smearing of Calvin's name for this matter cannot be upheld by historical study. Calvin warned Servetus not to come to Geneva, sought the reversal of his death penalty and sought to have a less painful method of execution employed. In every effort, Calvin failed, proving not his bloodthirsty tyranny but his lack of totalitarian control of Geneva. My defense of Calvin in this regard is neither meant to suggest that Calvin was a particularly nice character, nor is it to suggest that he did not believe the state could and should at times punish heretics. He was a sinful human being as well as a man of the sixteenth century, of course, even if he was not a particularly tyrannical leader or at blame for the death of Servetus. For the best analysis not only of the Servetus affair but of Calvin's character, see Bruce Gordon, *Calvin* (New Haven, CT: Yale University Press, 2009).

[73]Calvin, *First Epistle*, p. 33 (1 Cor 1:17); cf. nuances and qualifications on pp. 34-35.

[74]Ibid., p. 73 (1 Cor 3:10-15); cf. "He persists with the metaphor. It was not sufficient that the foundation had been laid, if the whole superstructure did not conform to it. . . . We have to continue to teach Christ, until the building is completed" (Ibid., p. 75 [1 Cor 3:12]; cf. p. 66 [1 Cor 3:1], p. 97 [1 Cor 4:15]).

thing—but he never mandates this as a universal Christian practice: "Let him be a warning to us, so that, if we are powerfully blessed with some particular gift, we may not be over-exacting in requiring it of others, who have not yet reached that level."[75] Calvin finds those who fail in this regard to be "overscrupulous people"—whether papists or fanatics—who expect their every action or gift to be binding for imitation.[76] One particular manifestation of this problem is the overly rigorous requirements of some in the early church regarding penance. When he comes to 2 Corinthians 2:6, Calvin notes that some of the bishops' approaches bound the consciences of their people unfairly, extending beyond any warrant found in Holy Scripture.[77] On the contrary, though, "it is the duty of a good pastor not only to restrain every desire to domineer but to regard the service of the people of God as the highest honour to which he may aspire."[78] Indeed, "the whole authority of ministers is based upon the Word, and in such a way that Christ always remains Lord and Master."[79]

When Calvin comes to the remarkable claim that God not only reconciles a people to himself but also makes that people "ministers of reconciliation" (2 Cor 5:18), he feels compelled to affirm not only the authority of the minister but also the conditions for ministry: "To sum up: ministers of the Church are ambassadors for testifying and proclaiming the blessing of reconciliation only on condition that they speak from the Gospel as providing a legitimate warrant for what they say."[80] Ambassadors do have authority and power (they are often appointed "plenipotentiaries"), yet not of their own: "So we are ministers of the Spirit not because we hold Him bound or captive and not because at our own whim we can confer this grace upon all or upon whom we please, but because through us Christ enlightens men's minds, renews their hearts, and wholly regenerates them."[81]

---

[75]Ibid., p. 143 (1 Cor 7:8). Calvin views celibacy as a lifestyle that allows space for a supernatural commitment; thus it is not a matter of grace over against sin, but of supernatural life over against merely natural relations (ibid., pp. 61-62 [1 Cor 7:35]).
[76]Ibid., p. 227 (1 Cor 11:1-2); cf. pp. 294-95 (1 Cor 14:18-20).
[77]Ibid., pp. 29-30 (1 Cor 2:6).
[78]Calvin, *Second Epistle*, p. 57 (2 Cor 4:5).
[79]Ibid., p. 133 (2 Cor 10:8); cf. "By His Word, God alone sanctifies temples to Himself for lawful use. And if we rashly attempt anything without his command, strange inventions forthwith cling to the bad beginning and spread evil without measure" (*Institutes*, IV.1.5 [2:1019]).
[80]Calvin, *Second Epistle*, p. 79 (2 Cor 5:14).
[81]Ibid., p. 43 (2 Cor 2:6). Calvin even sees this instrumental understanding of pastors as reason to

In these three ways, then, we see the theology of the cross shaping the whole spectrum of faith and practice. The particular shape of God's revelation in the gospel of Jesus suggests much for the contours of the Christian life, the expectations for Christian ministry and the necessity of the means of grace. Calvin may not use the phraseology of the theology of the cross in the same way as Luther, but he shows a similar concern for this doctrinal matrix. It functioned powerfully in Paul's writing to the Corinthians, and it continues to speak powerfully through the witness of John Calvin.

---

support financially only those church staff who actually function as teachers of the Word and not a whole, independent bureaucracy that functions discretely from this teaching task (Calvin, *First Epistle*, p. 191 [1 Cor 9:13]).

8

The Text of 1 & 2 Corinthians and the Theology of Calvin

Dane C. Ortlund

W<small>E ARE NEITHER THE FIRST</small> nor the smartest to think Paul's thoughts after him. Yet one does not often get that impression amid the onslaught of books and articles on the apostle that continue to pour off the presses, interacting as they do with a range of scholarship almost entirely contemporary. A strange kind of tunnel vision informs too much Pauline scholarship today, in which pre–E. P. Sanders exposition of Paul's thought garners less attention than it should. As seminal a book as Sanders's *Paul and Palestinian Judaism* was, and as important a corrective as it offered, the riches of Paul's letters far outstrip dependence on a certain (contested) view of the Judaism from which Paul's thought emerged.[1] The church has not always had Sanders, but the church has always had the Spirit, not to mention one another. Sanders himself clearly acknowledged the shoulders of those on whom he stood, such as C. G. Montefiore, G. F. Moore and W. D. Davies (though disagreeing with each of them in various ways).[2]

Each generation must beware the danger of failing to identify its own

---

[1] I am grateful to Richard Gaffin, Eric Ortlund, Gavin Ortlund, Herman Selderhuis and Stephen Westerholm for their comments on an early draft of this chapter.

E. P. Sanders, *Paul and Palestinian Judaism: A Comparison of Patterns of Religion* (Minneapolis: Fortress, 1977).

[2] Ibid., pp. 4-11.

generational assumptions—assumptions that, by the nature of the case, can at times only be seen by studying the work of other generations. Perhaps much of what is assumed by the Pauline guild today will look naive to scholars in a hundred years, just as the work of scholars from a century ago often looks naive to scholars today.

We all stand on the shoulders of those who have gone before, and gratefully so. Among all the thinkers preceding Sanders, one whose shoulders are especially stable is John Calvin. The purpose of this essay is to facilitate a dialogue of sorts between Paul and Calvin in light of currents in New Testament study. Picture a table. At one end sits the scarred apostle, short, balding, with a penetrating gaze, but overall very unimpressive (2 Cor 10:10). At the other end sits the pointy-bearded French reformer, gaunt, thin, rather emaciated and equally physically unimpressive. We will listen in as Calvin tells us about the apostle—if we are able to hear him above the opinions of some of the newer voices at the table who seem not to notice the reformer. The letters to the Corinthians will be our point of entry.

The ultimate goal of this chapter is to commend Calvin to Christians today, especially students and scholars of the apostle. Calvin had his blind spots, but we have ours too. And if we are to minimize the "chronological snobbery" with which New Testament scholarship is at times plagued, we must allow for the possibility that John Calvin was, at times, a better reader of Paul than we are.[3] Calvin was historically and culturally located, but no more so than those who ignore him because of that fact. With Calvin as with any thinker from the past, we must swallow the meat while spitting out the bones, neither receiving everything uncritically nor ignoring everything wholesale.

Calvin is an ideal thinker to appropriate as we plumb the riches of church history to better understand Paul's letters to the Corinthians. With his Renaissance/humanistic training and amid the swirling debates of the Reformation, he was strategically positioned to read Paul afresh for his genera-

---

[3]The phrase "chronological snobbery" belongs to C. S. Lewis, who defines it as "the uncritical acceptance of the intellectual climate common to our own age and the assumption that whatever has gone out of date is on that account discredited" (C. S. Lewis, *Surprised by Joy: The Shape of My Earthly Life* [Orlando: Harcourt, 1955], p. 207). Two others who apply Lewis's axiom explicitly to the value of the reformers are David Steinmetz ("The Superiority of Precritical Exegesis," *Theology Today* 37 [1980-1981]: 27-38) and Timothy George (*Reading Scripture with the Reformers* [Downers Grove, IL: InterVarsity Press, 2011], pp. 21-43).

tion.⁴ He transparently sat under the text and sought to hear it as the Word of God under the illumination of the Spirit, doing so with a solid knowledge of Hebrew and Greek.⁵ Moreover, he was not only a teacher but (as Michael Allen has reminded us in his companion chapter) a churchman. As a preacher and even a church planter, his engagement with Paul was not doctrinal or ecclesial gamesmanship but an earnest pursuit of truth for the sake of the health of the church and the preservation of the gospel.⁶

And while Calvin regularly connects his exposition of the Corinthian correspondence with the issues at hand that day, not least the errors of late medieval Roman Catholicism, he self-consciously refused to import the debates of the day into his reading of Paul (despite being accused of this by modern Pauline scholars). At one point in his exposition of 2 Corinthians, for example, Calvin explains that "the god of this world" (2 Cor 4:4) was mistakenly taken to refer to God by Hilary of Poitiers, John Chrysostom and Augustine due to the debates in which each was locked (Hilary with Arianism, Chrysostom and Augustine with Manichaeism). With most exegetes today, Calvin believed this text refers to Satan, not God, and remarks: "This is an example of what can happen in the heat of controversy, for if all these men had read Paul's words with a calm mind it would never have occurred to them to twist them into a forced meaning in this way. But being hard pressed by their opponents they were more anxious to refute

---

⁴On which see John L. Thompson, "Calvin as Biblical Interpreter," in *The Cambridge Companion to John Calvin*, ed. Donald K. McKim (Cambridge: Cambridge University Press, 2004), pp. 58-59. N. T. Wright repeatedly appeals to Calvin (over against Luther) as a model reader of Paul in his *Justification: God's Plan and Paul's Vision* (Downers Grove, IL: InterVarsity, 2009), esp. pp. 22-23, 72-73, though Wright overplays the discontinuity between Luther and Calvin. Better is Karla Wübbenhorst, "Calvin's Doctrine of Justification: Variations on a Lutheran Theme," in Bruce L. McCormack, ed., *Justification in Perspective: Historical Developments and Contemporary Challenges* (Grand Rapids: Baker Academic, 2006), pp. 99-100.

⁵Witness, e.g., Calvin's philologically sophisticated comments on 2 Cor 9:4 (Calvin, *The Second Epistle of Paul the Apostle to the Corinthians and the Epistles to Timothy, Titus, and Philemon*, ed. David W. Torrance and Thomas F. Torrance, trans. T. A. Smail, Calvin's Commentaries [Grand Rapids: Eerdmans, 1964], p. 120).

⁶On Calvin as a church planter, see Michael G. Haykin and C. Jeffrey Robinson Sr., *To the Ends of the Earth: Calvin's Missional Vision and Legacy* (Wheaton, IL: Crossway, 2014). Calvin reiterates his earnest pursuit of the truth in the first few paragraphs of the dedication of his commentary on 1 Corinthians (John Calvin, *The First Epistle of Paul the Apostle to the Corinthians*, ed. David W. Torrance and Thomas F. Torrance, trans. John W. Fraser, Calvin's Commentaries [Grand Rapids: Eerdmans, 1960], p. 1).

them than to expound Paul."⁷ It is striking, in light of the accusations of eisegesis of which the reformers are often accused, that Calvin here explicitly alerts his readers to the dangers of skewing a text's meaning by importing the questions of current controversies.

On first reflection, the Corinthian correspondence may seem of peripheral importance to Calvin and the Reformation. After all, the Corinthian letters contain only a few references to justification, which Calvin famously dubbed "the main hinge on which religion turns."⁸ Yet these few references are themselves theologically loaded ones. And other points of debate in the time of the Reformation do indeed figure prominently in Corinthians, such as church government and the gifts of the Spirit.

In this chapter we will consider five reminders Calvin provides for readers of Paul today. Each reminder interacts with an emphasis of current Pauline scholarship. Justification will be a particular focus throughout, given its prominence in present Pauline discussions. We will then offer one key way in which Calvin's reading could itself be strengthened by Pauline scholarship today.

LISTENING TO CALVIN WHILE READING PAUL

The fundamental human dilemma. First, Calvin was relentless in his focus on human sin as fundamentally estrangement from God. Alienation from fellow human beings is not greater than but follows from this more basic matter. It is striking that in a day when so much theological disagreement was painfully reinforcing lines of ecclesial division, Calvin never allowed the background issue of horizontal reconciliation (between humans) to crowd out the more pressing issue of vertical reconciliation (between humans and God).⁹

---

⁷Calvin, *Second Epistle*, p. 54.
⁸John Calvin, *Institutes of the Christian Religion*, ed. John T. McNeill, trans. Ford Lewis Battles (Louisville: Westminster John Knox, 1960), III.11.1.
⁹Other recent Pauline scholars who use the categories "vertical" and "horizontal" as I am here include Douglas J. Moo, "Israel and the Law in Romans 5-11: Interaction with the New Perspective," in D. A. Carson, Peter T. O'Brien and Mark A. Seifrid, eds., *Justification and Variegated Nomism: A Fresh Appraisal of Paul and Second Temple Judaism* (Grand Rapids: Baker Academic, 2001, 2004), 2:186-87; Peter T. O'Brien, "Was Paul a Covenantal Nomist?," in *Justification and Variegated Nomism*, 2:291; James D. G. Dunn, "The Dialogue Progresses," in *Lutherische und Neue Paulusperspektive: Beiträge zu einem Schlüsselproblem der gegenwärtigen exegetischen Diskussion*, ed. Michael Bachmann, WUNT 182 (Tübingen: Mohr Siebeck, 2005), pp. 410-12; Francis Watson, *Paul, Judaism, and the*

The same cannot be said for much Pauline scholarship today. Though we are now generally in a post-"new perspective" era, the influence of the new perspective continues to be evident in much current Paul scholarship, especially in the way Jew-Gentile unity tends to dominate treatments of Paul's life and theology.[10] The question is not whether Paul was concerned with horizontal unity. He clearly was. The question is its relative importance and emphasis in Paul's letters, and how it relates to vertical concerns.

To stick with the Corinthian correspondence for the moment, vertical concerns predominate. In his recent book on justification, Stephen Westerholm notes that the Corinthian correspondence says virtually nothing about Jew/Gentile relationships.[11] On the contrary, Paul is at pains in the opening chapters of 1 Corinthians to show that both Jews and Gentiles are themselves in equal peril before a just God. The gospel of a crucified Christ is a stumbling block to both Jews and Greeks (1 Cor 1:23). Paul's supreme concern in these chapters is not Jews and Gentiles being reconciled to one another but both being reconciled to God.

Recent Pauline studies generally sounds a different note from this. I would call the tone of current Pauline study the *overhorizontalization* of his theology. On the one hand, we must be careful not to paint with so broad a brushstroke that we unfairly cast the discipline as a whole; yet on the other hand, it would be unwieldy to reproduce statement upon statement in Pauline scholarship to make this point. Nevertheless, generally speaking, there has been a push away from the undercurrents of anti-Semitism in the early decades of the twentieth century, to the degree that scholars now tend to see interethnic unity as Paul's overriding concern. Humanity's dilemma

---

Gentiles: Beyond the New Perspective (Grand Rapids: Eerdmans, 2007), p. 6; and Michael J. Gorman, *Inhabiting the Cruciform God: Kenosis, Justification, and Theosis in Paul's Narrative Soteriology* (Grand Rapids: Eerdmans, 2009), pp. 45, 48-53, 58, 61, 87-90, 102-3. My use of "vertical" and "horizontal" should not be confused with Douglas A. Campbell's use of these terms in a different realm of discourse (*The Deliverance of God: An Apocalyptic Rereading of Justification in Paul* [Grand Rapids: Eerdmans, 2009], pp. xxix-xxx).

[10]Brendan Byrne had already spoken of a "post-'New Perspective' perspective" in 2001 ("Interpreting Romans Theologically in a Post-'New Perspective' Perspective," *Harvard Theological Review* 94 [2001]: 227-41), and Bruce Longenecker wrote in 2005 that the new perspective "is beginning to look like a potential casualty to even 'newer' perspectives" ("On Critiquing the 'New Perspective' on Paul: A Case Study," *Zeitschrift für die neutestamentliche Wissenschaft und die Kunde der älteren Kirche* 96 [2005]: 264).

[11]Stephen Westerholm, *Justification Reconsidered: Rethinking a Pauline Theme* (Grand Rapids: Eerdmans, 2013), p. 9.

and the purpose of Christ's work are cast as disunity and corporate reconciliation, respectively, while the need for vertical reconciliation is generally acknowledged but quietly backgrounded. Representative of this tendency, and as influential as any New Testament scholar writing today, is James Dunn. "Paul's exposition of faith and not works," writes Dunn, "emerged in the context of his Gentile mission and as the defence of what was of fundamental importance to him: that the gospel was for all, for Gentile as well as Jew."[12] Paul's "basic insight" emerging from his Damascus Road experience, according to Dunn, was that God's grace "was open to all and not restricted in effect to Jews alone."[13]

Calvin certainly believed in the crucial importance of ecclesial unity. Indeed, this comes through clearly in his comments on the factiousness of the Corinthian church as evident in 1 Corinthians 1: "There is nothing more out of keeping for Christians than their being divided from each other."[14] Again: "the most important principle of our religion is this"—what would you expect John Calvin to say here?—"that we be in concord among ourselves."[15] Of believers he writes (on 1 Cor 6:8) that "we are all brothers who name the one Father in heaven."[16] Calvin himself even (wrongly, to my mind) interprets a key vertical text, 2 Corinthians 8:9, in mainly horizontal terms.[17]

But to Calvin's mind, gospel unity is best preserved when it is couched explicitly in the *reason* Christ's work generates unity—namely, that salvation by sheer grace empties all human boasting, including ethnic boasting (1 Cor 1:29, 31; 2 Cor 10:17). For Calvin, horizontal reconciliation can take place no further than the degree to which vertical reconciliation is held high and cherished. He broke with Rome precisely because clarity on the gospel trumped ecclesial unity, and he deemed the Roman Catholic gospel as

---

[12]James D. G. Dunn, *The New Perspective on Paul*, rev. ed. (Grand Rapids: Eerdmans, 2008), p. 96. Dunn's earlier scholarship was less nuanced than his more recent work, as he himself has acknowledged. But even his most recent work casts Jew-Gentile unity as Paul's driving concern—as I show in Dane C. Ortlund, *Zeal Without Knowledge: The Concept of Zeal in Romans 10, Galatians 1, and Philippians 3*, Library of New Testament Studies 472 (London: T&T Clark, 2012), pp. 11-15.
[13]Dunn, *New Perspective on Paul*, p. 375.
[14]Calvin, *First Epistle*, p. 25.
[15]Ibid.
[16]Ibid., p. 123.
[17]Calvin, *Second Epistle*, pp. 110-11.

defective. Note the way Calvin couches ecclesial unity in the relationship one has to Christ: "The unity of the Church rests mainly on this one thing: that we all depend on Christ alone."[18] Reflecting further on the connection between the gospel and unity, he writes: "Since the purpose of the Gospel is that we might be reconciled to God through Him, it is necessary first of all, that we should all be bound together in Him."[19]

Calvin takes us into the heart of Paul's concerns as an apostle, where we see that Paul cared deeply about Jew-Gentile unity (a concern some have unhelpfully downplayed in their resistance to the new perspective), yet that this concern, while generally the presenting issue, was not the supreme one.[20] The raising of interethnic unity is certainly politically and socially amenable to our age, in which racism, classism and tribalism are the superlative sins. Yet on this point, one suspects it is the contemporary scholar, not the reformer, who is reading Paul overly beholden to the spirit of the times. Commenting on "the ministry of reconciliation" of 2 Corinthians 5:18, Calvin writes: "Let us remember that this is the main purpose of the Gospel, that, although we are by nature children of wrath, the quarrel between God and us can be resolved and we can be received by Him into His grace."[21]

In all this one is struck by the way Calvin took with utter seriousness both doctrinal purity and ecclesial unity, both the vertical and the horizontal, both truth and love. This is a word in season to Pauline scholarship today, in which one of these poles often seems to rise in importance as the other falls.

The forensic nature of justification. Chief among the topics pursued by Pauline scholars today is what the apostle meant when he spoke of God *justifying* individuals—a question equally hot in Calvin's day.

An increasingly accepted view in current Pauline scholarship is the transformative nature of justification. One form of this view can be seen in a strand of German scholarship articulated by Adolf Schlatter, Ernst Käsemann and Peter Stuhlmacher. All three resist speaking of justification

---

[18]Calvin, *First Epistle*, p. 28.
[19]Ibid.
[20]For an example of one who has downplayed Jew-Gentile unity in Paul, see Vincent M. Smiles, *The Gospel and the Law in Galatia: Paul's Response to Jewish-Christian Separatism and the Threat of Galatian Apostasy* (Collegeville, MN: Liturgical Press, 1998).
[21]Calvin, *Second Epistle*, p. 77.

as a bare declaration. Rather, justification does something dynamically. It is a power.[22] While one might puzzle over whether this strand of German teaching captures exactly what Paul meant, there is much to be commended and received here, and the forensic nature of justification is upheld even as the transforming results of justification are emphasized.

More at odds with Calvin's view is the work of Michael Gorman. Through several recent works, Gorman has set forth a view of justification that includes transformational cocrucifixion with Christ, or what Gorman calls "cruciformity."[23] To be sure, Protestant Pauline scholars ought not to shy away (as Calvin did not) from readings of Paul that reflect at length on the participatory side of Paul's soteriological thinking. One thinks, for example, of the recent work of Ben Blackwell, who intriguingly suggests "Christosis" as a more accurate term than "theosis" for capturing Paul's soteriological goal.[24] David Litwa, drawing heavily on Greco-Roman sources, has pursued a similar theme, arguing that Paul did indeed argue for a form of "deification," rightly understood.[25]

What sets off Gorman's work is his attempt to include participatory cruciformity within the definition of justification—"inherent within the

---

[22]See Adolf Schlatter, *The Theology of the Apostles: The Development of New Testament Theology*, trans. Andreas J. Köstenberger (Grand Rapids: Baker Academic, 1998), pp. 228-39; Ernst Käsemann, "'The Righteousness of God' in Paul," in *New Testament Questions of Today* (Philadelphia: Fortress, 1969), pp. 168-82; cf. Paul F. M. Zahl, *Die Rechtfertigungslehre Ernst Käsemanns*, Calwer Theologische Monographien, Reihe B: Systematische Theologie und Kirchengeschichte 13 (Stuttgart: Calwer, 1996); Peter Stuhlmacher, *Gerechtigkeit Gottes bei Paulus*, 2nd ed., Forsuchungen zur Religion und Literatur des Alten und Neuen Testaments 87 (Göttingen: Vandenhoeck & Ruprecht, 1966), passim; Stuhlmacher, *Revisiting Paul's Doctrine of Justification: A Challenge to the New Perspective*, trans. D. P. Bailey (Downers Grove, IL: InterVarsity Press, 2001), pp. 62-67; Stuhlmacher, *Biblische Theologie des Neuen Testaments* (Göttingen: Vandenhoeck & Ruprecht, 2005), pp. 332-34. Similarly E. Jüngel, *Justification: The Heart of the Christian Faith* (Edinburgh: T&T Clark, 2001), pp. 208-11, 259.
[23]Michael J. Gorman, *Cruciformity: Paul's Narrative Spirituality of the Cross* (Grand Rapids: Eerdmans, 2001); *Apostle of the Crucified Lord: A Theological Introduction to Paul and His Letters* (Grand Rapids: Eerdmans, 2004); *Inhabiting the Cruciform God*.
[24]Ben C. Blackwell, *Christosis: Pauline Soteriology in Light of Deification in Irenaeus and Cyril of Alexandria*, WUNT 2/314 (Tübingen: Mohr Siebeck, 2011).
[25]M. David Litwa, *We Are Being Transformed: Deification in Paul's Soteriology* (Berlin: de Gruyter, 2012). Litwa's work is, however, fraught with problems. To take one: whereas for Blackwell deification never allows the individual human being to be lost, Litwa is comfortable with a kind of sharing in identity that goes beyond what Calvin would be comfortable with. Any attribution of deification to Paul's theology, Calvin would say, must emphasize (as Blackwell does) the restoration of the divine image as the content of our transformation, maintaining the Creator/creature distinction—the very distinction Calvin was keen to maintain in his engagement with Osiander.

very notion of reconciliation/justification are both participation and transformation."²⁶ This creates a point of contact between Gorman and the new Finnish interpretation of Luther, which, arising out of ecumenical dialogue between the Finnish Lutherans and the Russian Orthodox Church, likewise views justification itself as including a transformative element.²⁷ Calvin himself engaged something close to a participatory view of justification in his interaction with Andreas Osiander.²⁸

For Gorman and others, an appropriate concern for authentic transformation of life leads to bringing transformation *into the definition of justification*. For Calvin, however, it is precisely by keeping personal transformation out of justification that this transformation is assured. Calvin resolutely insisted that all true believers will be transformed; but this is not part of what justification specifically means. Commenting on Christ becoming our "sanctification" in 1 Corinthians 1:30, he remarks that forgiveness of sins and a transformed life of holiness are inseparable. Yet he then follows up quickly to add that, while inseparable, the two are distinct: "While those two offices of Christ are united, they are yet distinguishable from each other. Therefore we are not at liberty, indeed it would be wrong, to confuse what Paul expressly separates."²⁹ This is a liberty that Gorman and others, however, take. Justification is nevertheless forensic—"'to justify,'" writes Calvin, "means nothing else than to acquit of guilt him who was accused"—and it is by preserving this that the life-changing implications of justification are most decisively assured.³⁰ Reflecting on 1 Corinthians 6:11, Calvin says that "purity" and "true holiness" are "the purpose for which God reconciles us to Himself by the free remission of sins."³¹ That is, it is the very

---

²⁶Gorman, *Inhabiting the Cruciform God*, p. 163.
²⁷See, e.g., Tuomo Mannermaa, *Christ Present in Faith: Luther's View of Justification* (Minneapolis: Fortress, 2005); or Veli-Matti Kärkkäinen's contribution in James K. Beilby and Paul Rhodes Eddy, eds., *Justification: Five Views* (Downers Grove, IL: InterVarsity Press, 2011).
²⁸See Julie Canlis, "Calvin, Osiander and Participation in God," *International Journal of Systematic Theology* 6 (2004): 169-84; Timothy Wengert, *Defending Faith: Lutheran Responses to Andreas Osiander's Doctrine of Justification, 1551–1559*, Spätmittelalter, Humanismus, Reformation 65 (Tübingen: Mohr Siebeck, 2012). I am grateful for Herman Selderhuis's interaction with me on this point.
²⁹Calvin, *First Epistle*, p. 46. Calvin is similarly keen to distinguish between the juridical nature of justification and the transformative nature of sanctification in his comments on 1 Cor 6:11 (ibid., p. 126).
³⁰Calvin, *Institutes*, III.11.3.
³¹Calvin, *First Epistle*, p. 126.

freeness of grace in its forensic sharpness that ensures true integrity of life.

One can warmly appreciate, as Calvin would, the recent emphasis among Pauline scholars that is seeking to reassert the participatory dimension of salvation. The question, however, is whether participation (especially as transformative) is what Paul is talking about *when he speaks of justification.* To be sure, believers are caught up into the triune life of God. But Calvin would assert that this is not what justification itself means. Justification is fundamentally forensic.[32] It takes place "before God's judgment seat," as sinners are "reckoned righteous in God's judgment."[33]

For Calvin, the participationist dimension to salvation is best captured in the theological rubric of union with Christ (on which more below), the umbrella soteriological category within which both the forensic and the transformational are subsumed without being confused.

Imputation? Before leaving the subject of justification, there is one more matter worth considering. Calvin reminds those ready to abandon or reconfigure the classic teaching on imputation that this doctrine arises unavoidably from texts within the Corinthian correspondence.[34]

The imputation of the righteousness of Christ has undergone much reassessment in recent years among Pauline scholars for at least two reasons. First, nowhere in Paul's letters does he say outright that we are given Christ's righteousness.[35] Second, this doctrine has at times been expressed in unhelpful ways, such as articulating the doctrine in a crassly formulaic way, in which the righteous standing of Christ is passed over to my account as funds would be transferred from a rich person's account to a poor person's.[36] (A

---

[32]Wübbenhorst, "Calvin's Doctrine of Justification," pp. 107-9.
[33]Calvin, *Institutes*, III.11.2.
[34]By the classic teaching I mean the teaching on imputation as formulated in the Reformed confessions and catechisms.
[35]As noted by Mark Seifrid, whose view of justification nevertheless nets out as essentially what I am describing as imputation (Mark A. Seifrid, *Christ, Our Righteousness: Paul's Theology of Justification*, New Studies in Biblical Theology 9 [Downers Grove, IL: InterVarsity Press, 2000], pp. 174-75). Seifrid believes imputation as generally articulated is insufficiently Christ-centered, yet Calvin's placing of imputation squarely in terms of union with Christ would, it seems to me, alleviate Seifrid's otherwise valid concern at this point. The lack of an explicit formulation of imputation in Paul's letters leads Robert Gundry, more strongly, to reject imputation outright (Robert H. Gundry, "The Nonimputation of Christ's Righteousness," in Mark Husbands and Daniel J. Treier, eds., *Justification: What's at Stake in the Current Debates?* [Downers Grove, IL: InterVarsity Press, 2004], pp. 17-45).
[36]As leveled by N. T. Wright, *What Saint Paul Really Said: Was Paul of Tarsus the Real Founder of*

third possible reason, which will not be explored at this juncture since we have already discussed it above, is the trend in Pauline scholarship away from the juridical toward the participatory.)

I am sympathetic to both of these concerns. They are understandable. But neither objection is enough to require a major recasting of the doctrine that Calvin held so dearly, and which he founded, in large part, on the Corinthian correspondence. Take the first objection (that Paul nowhere articulates imputation explicitly). It is a charge that could equally be leveled at other more central doctrines, such as that of the Trinity. In the cases of both imputation and the Trinity, the doctrine represents a synthetic formulation of a constellation of texts and the theological ligaments that must be understood to hold them together. A truth may not be explicitly couched in the articulations of later theology yet still be present in the biblical text.[37]

What about the second objection, that imputation is an overly formulaic way of expressing how justification works? Again, at times the doctrine has indeed been stated in unhelpful ways. The righteousness of Christ is not a "thing" out there that, in salvation, is sent over to me and somehow downloaded into some merit account on my behalf. Rather, we are counted righteous *in Christ*. It is in union with Christ that I am given his righteousness.[38] Christ's righteousness comes to me as a wholly alien righteousness but becomes my own through union. It is only externally available; but it is only internally appropriated. And imputation is never ethically irrelevant because, as Calvin programmatically explained, the union that grants us righteousness at the same time necessarily grants us sanctification. This is plain, for example, in 1 Corinthians 6:11, on which Calvin comments, "From His death and resurrection we obtain righteousness and sanctification.... Christ, therefore, is the source of every blessing to us."[39]

What did Calvin say specifically about imputation? While Martin Luther

---

Christianity? (Grand Rapids: Eerdmans, 1997), p. 98.

[37]So D. A. Carson, "The Vindication of Imputation: On Fields of Discourse and Semantic Fields," in Husbands and Treier, *Justification*, pp. 46-78; Henri Blocher, "Justification of the Ungodly (Sola Fide): Theological Reflections," in *Justification and Variegated Nomism*, 2:498-99; Ben C. Dunson, "Do Bible Words Have Bible Meaning? Distinguishing Between Imputation as Word and Doctrine," *WTJ* 75 (2013): 239-60.

[38]As indicated in the title (and taken from Gal 2:17), this is the burden of the book *Justified in Christ: God's Plan for Us in Justification*, ed. K. Scott Oliphint (Fearn, UK: Christian Focus, 2007).

[39]Calvin, *First Epistle*, p. 127.

is famous for using the language of marriage to describe the "happy exchange" of imputation, Calvin preferred the language of clothing.[40] In justification, a sinner is "clothed with Christ's righteousness as if it were his own."[41] Commenting on the early verses of 2 Corinthians 5, Calvin speaks of believers as those "who are clothed with Christ and adorned with His righteousness."[42] Our comments just above about imputation itself residing within the broader soteriological orbit of union with Christ are given lovely expression in the following statement from Calvin:

> That joining together of Head and members, that indwelling of Christ in our hearts—in short, that mystical union—are accorded by us the highest degree of importance, so that Christ, having been made ours, makes us sharers with him in the gifts with which he has been endowed. We do not, therefore, contemplate him outside ourselves from afar in order that his righteousness may be imputed to us but because we put on Christ and are engrafted into his body; in short, because he deigns to make us one with him.[43]

Commenting on 1 Corinthians 1:30, Calvin writes that "we are accepted by God, because [Christ] atoned for our sins by His death, and His obedience is imputed to us for righteousness. For since the righteousness of faith consists in remission of sins and free acceptance, we obtain both through Christ."[44] And on 2 Corinthians 5:21, perhaps the cornerstone text of the doctrine of the imputation of Christ's righteousness, Calvin says that we are justified "not because we have satisfied God's judgment by our own works, but because we are judged in relation to Christ's righteousness which we have put on by faith, that it may become our own."[45] One might note, interestingly, that Calvin does not view "the righteousness of God" in this text as a righteousness that God gives us, but instead as a righteousness that renders sinners worthy of

---

[40] Noted by Blocher, "Justification of the Ungodly," p. 499.
[41] Calvin, *Institutes*, III.17.8; similarly, III.14.12.
[42] Calvin, *Second Epistle*, p. 67.
[43] Calvin, *Institutes*, III.3.11.
[44] Calvin, *First Epistle*, p. 46.
[45] Calvin, *Second Epistle*, pp. 81-82. On 2 Cor 5:18, Calvin writes that "Christ made a guilt-offering for our sins and procured righteousness for us" (ibid., p. 77). Imputation was so precious to Calvin that he occasionally raises it in his Corinthian commentaries when it is not raised in the text, such as at 2 Cor 5:16 (ibid., p. 75). At other times, though, when righteousness is explicitly mentioned, he does not make any reference to imputation—such as regarding "justified" in 1 Cor 4:4 (*First Epistle*, pp. 88-89) or "the armor of righteousness" at 2 Cor 6:7 (*Second Epistle*, p. 87).

being accepted and embraced.[46] This is one more small indication that Calvin's doctrine of imputation is not a bare, abstract notion.[47]

Calvin would discourage us from placing either imputation or union with Christ out ahead of the other, or at the expense of the other—as, to take one example, Don Garlington does.[48] Karla Wübbenhorst even detects a slight change in Calvin from the 1539 Romans commentary to the 1546 commentary on 1 Corinthians, the former speaking of sanctification as necessarily following on justification in a more linear way, the latter speaking of sanctification and justification as both simultaneous gifts of union with Christ.[49] In any case, it is the latter articulation of a *duplex gratia* within union with Christ that surely captures Calvin's mature and most consistent way of formulating salvation.

To draw all this together: for Calvin, the imputing of the righteousness of Christ to the believer is an inescapable synthesizing of biblical teaching. The reformer would agree with Wright and others that Christ's righteousness is not "a substance or a gas which can be passed across the courtroom."[50] Calvin would reject such a presentation as strongly as Wright does. But Calvin found imputation in Paul, while Wright does not. Why? Because Calvin sees that Christ's righteousness becomes ours through vital union with Christ.[51] United to Christ by the Holy Spirit, Christ himself becomes our righteousness. This emphasis on the Holy Spirit as integrally involved in uniting a sinner to Christ is another emphasis of Calvin's and is one more way we see that he did not view imputation as a bare, dry transaction. (One sees this emphasis in his comments on 1 Cor 6:11.[52]) One also finds *adoption* often close at hand in Calvin's discussion of justification.

---

[46]Calvin, *Second Epistle*, p. 81.
[47]Wübbenhorst, "Calvin's Doctrine of Justification," pp. 110-11.
[48]E.g., Don Garlington, *Studies in the New Perspective on Paul: Essays and Reviews* (Eugene, OR: Wipf and Stock, 2008), pp. 181-82.
[49]Wübbenhorst, "Calvin's Doctrine of Justification," pp. 111-14. For more on imputation as taking place in union with Christ, see R. Michael Allen, *Justification and the Gospel: Understanding the Contexts and the Controversies* (Grand Rapids: Baker Academic, 2013), pp. 103-6.
[50]Wright, *What Saint Paul Really Said*, p. 98.
[51]Jonathan A. Linebaugh makes the same point in *God, Grace, and Righteousness in Wisdom of Solomon and Paul's Letter to the Romans*, NovTSup 152 (Leiden: Brill, 2013), p. 170 n. 155. For a sustained reflection on imputation as attributing righteousness to those united to Christ, see Mark A. Garcia, "Imputation and the Theology of Union with Christ: Calvin, Osiander, and the Contemporary Quest for a Reformed Model," *WTJ* 68 (2006): 219-51.
[52]Calvin, *First Epistle*, p. 127.

This is helpful because adoption captures both the warmth of filial acceptance and the clarity of forensic declaration.[53]

If contemporary Paul scholarship is going to reject imputation, may it do so on the other side of weighing Calvin's reflections.

"Justification theory." Those who have not read Calvin often swallow the stereotype that he was a cold, hard, unfeeling man who bequeathed to the Western church a rigid soteriological system in which the fateful ordaining of a callous God determines all things and exacts precise retribution from those who have incurred guilt against him. Given that this is precisely the kind of God from whom Douglas Campbell is seeking to liberate the church in his 2009 book *The Deliverance of God*, it is striking that when one actually gets into Calvin one is delighted to discover a thinker who held God's goodness and grace just as high as God's sovereignty and justice. Calvin himself, then, is a useful dialogue partner for Campbell's wholesale dismissal of "justification theory," the alleged mistake made by centuries of Western Christianity in which the benevolent God of the New Testament is neglected and replaced with the coldly just God of "justification theory" who waits for the initiative of human "faith" to trigger the arid transaction in which the believer is suddenly acquitted and counted righteous.

We can only briefly interact with Campbell. Perhaps I could put Calvin in dialogue with Campbell at just two points, among several on which the two would disagree.[54] In both cases, Campbell sets forth an either/or when a both-and is, for Calvin, a more satisfying way to read Paul. The first has to do with the character of God, and the second with human faith.[55]

---

[53]For adoption in the Corinthian correspondence, see, e.g., Calvin's comments on 2 Cor 1:20 (Calvin, *Second Epistle*, p. 22). Kevin Vanhoozer suggests that adoption is the key Pauline metaphor for mediating old and new perspectives in Vanhoozer, "The State of the Union with Christ in St. Paul and Protestant Soteriology," in Nicholas Perrin and Richard B. Hays, eds., *Jesus, Paul and the People of God: A Theological Dialogue with N. T. Wright* (Downers Grove, IL: InterVarsity Press, 2011), pp. 235-58, esp. pp. 254-57.

[54]Campbell interacts directly with Calvin in *Deliverance of God*, pp. 261-64, 270-77. For shorter articulations by Campbell of his view of Paul, see his summary of *Deliverance of God* in Douglas A. Campbell, "An Apocalyptic Rereading of 'Justification' in Paul: Or, an Overview of the Argument of Douglas Campbell's *The Deliverance of God*," *Expository Times* 123 (2012): 382-93; and also his contribution to Michael Bird, ed., *Four Views on the Apostle Paul* (Grand Rapids: Zondervan, 2012), pp. 113-58.

[55]For a substantive engagement with *Deliverance of God*, see R. Barry Matlock, "Zeal for Paul but Not According to Knowledge: Douglas Campbell's War on 'Justification Theory,'" *Journal for the Study of the New Testament* 34 (2011): 115-49.

First, Campbell sets forth God as kind and gracious and not concerned with exacting justice in a "retributive" sense. That is, God is not "contractual," operating in terms of "strict desert-based acquittal."[56] In "justification theory," "the critical attribute of God is retributive justice," while Campbell's own alternative "has a fundamentally different view of God" in which "God is inherently benevolent."[57] This kind of contractual/transactional view of God and salvation is the same basic accusation lodged by James Torrance at the Puritans and other post-Reformation thinkers—over against (intriguingly for our purposes) a more relational/covenantal view associated with Calvin.[58] Whether Torrance is right or not is for the historians to deal with.[59] I am concerned with how Campbell and Calvin read Paul. And both the apostle and the reformer would ask of Campbell: why must one exalt one of these (benevolence *or* justice, the relational *or* the transactional) over the other as that which really gets at who God is?[60]

Calvin understands that the divine character as revealed in Paul is inescapably both benevolent and just, and that the two are not in tension but mutually reinforcing. While the classic text for this both-and is Romans 3:26 (God is both *just* and, in benevolence, *justifier*), we see both dimensions in Calvin's comments on the Corinthian correspondence.

On the one hand, to be sure, we find in these two epistles a God of benevolence. Though he may not be known for it in popular discourse, Calvin freely exults in "the wonderful love that Christ has shown us in His death."[61] But it is because of God's divine wrath and justice that such love in Jesus Christ shines all the more brightly, as Calvin's comments repeatedly make clear. He brings God's benevolence and his justice together beautifully in

---

[56]Campbell, *Deliverance of God*, p. 15.
[57]Ibid., p. 75.
[58]James B. Torrance, "Covenant or Contract? A Study of the Theological Background of Worship in Seventeenth-Century Scotland," *SJT* 23 (1970): 51–76; Torrance, "Calvinism and Puritanism in England and Scotland—Some Basic Concepts in the Development of 'Federal Theology,'" in William H. Neuser, ed., *Calvinus Reformator: His Contribution to Theology, Church, and Society* (Potchefstroom: Potchefstroom University for Christian Higher Education, 1982), pp. 264-89, esp. pp. 267-70.
[59]See, e.g., Allen, *Justification and the Gospel*, pp. 40-45, and sources cited.
[60]Campbell's pitting against each other of divine justice and divine benevolence is the heart of Stephen Westerholm's critique of *Deliverance of God* in Westerholm, *Justification Reconsidered*, pp. 87-94.
[61]Calvin, *Second Epistle*, p. 74 (on 2 Cor 5:14).

commenting on 2 Corinthians 5:19: "Although Christ's coming had its source in the overflowing love of God for us, yet, until men know that God has been propitiated by a mediator, there cannot but be on their side a separation which prevents them from having access to God."[62] Here we find divine benevolence ("the overflowing love of God") and divine justice (the need for a propitiating mediator) interlocked and mutually clarifying.

We see this balance again in his comments on 1 Corinthians 10:11, where Calvin rejects the idea that the God of the Old Testament was harsher and more inclined to punish than the God of the New Testament. "If God inflicted punishments on them, no more will He let us off with anything. No more, then, of the mistaken view, that God is now more lax about punishing sins!" And this highlights—not denies—"the goodness of God that has been poured out on men much more gloriously and richly with the coming of Christ."[63]

Second, Campbell rejects what he considers the "voluntarism" of most readings of Pauline "faith."[64] In one of many moves in which his strong Barthianism comes through, Campbell casts God's righteous deliverance as utterly unconditional. But Campbell argues here for a kind of hypermonergism that flies in the face of the Corinthian evidence and which Calvin, despite stereotypes of him, would resist. Following the apostle, Calvin presents a more holistic and compatibilist depiction of divine and human agency in salvation. God's sovereignty in justifying, on the one hand, and human responsibility in exercising meaningful faith that receives this free gift, on the other hand, both exist as happily compatible realities (though both are finally due to God's sovereign grace).[65] In his treatment of Calvin's view of faith, Campbell suggests that faith must be either "voluntary" or "a gift."[66] But why?

Consider, for example, Calvin's comments on the difficult issue of judgment according to works, which comes up in 2 Corinthians 5:10. "There is no inconsistency in saying that He rewards good works provided we un-

---

[62]Ibid., p. 78.
[63]Calvin, *First Epistle*, p. 212.
[64]Campbell, *Deliverance of God*, pp. 57-60.
[65]Stephen Westerholm zeroes in on this issue in Calvin through a consideration of Calvin's reading of the Joseph story (Stephen Westerholm, *Perspectives Old and New on Paul: The "Lutheran" Paul and His Critics* [Grand Rapids: Eerdmans, 2004], pp. 42-46).
[66]Campbell, *Deliverance of God*, p. 261.

derstand that this implies no denial of the fact that it is by free grace that we obtain eternal life."[67] Note the both-and here. Calvin does not allow divine grace and human reward to cancel each other out. He elegantly expresses the compatibility of divine sovereignty with human responsibility once more in his comments on 1 Corinthians 15:11.[68]

One might also point out that not only does Calvin believe firmly in meaningful human agency when it comes to faith, but "voluntarism" is an unhelpful way of expressing this act of believing. Faith, for Calvin, is itself wholly a gift of grace. We believe only because God has already moved toward us; our belief does not ultimately activate such divine condescension. Calvin is more Calvinistic than Campbell allows for. Calvin saw in Paul the "true faith" that "allows us to rest in God's grace, not with a dubious opinion but with firm and steadfast assurance."[69] Faith is integral to how salvation works. It is "firm and steadfast assurance," exercised by the human agent, that accesses the saving righteousness of God. It is one thing to acknowledge utter human inability and moral death apart from Christ (as Calvin does); it is another to eliminate meaningful human agency in redemption (as Campbell does).[70]

Campbell's work is useful because it is so fresh, so upending of a long-held paradigm. One is forced to rethink things from the ground up. One also appreciates his desire to remarry the two-hundred-year-old divorce between exegesis and constructive theology. But his work is yet another example of modern Pauline scholars going beyond fresh creativity into unhelpful idiosyncrasy. Calvin is more satisfying, avoiding unnecessary false dichotomies in reading Paul.

The folly of academic preening and parading. In his companion essay, Michael Allen has reflected on Calvin's desire to strengthen the church first and foremost. This final point I wish to make is similar, though a bit more

---

[67]Calvin, *Second Epistle*, p. 72.
[68]Calvin, *First Epistle*, pp. 317-18.
[69]Calvin, *Second Epistle*, p. 173.
[70]A third area that could be fruitfully explored is the relationship between forensic justification and vital participation, as Campbell's work is part of a broader trend that continues to recentralize the latter. Here too we could find a both-and in Calvin (made coherent through union with Christ) where Campbell erects an either/or. (See the both-and work here of Allen, *Justification and the Gospel*, chap. 2.) But as we have already broached the forensic nature of justification in Calvin's thought above, we will pass on this for now.

delicate to handle and certainly more subjective than other points I have made above. In his Corinthian commentaries as much as anywhere in his writings we see Calvin tearing down intellectual pride cloaked as Bible scholarship. Given the pride Paul himself was clearly tackling in these two letters, one is not surprised. This is worth reflection by Christian teachers and leaders.

Throughout his Corinthian commentaries, Calvin speaks of Paul's concern to "dethrone all the haughtiness and superiority of that [worldly] wisdom."[71] Real wisdom renounces our "own understanding of things, and all the wisdom of the world."[72] "The characteristic work of the Gospel is to bring down the wisdom of the world in such a manner, that, deprived of our own understanding we become completely docile."[73] Do Calvin's words here characterize contemporary biblical scholarship?

Calvin did not take these two epistles to say that we should therefore resist learning and scholarship. He was himself a product of the resurgence of the scholarly side of the humanistic movement. Indeed, his own personal ambition early on was to hole up as a thinker and writer, until Farel frightened him into the throes of civic and ecclesial leadership. Commenting on 1 Corinthians 8:1 ("'Knowledge' puffs up, but love builds up"), Calvin reflects on the vanity of learning without love for others.[74] But he then writes: "Paul, however, did not mean that this fault should be laid at the door of erudition. . . . Again, he did not mean that learning, by its very nature, breeds arrogance. He simply wanted to show the effect that knowledge has on men, when fear of God and love of the brethren are lacking."[75] Calvin returns to the fraudulence of knowledge without love in his comments on 1 Corinthians 13:1-3.[76] And the folly of intellectual pride is a theme right through Calvin's commentary on 2 Corinthians. Even a text such as 2 Corinthians 5:17 is applied by Calvin to the issue of pride and humility among Christian leaders.[77]

It would be a strange intellectual asceticism that takes Paul's hammering

---

[71]Calvin, *First Epistle*, p. 32.
[72]Ibid., pp. 32-33.
[73]Ibid., p. 34.
[74]Unless otherwise indicated, all Scripture quotations are from the ESV.
[75]Calvin, *First Epistle*, p. 171.
[76]Ibid., pp. 274-75.
[77]Calvin, *Second Epistle*, pp. 75-76.

away at fleshly "wisdom" to mean that Christians should withdraw from the world of scholarship, as Calvin himself made clear. But the reformer's words, resting on Paul's, remain a word in season to biblical scholarship. Paul is such a fascinating thinker, and the literature on this thinker is so vast, that one could easily devote several lifetimes over to the study of him *only* at a technical level. The apostle would himself, however, cringe at such aspirations.

To be sure, this academic gamesmanship is a slippery matter to diagnose, and one must tread carefully. But as the Pauline guild considers what we can learn from Calvin, it is difficult to ignore the distinct difference in flavor between a typical monograph on Paul and Calvin's writings on Paul, such as his Corinthian commentaries. Scholars we must have, including scholars who spend their entire lives devoted to the academic study of Paul; but Calvin reminds even those called to such vocations that all study of the apostle must finally funnel down into the clear holding forth of the gospel, the health of the church and the majesty of God.

What Did Calvin Miss?

There are many ways we today can learn from Calvin. I close by suggesting one way our reading of Calvin could benefit from more recent biblical scholarship. A strand of Pauline teaching has emerged with special clarity in the past century or so, seen especially in the work of Geerhardus Vos and Oscar Cullmann, among others. This strand of teaching is the reality of inaugurated eschatology, by which Paul is seen to have viewed Christ (and especially his resurrection) as climactic to all of human history, launching the long-hoped-for new creation. I am referring to the Pauline teaching that all that the Jews looked for at the end of the age has, in Christ, been decisively inaugurated. What was expected to happen at the end of history has taken place in the middle of history, so that we are now living in the last days.

For our present purposes, I will call Calvin's reading of Paul as tending toward a personal-soteriological model and neglecting what we might call a cosmic-eschatological model. The point is not that we should opt for one over against the other. But Calvin tends to neglect here the cosmic-eschatological dimension of Paul's hermeneutic, a dimension that has been especially clarified for us in recent years by scholars such as Herman Ridderbos, George Ladd, Meredith Kline, Richard Gaffin, C. Marvin Pate and G. K.

Beale.[78] These writers (and others) have reminded us that Christ not only accomplished salvation but also launched the new age. The new order of humanity, the final world, has dawned.[79] Paul's gospel addresses not only a *what* question (what is the human dilemma?) but also a *when* question (in what age do we now live?).

One of the striking things about the Corinthian correspondence is that despite being among Paul's most contextually situated letters, Paul addresses the various issues in Corinth with some of the New Testament's most eschatologically charged discourse. Yet Calvin repeatedly interprets these texts in personal-soteriological ways.

Thus 2 Corinthians 1:20 ("all the promises of God find their Yes in him") is interpreted primarily as testimony to Christ's sufficiency as mediator, not the fulfillment of the sweep of God's promises that tumble down through salvation history.[80] The eschatologically loaded descriptor of the Spirit as "a guarantee" (ἀρραβών) in 2 Corinthians 1:22 is interpreted as covenantal ratification; not untrue, but quite incomplete—the ἀρραβών is the installment now of the superlative gift (the Spirit) of the new age (cf. Eph 1:14).[81] The same Greek word is used in 2 Corinthians 5:5, and while Calvin calls the Spirit "an earnest and foretaste of what is to come," he immediately explains that the Spirit has two main functions—to show us what we should desire and to incline us to choose it, neither of which gets at the eschatological significance of

---

[78]Herman Ridderbos, *Paul: An Outline of His Theology*, trans. John Richard de Witt (Grand Rapids: Eerdmans, 1975); George Eldon Ladd, *The Presence of the Future: The Eschatology of Biblical Realism* (repr., Grand Rapids: Eerdmans, 1996); Meredith G. Kline, *Images of the Spirit* (Grand Rapids: Baker Academic, 1980); Kline, *Kingdom Prologue: Genesis Foundations for a Covenantal Worldview* (Eugene, OR: Wipf and Stock, 2006); Richard B. Gaffin, *Resurrection and Redemption: A Study in Paul's Soteriology* (Phillipsburg, NJ: P&R, 1987), pp. 33-36; Gaffin, *By Faith, Not by Sight: Paul and the Order of Salvation* (Waynesboro, GA: Paternoster, 2006); C. Marvin Pate, *The End of the Age Has Come: The Theology of Paul* (Grand Rapids: Zondervan, 1995); G. K. Beale, *A New Testament Biblical Theology: The Unfolding of the Old Testament in the New* (Grand Rapids: Baker Academic, 2011).

[79]I am not thinking so much here of the "apocalyptic" strand of Pauline scholarship of which J. Louis Martyn might be seen as representative, because this strand emphasizes discontinuity between the Testaments to the neglect of continuity. The New Testament, however, teaches both that something entirely new has arrived and that this new thing is, on reflection, precisely what was anticipated all along; on which see D. A. Carson, "Mystery and Fulfillment: Toward a More Comprehensive Paradigm of Paul's Understanding of the Old and the New," in *Justification and Variegated Nomism*, 2:393-436.

[80]Calvin, *Second Epistle*, pp. 21-22.

[81]Ibid., p. 23.

the coming of the Spirit.[82] The eschatological significance of the dawning of the "new creation" in 2 Corinthians 5:17 is missed, as is "the day of salvation" (quoting Is 49:8) in 2 Corinthians 6:2.[83] And so on.

I have started with 2 Corinthians here because perhaps the most eschatologically loaded text in the New Testament, the place where inaugurated eschatology is thickest on the ground, is 1 Corinthians 15. What then of the New Testament's great resurrection chapter? A close look at the text is beyond the scope of this chapter, but it is fair to say that post-Vos Pauline scholarship has perceived with greater clarity than Calvin Paul's line of argument—in which the cosmic-eschatological and not the personal-soteriological is in the foreground. Paul refers to the soteriological dimension of Christ's work early in the chapter (1 Cor 15:1-5), but then extracts the quick reference to Christ's resurrection in the gospel formula of 1 Corinthians 15:3-4 and dwells on it at length. That is, Paul spends the rest of the chapter expanding out from the benefits sinners receive in Christ to the eon in which we now live in Christ. Soteriology is never left behind (1 Cor 15:17), but it is not the driving thrust of the passage.

Paul then speaks of Christ as the "firstfruits" (1 Cor 15:20, 23), perhaps the key word of the entire chapter, by which he means that Jesus' bodily resurrection is the first ingathering of one single harvest. We are united to Christ, so that when we look at the resurrected Christ, we look on the first instance in human history of what we ourselves will one day enjoy—and already, at some level, do (Eph 2:6). Especially noteworthy here is the work of Richard Gaffin.[84] In Christ, the new day has dawned. He is the last Adam, *the* eschatological man (ὁ ἔσχατος Ἀδάμ; 1 Cor 15:45), the first instance of the new order of humanity.

Does Calvin track with Paul in all this? Less than one would wish. At least twice in his treatment of 1 Corinthians 15 Calvin raises the error of Hymenaeus and Philetus, who mistakenly said "that the resurrection has already happened" (2 Tim 2:18), and one wonders whether Calvin is overly fearful of committing the same error in his reading of 1 Corinthians 15.[85]

---

[82]Ibid., p. 68.
[83]Ibid., pp. 75-76, 84-85.
[84]Gaffin, *Resurrection and Redemption*, pp. 33-36; also Vos, *Pauline Eschatology*, pp. 44-49.
[85]Calvin, *Second Epistle*, pp. 312, 321.

His (appropriate) soteriological focus on Christ's resurrection in commenting on 1 Corinthians 15:3—"as sin was destroyed by the death of Christ, so righteousness was procured by His resurrection"[86]—remains (inappropriately) his focus throughout the chapter. Thus Calvin explains the close connection between Christ's resurrection and ours in 1 Corinthians 15:12-19 in rather pallid terms of logical salvific coherence ("someone who has been completely conquered by death cannot effect the salvation of others"), and not the fact that in Christ's resurrection the general resurrection (and thus the latter days) has already begun in the middle of history.[87] This neglect of the eschaton-inaugurating effect of Christ's resurrection comes out again when Calvin deals with the "firstfruits" text, reading ἀπαρχή as underscoring "the power of Christ's resurrection" as "extended to all of us."[88] And Christ as "the last Adam" in 1 Corinthians 15:45 is again treated in strictly soteriological, not eschatological, terms.[89]

Conclusion

Calvin's dictum in commentary writing of *perspicua brevitas* (lucid brevity) stands in stark contrast to much of what comes to us from the Pauline guild in the twenty-first century. But beyond how he writes, what he writes merits consideration by today's Pauline scholars.

Calvin was a man of his times as we are of ours, but we will only see how much this is the case for ourselves as we are willing to engage with those of another age—which was Calvin's own method, drawing extensively throughout his writings on the church fathers. As we do so, we will find in John Calvin a reader of Paul possessing an unusual ability to follow the mind of the apostle. We will not follow him on everything, nor should we, as we have just seen above. But the net effect of engaging with him as we seek to read Paul today will be a sharper, more coherent and more penetrating understanding of the apostle.

---

[86]Calvin, *First Epistle*, p. 314.
[87]Ibid., p. 319.
[88]Ibid., p. 322.
[89]Ibid., p. 339.

The Letters of Paul and Thomas Cranmer

9

Thomas Cranmer's Reading *of* Paul's Letters

Ashley Null

In the famous Gerlach Flicke painting found today in London's National Portrait Gallery, Thomas Cranmer looks out at us as if we had just walked in on him unexpectedly in his study.[1] He is seated at a richly carpeted desk. The billowing curtain behind him is drawn back, enabling the sun to provide plenty of good light for the archbishop's reading, which we have evidently interrupted. Two books and a letter lie on top of the table, evidencing his engagement in study. Yet in his long, slender and rather pale scholar's hands is the particular, still open book from whose consideration we have just distracted him. Due to its helpful labeling, we can see that the archbishop has been reading from the Scriptures.

Undoubtedly Cranmer is seeking to make a statement. He wants to be remembered as an archbishop whose most characteristic act was to read the Bible. Equally clear, in the context of his times, such a depiction is a polemical declaration of allegiance to church reform. If the Flicke painting were intended to be hung in Lambeth Palace next to Hans Holbein the Younger's portrait of William Warham, Cranmer's immediate predecessor, this message would have only been even more obvious. Both archbishops are dressed in white rochet and black chimere, wearing fur stoles and black

---

[1]Number 535, National Portrait Gallery, London.

caps, and seated at a table in front of a richly woven curtain. Yet, instead of an open Bible, beside Warham lies a prayer book open to the litany of the saints. Moreover, unlike Warham, Cranmer has pulled back the curtain to let in fresh light, an act that has in fact revealed three chipped window panes needing repair. Cranmer, unlike Warham, knows he has restoration work to do, and for inspiration and strength for the task he looks to God's Word rather than to his now-deceased servants.

Of course, Cranmer does not have the whole Bible in his hands. The first complete text of the Holy Scriptures in quarto size would be the work of the Genevan exiles fifteen years later. Of the two Testaments, as a Christian leader Cranmer naturally chose to be seen reading from the second. Still, somewhat unexpectedly, he is not depicted with a full New Testament, despite the recent publishing advances associated with it. Cranmer holds neither Desiderius Erasmus's *Novum Instrumentum* (1516), the landmark reworking of the Vulgate's Latin against the Greek whose eloquence drew Thomas Bilney to solifidianism, nor William Tyndale's *Newe Testament as it was written* (1526) whose catalogue of ear-pleasing English phrases, freshly minted from the original, eventually made their way into the Great Bible for which Cranmer himself wrote a preface (1540). In the Flicke portrait, the primate of all England is seen reading from a volume containing only a portion of the New Testament. From someone so deeply inspired by the Erasmian principle that Christ was the *scopus* of the Scriptures, not to mention the archbishop's abiding interest in liturgy, one could then reasonably expect him to be holding a book of the Gospels. Yet such is not the case. The volume open in Cranmer's hand is labeled as Paul's letters.[2] Flicke has exercised some artistic license. No such book was ever published in England during this period.[3] Yet no embellishment could more clearly convene the key to Cranmer's understanding of the Christian life in general and his work as bishop in particular. Literally, as well as figuratively, Cranmer's handbook is the writings of Paul.

Such was the case even before Cranmer had made the decisive turn to

---

[2] Flicke's inscription is in abbreviated Latin: "Pauli e*pistolae*." Omitted letters are in italics.
[3] A. W. Pollard, G. Redgrave, W. A. Jackson et al., eds., *A Short-Title Catalogue of Books Printed in England, Scotland, & Ireland and of English Books Printed Abroad, 1475–1640*, 2nd ed. (London: Bibliographical Society, 1986), 1:129.

solifidianism (justification by faith), an event most likely to be associated with his German embassy of 1532, when he married into the household of the angular Nuremberg reformer Andreas Osiander. Cranmer rejected medieval ecclesiology before he came to abandon scholastic soteriology, and he looked to the Pauline epistles for his reforming approach to the office of a bishop as much as he would later do for his reconsideration of the nature of salvation.

Paul for Cranmer the Erasmian Humanist

We can see this distinction between Cranmer's Erasmian and evangelical phases in the earliest stratum of his annotations to a copy of Jacques Merlin's *Concilia*.[4] In green ink, Cranmer has carefully underlined material in the text of the Eighth Session of the Council of Constance (1415) where numerous heresies held by John Wycliffe are listed: "The Roman church is the synagogue of Satan. The Pope is not the immediate and next-in-line vicar of Christ and the apostles. . . . [Wycliffe's doctrine is in error because] it would deny the pope's primacy over other individual churches."[5] Note that Cranmer carefully underlined passages which clearly rejected Petrine authority but not Roman soteriology. Later as a convinced evangelical, Cranmer will accuse Rome of departing from Scripture and, thus, belonging to the synagogue of Satan.[6] However, at the time of the green-ink underlinings, he showed no interest in this charge.

Further green-ink underlinings in Cranmer's copy of the *Concilia* show that his initial attack on Roman ecclesiology was grounded in a humanist's historical comparison of the New Testament witness with later claims for a papal authority. His annotations to one document are particularly helpful,

---

[4]Jacques Merlin, ed., *Quatuor conciliorum generalium* (Paris: Jean Conrilleau for Galliot du Pré, 1524). Cranmer's copy of the first edition of Merlin is now part of the Karpeles Manuscript Libraries in Santa Barbara, California. I am very grateful for the many kindnesses that Dr. Karpeles has shown me in giving me unimpeded access to this volume.

[5]"Ecclesia Romana est synagoga sathanae; *nec papa est proximus et immediatus vicarious christi & Apostolorum* . . . *negaret primatum summi pontificis super alias ecclesias particulars*" (*Cranmer's Concilia*, vol. 2, fol. 158v). Quotations from *Cranmer's Concilia* adhere to the following conventions: Letters omitted in Cranmer's original abbreviated marginalia are supplied in the quotation in italics, and where he underlined the printed text, the quotation is also underlined.

[6]See "Cranmer's Great Commonplaces," BL Royal MS 7.B.XI, fol. 22v. For a posthumous editor's translation of this passage, see John Cox, ed., *Miscellaneous Writings and Letters of Thomas Cranmer* (Cambridge: Parker Society, 1846), p. 52.

the Clementine forgery purported to be a letter to James, the brother of Jesus, in which Clement described his appointment by Peter as his successor. To Pseudo-Clement's claim that Peter "was set apart to be the foundation of the Church,"[7] Cranmer countered by quoting Paul from 1 Corinthians 3:11: "This statement is contrary to the plain words of Scripture that 'no one is able to lay another foundation other than that which has been laid, that is Jesus Christ.'"[8] Beside the assertion that Peter was also the "first to whom God the Father revealed the Son,"[9] Cranmer wrote, "Now the Son was revealed to John when he said, 'Behold, the Lamb of God who takes away the sins of the world.'"[10] Finally, Cranmer dismissed Pseudo-Clement's statement that Peter "was commanded to enlighten the darker region of the western world"[11] by asking: "How can this be so, since according to Paul's letter to the Galatians it seems rather that Peter was commanded to enlighten the Jews, for whose sake the Gospel was entrusted to him."[12]

At a later date, Cranmer read through the forged letter again, and this time he underlined key passages in black ink while making further marginal comments in a relatively small hand. These annotations exhibit a strong commitment to the primacy of Scripture and the ministry of the Word. Cranmer underlined the statement "let every church believe and obey only [the Savior's] decrees and commands."[13] He also marked Peter's description of apostolic succession: "I pass on the chair of my preaching and teaching to [Clement] alone."[14] In the accompanying *marginalium*, however, Cranmer made a small but significant transposition, which stressed the preeminence of the ministry of the Word: "He passed on only the chair of preaching and

---

[7] "[F]undamentum esse ecclesiae definitus est" (*Cranmer's Concilia*, vol. 1, part 1, fol. 3v). Note that the two parts of volume one of *Cranmer's Concilia* have been misbound at a later date. Currently, part 2 precedes part 1. However, I have followed the original publication order in my citations.
[8] "Hoc est contra manifesta scripturae verba Fundamentum aliud nemo potest ponere praeter id quod positum est, quod est Christus Ihesus" (ibid.).
[9] "[C]ui et primo, deus pater filium revelauit" (ibid.).
[10] "Nunc Johanni revelatus est filius cum diceret Ecce agnus dei qui tollit peccata mundi, etc." (ibid.).
[11] "Qui obscuriorem mundi plagam occidentis velut omnium potentior illuminare praeceptus est" (ibid.).
[12] "Ubi Unde hoc constat cum ex paulo ad Galatas potius videatur praeceptus illuminare Judaeos, erga quos creditum erat ei evangelium" (ibid.).
[13] "[Salvatoris] solius praeceptis, ac iussis credat, et obediat omnis ecclesia" (ibid., fol. 5r).
[14] "[C]ui soli meae praedicationis et doctrinae cathedram trado" (ibid., fol. 3v).

teaching."[15] When Peter urged Clement to keep himself free from worldly concerns so as to be able to teach Scripture without interruption, Cranmer commented, "Why then do bishops now abandon the Word of God?"[16] When Peter encouraged presbyters to engage in a series of corporal works of mercy derived from Matthew 25, Cranmer added in the margin, "Why indeed did he overlook only the obligation to preach which is the unique special duty of priests?"[17] While Protestants on the Continent would no doubt have agreed with these remarks, Cranmer still characterized good works as the best source of charity.[18] Hence, the Cranmer who made the smaller black-ink annotations beside the black underlinings would still seem to have been an Erasmian humanist.[19]

To whom, then, did this Cranmer turn to serve as the apostolic ideal to counter the über-ecclesiastical claims of the Pseudo-Clementine literature? The apostle Paul as recorded in Scripture. When Peter was alleged to have counseled against serving as a surety, Cranmer wrote in the margin, "Why then did Paul stand ready to pay Philemone's debts?"[20] When Peter warned Clement against any involvement in secular affairs, Cranmer retorted, "Why then did Paul call emperors and princes to his tribunal?"[21] Peter also argued that because priests led superior holy lives to those of laypeople, the former were not accountable to the latter. When Peter quoted in support Paul's statement that the apostle was not interested in the judgments of other people about his ministry (1 Cor 4:3), Cranmer dismisses the purported evidence out of hand: "He misuses this Pauline verse."[22] Most telling of all, however, is an annotation beside Peter's description of bishops carrying on

---

[15] "Et cathedram praedicationis ac doctrinae solum tradidit" (ibid.).
[16] "Cur ergo nunc pontifices deserunt verbum dei?" (ibid., fol. 4r).
[17] "Immo cur, solum praedicandi officium praetermisit, quod unicum esset praecipuum sacerdotum officium" (ibid., fol. 4v).
[18] "Charitatis maximum fomentum est, promixos ad mensam tuam adhibere" ("The greatest kindling for love is showing hospitality to neighbors," ibid.).
[19] Only the black-ink comments written in a much larger hand should be associated with MacCulloch's observation that some of Cranmer's marginalia in this section of Merlin must date from his preparation for his Answer (1551) to Gardiner's critique of his mature eucharistic doctrine outlined in the Defence. See Diarmaid MacCulloch, "Two Dons in Politics: Thomas Cranmer and Stephen Gardiner, 1503–1533," Historical Journal 37 (1994): 1-22, at pp. 8-9. Cf. Peter Newman Brooks, Cranmer in Context (Cambridge: Lutterworth, 1989), pp. 20-22.
[20] "Cur ergo fideiubebat Paulus pro Philemone?" (Cranmer's Concilia, vol. 1, part 1, fol. 4r).
[21] "Cur ergo Paulus Imperatores et principes vocat ad tribunal suum?" (ibid.).
[22] "Locus Pauli detorquetur" (ibid., fol. 6v).

the office of the apostles. In this context, Peter instructs Clement not to appoint bishops for anything less than a major city, lest he lessen episcopal dignity. Cranmer derisively retorts, "But Paul did not feel it beneath himself to be considered as the excrement of the world."[23] Note that Cranmer chose to follow Erasmus's harsher rendering of Paul's statement in 1 Corinthians 4:13 than the Vulgate's milder "refuse" (*purgamenta*).[24]

PAUL FOR CRANMER THE SOLAFIDIAN

So apostolic succession for Cranmer was the handing on of apostolic teaching with apostolic humility. At some point in the early 1530s, Cranmer came to a new understanding of what exactly was the apostolic understanding of salvation. The Flicke portrait also gives us a significant clue to the intellectual process behind this decision. On the desk before Cranmer lies a copy of Augustine's *De fide et operibus*. A product of Augustine's later affective theology, probably written in 413, *On Faith and Works* outlined his mature understanding of the relationship between the two. On the one hand, Augustine clearly stated that Paul's teaching on justification by faith meant that good works could not precede justification, but followed it, because only people who had received the Holy Spirit could perform works out of love for righteousness. On the other hand, once Christ dwelt in the believer's heart by faith, this living faith necessarily produced good works performed out of love for God. In short, a good life was inseparable from faith, because a life could not be good without faith, and true faith could not but bear the fruit of a good life. Thus the Flicke portrait suggests that Cranmer's reading of Augustine pointed him toward the Protestant interpretation of Paul on justification.

However, once again, it was the apostle's own writings that were the decisive factor. The first extensive evidence we have for Cranmer's new theological orientation is his annotations to Henry VIII's corrections to the Bishops' Book (1538).[25] The latter was a compromise formulary devised by

---

[23]"Sed Paulus non est dedignatus tamquam excrementum mundi haberi" (ibid.).
[24]"[V]eluti excrementa mundi facti sumus" (*Novum Instrumentum*, in Erasmus, *Opera omnia Desiderii Erasmi Roterodami*, ed. J. Leclerc [Leiden: Pieter van der Aa, 1703-1706], VI.676). Cf. also Erasmus's use of *haberi* in his Latin paraphrase of 1 Cor 4:13: "ut rejectamenta habemur huius mundi" (ibid., VI.871).
[25]Cox, *Miscellaneous Writings*, pp. 83-114.

a committee composed of both traditionalist and evangelical bishops under the watchful eye of Thomas Cromwell, the king's vicegerent for spirituals. Henry, however, did not personally review the text until after its publication in September 1537—hence the reason for both the common name of the formulary and Henry's later corrections sent to Cranmer. Since the book's short descriptions of Christian basics were intended for use as a series of parish sermons, for all the donnish comments that Cranmer also made about the king's diction and syntax, the substance of the debate between them was not merely academic.[26]

In his entries Cranmer defended the description of the Christian life in the Bishops' Book based on his reading of Romans 8. In so doing, he clearly recast the narrative of justification from the medieval longer-than-life quest to gain personal merit to an evangelical wonder at the transforming power of the heavenly Father's never-ending love for his wayward children. With his usual acuteness, Stephen Gardiner, the leading traditionalist bishop at the Henrician court, grasped the essential difference between these two approaches. He emphasized that the "contention is not of the preciousnes, validitie and effecte of christes passion, but of the vse of it."[27] It seemed patently obvious to him that the cross's effectiveness in any individual's life depended on whether that individual had fulfilled the conditions on which God promised salvation.[28] As Gardiner read his Bible, those conditions included making use of the sacraments of baptism and penance as means of justifying grace, believing in the articles of the faith and showing forth love by doing good works.[29] Consequently, he thought it perfectly acceptable to talk of meriting salvation, since such language simply "signifieth the due vsing of the benefite offred," that a person was "worthely, fully, and holly to deserue, none otherwyse then a workeman deserueth his wages, for his labour and trauayle."[30] Concisely summarizing his quid pro quo understanding of God's relationship with human beings, Gardiner argued that

---

[26]See Ashley Null, "Official Tudor Homilies," in *The Oxford Handbook of the Early Modern Sermon*, ed. Peter McCullough, Hugh Adlington and Emma Rhatigan (Oxford: Oxford University Press, 2011), pp. 348-65, at p. 349.
[27]Stephen Gardiner, *A Declaration of such true articles as George Ioye hath gone about to confute as false* (London: Johannes Herford for Robert Toye, 1546), fol. 12r.
[28]"They that wyll enioye the effecte of Christes passion, must fulfyll the condicion" (ibid., fol. 17r).
[29]Ibid., fol. 49.
[30]Ibid., fol.12v; fol. 11v.

"He is worthy [of] loue and fauour, that wil seke for it, and do his dutie to atteyne it."[31] Of course, comparing salvation to the payment of a hired hand's wages is not without biblical precedent—the parable of the vineyard in Matthew 20:1-16 does just that. Cranmer, however, found in Paul's language of sonship a completely different explanation for God's relationship with the saved—divine love made known in unmerited adoption.

Romans 8 begins and ends with an unconditional affirmation of God's love for the justified. God will never condemn them (Rom 8:1), despite their ongoing infirmity of the flesh (Rom 8:3), nor will he let anything in all creation drive a wedge between them and his love (Rom 8:38-39). Cranmer also rooted the salvific process in the power of God's love to save: "The favour and love of the Father of heaven towards us is the mean whereby we come to his favour and love . . . his love was the original and beginning of our salvation."[32] Yet he was equally clear that justification was not ultimately dependent on human responses to that divine initiative: "Our faith and trust that we be in God's favour and his own children hangeth not of our own merits and applying of our will to his motions: for, insomuch as many times the good men do the contrary, that were the ready way to desperation."[33] Rather, humanity was essentially passive in the reception of salvation, for sinners were held captive by Satan. When the Bishops' Book stated that Christ "hath spoiled [his enemies] of the possession of mankind," Henry had wanted to add an important condition "[of those] willing to return to him." Cranmer rejected the qualification out of hand:

> It is good to speak of our redemption after the fashion of the scripture, which useth ever to say, that Christ hath spoiled the devils, and redeemed the world, without this or any like addition: ["He,"] saith the scripture, ["spoiled the principalities and powers," and "He suffered for our sins, and not for ours only but for those of the whole world"].[34]

For Cranmer, salvation was not the result of human choices but God's.

According to Romans 8:30, those whom God "has predestined, he also called; those he called, he also justified, those he justified, he also glorified."

---

[31]Ibid., fol. 12v.
[32]Cox, *Miscellaneous Writings*, p. 113.
[33]Ibid., p. 94.
[34]Ibid., p. 88.

Hence those whom he has made sons through justification will also one day inherit the kingdom (Rom 8:17). Cranmer interpreted these passages to mean that all those who were justified were also the elect. Nothing makes Cranmer's coterminous understanding of the two groups any clearer than his response to Henry's desire to insert "only" and "chiefly" into a sentence in the Bishops' Book. The king's revision would have read "not *only* for the worthiness of any merit or work done by the penitent, but *chiefly* for the only merits of . . . Jesus Christ." Cranmer responded, "These two words may not be put in this place in any wise: for they signify that our election and justification cometh partly of our merits, though chiefly it cometh of the goodness of God."[35] Of course, the archbishop's primary point was that justification was not merited through inherent righteousness. However, one should not fail to notice that someone as careful with diction as Cranmer treated the phrase "election and justification" as a single process of salvation to which he then could refer in the dependent clause with the singular neuter pronoun "it."

Despite his great debt to Augustine, on this point Cranmer's reading of Romans 8 caused him to depart from his favorite patristic authority. Augustine had taught that the justification that was brought about by baptismal regeneration was not automatically effectual for eternal life in heaven. A second, additional grace of perseverance was needed for salvation from hell, and this grace was God's unmerited gift to a smaller group of the elect.[36] All medieval penitential theology was based on this distinction between the initial, amissable justification brought about by baptism and then renewed by penance, i.e., a temporary state of grace, and the perseverance of the elect to saving final justification in the hour of their deaths. Here is the theological foundation for Gardiner's insistence on the conditional nature of salvation. Since human beings could never be certain that they would die in a state of grace, all the energies of medieval penitential theology were directed at pricking the human will to fight the good fight until the very end.

Hence, in one of his first corrections, Henry VIII amended the text to read "as long as I persevere in his precepts and laws, [I am] one of the right inheritors of his kingdom." Cranmer, however, rejected the change, arguing

---

[35]Ibid., p. 95.
[36]J. Patout Burns, *The Development of Augustine's Doctrine of Operative Grace* (Paris: Études Augustiniennes, 1980), pp. 175-78.

on the basis of Paul's filial language that those with saving faith would naturally seek to serve God and would indeed enjoy salvation in the end:

> He that had this faith, converteth from his sin, repenteth him, that he like [the prodigal son] vainly consumed his will, reason, wits, and other goods, which he received of the mere benefit of his heavenly Father, to his said Father's displeasure; and applieth himself wholly to please him again, and trusteth assuredly, that for Christ's sake he will and doth remit his sin, withdraweth his indignation, delivereth him from hell, from the power of the infernal spirits, taketh him to his mercy, and maketh him his own son and his own heir: and he hath also the very christian hope, that after this life he shall reign ever with Christ in his kingdom. For St Paul saith: ["If we are sons, then also heirs, indeed heirs of God and co-heirs with Christ"].[37]

Because Romans 8:17 taught that those with justifying faith would also inherit the life of glory, Cranmer insisted that believers should be confident that they would persevere in repentance and amendment of life until the very end. Cranmer would return again and again to this notion of assurance:

> And the true faithful man endeavoureth himself to conform his will to God's will in all things, and to walk right forth in all his precepts. And where by infirmity he chanceth to take a fall, he lieth not still, but by God's help riseth again. And his trust is so much in God, that he doubteth not in God's goodness toward him, but that, if by fragility and weakness he fall again, God will not suffer him so to lie still, but put his hand to him and help him up again, and so at the last he will take him up from death unto the life of glory everlasting.[38]

> The elect, of whom is here spoken, will follow Christ's precepts, and rise again when they fall; and the right faith cannot be without following of Christ's precepts, and repentance after falling.... Therefore in my judgment it were better to say thus: "The elect shall follow Christ's precepts, or when they fall, they shall repent and rise again, and obtain remission."[39]

> This article speaketh only of the elect, in whom finally no fault shall be, but they shall perpetually continue and endure.... Likewise the elect shall not wilfully and obstinately withstand God's calling.[40]

---

[37]Cox, *Miscellaneous Writings*, p. 84.
[38]Ibid., p. 93.
[39]Ibid., p. 92.
[40]Ibid., p. 91.

So that it pertaineth as well to our faith, that we should so die, as that we should be saved.[41]

Assurance lay at the heart of Cranmer's soteriology, for he believed that only such certitude made an ongoing renewal of human affections possible.

Both the scholastics and the reformers believed fear and hope were essential for the restoration of a sinner to God. According to the medieval penitentials, like the upper and lower millstones used to grind wheat, the fear of damnation and the hope of salvation shattered hardened human hearts so that the tears of contrition would flow.[42] Likewise, Cranmer thought fear of punishment preceded hope of forgiveness.

> And, for a further declaration to know how we obtain our justification, it is expedient to consider first, how naughty and sinful we are all, that be of Adam's kindred; and contrariwise, what mercifulness is in God, which to all faithful and penitent sinners pardoneth all their offences for Christ's sake.... The commandments of God lay our faults before our eyes, which putteth us in fear and dread, and maketh us see the wrath of God against our sins, as St Paul saith, ["The recognition of sin comes through the law," and, "The law works wrath,"] and maketh us sorry and repentant, that ever we should come into the displeasure of God and the captivity of the devil. The gracious and benign promises of God by the mediation of Christ sheweth us, (and that to our great relief and comfort,) whensoever we be repentant, and return fully to God in our hearts, that we have forgiveness of our sins, be reconciled to God, and accepted, and reputed just and righteous in his sight.[43]

Since the scholastics considered justification to be regularly amissable until the point of death, fear of punishment remained a necessary attitude throughout a Christian's life. On the one hand, dread of damnation began the process that led to a renewed state of grace. On the other, even when temporarily justified, Christians were to keep fear of hell ever before their eyes as the best aid against the presumption of salvation. For a false assurance would only lead to moral laziness and its inevitable consequence of

---

[41]Ibid., p. 89.
[42]See Ashley Null, *Thomas Cranmer's Doctrine of Repentance: Renewing the Power to Love* (Oxford: Oxford University Press, 2000), pp. 40-42.
[43]Cox, *Miscellaneous Writings*, p. 113.

being caught unaware by a demonic, eternal death–inducing temptation.[44]

Cranmer's reading of Romans 8 meant that he had a very different approach. First, he did not think personal salvific certitude was presumptuous but instead necessary. Second, saving justification came in a moment of belief, not as the result of an oft-repeated process. Once again, Gardiner grasped this point: "The deuyll hath excogitate, to offre heauen without workes for it, so frelye that men shall not nede for heauen to worke at al . . . but onely belefe, onely, onely, nothinge els."[45] Thirdly, according to Romans 8:15, since the justified had received the "Spirit of sonship," they were no longer slaves to fear. Rather, they warmly addressed God Almighty by the most privileged expression of intimate, filial love: "Abba, Father." Consequently, for Cranmer, fear of damnation was merely preparation for conversion; assurance of salvation and the loving gratitude that it birthed characterized the normal life of a child of God thereafter. Although believers could expect to experience earthly adversities sent from God to help them learn to crucify their sinful desires, Cranmer argued that for the justified these corrections were simply manifestations of his fatherly love for his children.[46]

> Verily, although we ever deserve as much punishment as is laid upon us, and much more, yet no part of this is afflict[47] unto us by the will of God; yea, and as touching [us,] which are so taken into his favour that through Christ we be made his children, though it seem never so grievous, it is done of his most beneficial and fatherly good-will, that he beareth towards us, which chasteth, as St Paul saith, all those that he loveth.[48]

Finally, in Romans 8, Paul contrasts those who are led by the sinful nature with those who are led by the Holy Spirit. The justified show themselves sons of God by how they live according to the Spirit (Rom 8:14), i.e., setting their minds on what the Spirit desires (Rom 8:5), choosing to put to death the

---

[44]Null, *Thomas Cranmer's Doctrine of Repentance*, pp. 41-42.
[45]Gardiner, *Declaration of True Articles*, fol. 6r.
[46]"Endue vs with thy grace, that we maye gladly suffre all diseases, pouertie, dispisinges, persecutions, and aduersities, knowyng that it is thy wyl, that we shuld crucifie, and mortifie our wyls" (*The Institution of a Christen Man* [i.e., The Bishops' Book] [London: Thomas Berthelet, 1537], fol. 83v).
[47]That is, "affliction" or "misery."
[48]Cox, *Miscellaneous Writings*, p. 107.

misdeeds of the body (Rom 8:12-13) so as to enjoy life and peace instead (Rom 8:6).

Cranmer was very clear that the certitude of forgiveness in the justified led to the advent of divine love in their hearts, which they then expressed in godly way of life.

> But, if the profession of our faith of the remission of our own sins enter within us into the deepness of our hearts, then it must kindle a warm fire of love in our hearts towards God, and towards all other for the love of God,—a fervent mind to seek and procure God's honour, will, and pleasure in all things,—a good will and mind to help every man and to do good unto them, so far as our might, wisdom, learning, counsel, health, strength, and all other gifts which we have received of God, will extend,—and, *in summa*, a firm intent and purpose to do all that is good, and leave all that is evil.[49]

Scholasticism taught that faith had to be combined with the infused divine gift of sanctifying love (*fides charitate formata*) in order for penitents to receive forgiveness of their sins. In the passage above, however, Cranmer clearly reversed the order: first certitude of forgiveness, then the stirring of love in the heart for God, his will and others. Here was Cranmer's answer to the charge that a salvation that lacked conditions would only lead to lawlessness. Once again, Gardiner grasped the difference:

> There is no forward in the newe teaching, but al backwarde ... in so moch as he must lerne to say his [Lord's Prayer] backward, and where we sayd, forgiue vs our debtes, as we forgyue our debters, now it is, as thou forgiuest our debtes, so I wyll forgyue my debters, and so God must forgyue fyrst, and al I sayd is turned backewarde.[50]

> They wold perswade to the world, that we can do no maner of good dedes tyll we haue no nede of them for our saluacion, that is to say, tyl we be iustified, and clearly in gods perfit favour, and assured by our owne belefe of life euer lastynge, and as though we shulde say to god: Gyue me my wages aforehand, and make me sure that I shall haue heauen, and then I professe I will forgeue my neyghbour. Then I wil fast the true fast from synne. Then I wyl pray. Then I wyll do almose. Then I wyll loue myne enemye. For then I can do it.[51]

---

[49]Ibid., p. 86. Cf. ibid., p. 114.
[50]Gardiner, *Declaration of True Articles*, fol. 5v.
[51]Ibid., fol. 21r.

Gardiner was spot-on that Cranmer taught that only assurance of salvation enabled the justified to begin to do good works. Cranmer, however, would have undoubtedly pointed out to Gardiner that only assurance drove out fear and so enabled love to reorient the will of the justified toward desiring to please God.

Cranmer's Public Proclamation

Cranmer's annotations to Henry's corrections of the Bishops' Book had defended a Pauline description of the Christian life that resulted from holding justification by faith without directly addressing the issue itself. No doubt such an approach was only politic in the light of the compromise nature of the formulary, not to mention the king's own lifelong opposition to solifidianism. Nevertheless, even this limited evangelical advance was thoroughly routed in its successor text, the King's Book, published with royal authority in 1543.[52] Famously, the article on justification specifically repudiated both solifidianism and "all phantastical imagination, curious reasoning, and vain trust in predestination," encouraging instead that people remember Paul's warning, "He that standeth, let him take heed that he fall not."[53] With the advent of the King's Book, denouncing Cranmer's understanding of salvation had become the standard staple of English parochial preaching.

Nevertheless, everything would change again in only a few years. In his will, Henry appointed a regency council that would govern after his death on behalf of his nine-year-old heir. When two leading traditionalist peers earned the king's wrath and were stricken from the list in December 1546, the council was left dominated by supporters of doctrinal reform.[54] Not surprisingly, then, with the accession of Edward VI on January 28, 1547, the new government embraced indisputably Protestant teaching with revolutionary fervor. Within six months—on July 31, 1547—another formulary for parish preaching was introduced. The *Book of Homilies* was designed to be both a manifesto of the Edwardian regime's theological agenda and the means of implementation. Its sermons established an official epitome of scriptural teaching on the way of salvation that served as the doctrinal standard for the government's Protestant

---

[52]T. A. Lacey, *The King's Book* (London: SPCK, 1932).
[53]Ibid., pp. 151-57, at pp. 155-56.
[54]MacCulloch, *Cranmer*, pp. 358-60.

makeover of the faith and practice of the English church.[55] Not surprisingly, at the heart of the "Homily on Salvation" was Cranmer's clear defense of justification by faith based on his reading of the Pauline epistles.

In his theological research recorded in his "Great Commonplaces" and "Notes on Justification," Cranmer had already delineated in private his commitment to the Protestant interpretation of Pauline soteriology—including the key doctrine of forensic justification.[56] Now at last, in the "Homily on Salvation," he was able to argue for solifidianism publicly and with the full authority of the crown. Cranmer opened the sermon by insisting that human beings needed an alien righteousness for their justification: "Because all men be sinners and offenders against God . . . every man of necessity is constrained to seek for another righteousness, or justification, to be received at God's own hands." However, unlike Gardiner, Cranmer made clear that the righteousness given to the believer through Christ was not true inherent righteousness but merely "taken, accepted, and allowed of God for our prefect and full justification."[57] Because of the sinful nature of ever-present concupiscence that tainted any inner goodness, the only possible means of salvation was the imputation of an extrinsic saving righteousness by faith: "Christ is now the righteousness of all them that truly do believe in him . . . forasmuch as that which their infirmity lacketh, Christ's justice hath supplied."[58]

To defend and expand on these propositions, Cranmer naturally turned to the writings of Paul. He did so, however, in the typical early modern manner, by the *loci communes* method of biblical exegesis. In antiquity, these "commonplaces" were conceived as "pigeon-holes" to store material connected either by a similar theme or its opposite. Such organization by "topics" (from τόπος, Greek for "place") enabled an orator more easily to recall his persuasive arguments and enrich his style. In Erasmus's description of theological method, *Ratio seu methodus compendio perveniendi ad veram theologiam* (1519), he added a hermeneutical function by merging his commonplace method of reading literature with

---

[55]See Null, "Official Tudor Homilies," pp. 351-57.
[56]See Null, *Thomas Cranmer's Doctrine of Repentance*, pp. 157-212.
[57]Cox, *Miscellaneous Writings*, p. 128.
[58]Ibid., p. 130.

Augustine's insistence in the *De doctrina christiana* that the more difficult places of Scripture could be understood in the light of the clearer passages.[59] As an expert on rhetoric himself, Philipp Melanchthon used this commonplace method in his groundbreaking explanation of Protestant theology. As its title suggests, *Loci communes theologici* (1521) gathered all the pertinent biblical passages on such key doctrines of Christian theology as sin, law, gospel, grace and justification by faith so that Scripture could interpret Scripture. Naturally, being now a Protestant humanist, Cranmer did likewise.

Initially he used just two verses to buttress his argument that sinners were not justified through personal efforts to do good. The first was a composite of parts of Romans 3:20, 22: "No man is justified by the works of the law, but freely by faith in Jesus Christ." The second is Galatians 2:16: "We believe in Christ Jesu, that we be justified freely by the faith of Christ, and not by the works of the law, because that no man shall be justified by the works of the law."[60] Note that in both quotations attributed to Paul, Cranmer translated rather freely by inserting the word *freely*, which is found neither in the Greek original nor in the Vulgate nor in Erasmus's Latin translation. Its insertion in both verses clearly had polemical force, for the King's Book had explicitly rejected Cranmer's understanding of "freely" as meaning "apart from human effort": "although such works of penance be required in us towards the attaining of remission of sins and justification, yet the same . . . is the free gift of God, and conferred unto us gratis, that is to say, of the grace of God."[61]

Cranmer then proceeded to explain that even if justification came freely to humankind, it did not come freely in the sense that no one had to pay a price for it. Jesus' blood paid the ransom for our release from captivity to the devil even as his life perfectly fulfilled the law. To support the essential passivity of humanity in salvation, Cranmer added another commonplace

---

[59]Otto Schottenloher, "Zur Funktion der loci bei Erasmus," in *Hommages à Marie Delcourti* (Brussels: Collection Latomus 114, 1970), pp. 317-31.

[60]Cox, *Miscellaneous Writings*, pp. 128-29. Jesu is the traditional Latin vocative for "Jesus" used in medieval prayers to convey a sense of intimacy with the Savior; Cox, *Miscellaneous Writings*, p. 128.

[61]Lacey, *King's Book*, p. 160.

of Scripture verses, all his own translation from Romans.[62] This time, however, the "freely" found in Romans 3:23 was not Cranmer's insertion:

> All have offended, and have need of the glory of God, justified freely by his grace, by redemption which is in Jesu Christ, whom God hath set forth to us for a reconciler and peace-maker, through faith in his blood, to shew his righteousness. [Rom 3:23-25]
>
> Christ is the end of the law unto righteousness to every man that believeth. [Rom 10:4]
>
> That which was impossible by the law, inasmuch as it was weak by the flesh, God sending his own Son in the similitude of sinful flesh, by sin damned sin in the flesh; that the righteousness of the law might be fulfilled in us, which walk not after the flesh, but after the Spirit. [Rom 8:3-4]

According to Cranmer, these passages show that Paul taught that justification involved three factors: (1) God's mercy and grace, (2) Christ's justice and (3) humanity's personal faith. In keeping with the Scripture verses chosen, Cranmer was careful to define Christ's righteousness both as "the satisfaction of God's justice, or price for our redemption, by the offering of his body and shedding of his blood" and as the "fulfilling of the law perfectly and thoroughly." Cranmer, however, also clarified that justifying faith on the part of a sinner was "the gift of God, and not man's only work without God."[63] Yet, of course, he did not want to leave the English people with the impression that human passivity in the reception of salvation meant inactivity thereafter. Therefore, Cranmer concluded this first section of the sermon by arguing that only faith justified, but faith was not alone in the justified:

> Faith ... doth not exclude the justice of our good works, necessarily to be done afterward of duty towards God, (for we are most bounden to serve God in doing good deeds, commanded by him in his holy scripture, all the days of our life;) but it excluded them, so that we may not do them to this intent, to be made good by doing them.[64]

As first noticed in the nineteenth century by R. C. Jenkins, and confirmed by the "Great Commonplaces," Cranmer's exegesis of his Romans common-

---

[62]Cox, *Miscellaneous Writings*, p. 129.
[63]Ibid.
[64]Ibid.

place on justification—both the three parts involved as well as the exclusion of good works beforehand but not afterward—was cribbed from Cajetan's commentary on the epistle.[65]

Having laid out his basic arguments for solifidinism, Cranmer now revisited the key issues more thoroughly by using his preferred theological method—Scripture, tradition and then arguments reasoned from them.[66] Consequently, the second section of the homily begins with another Pauline commonplace proving that justification cannot come through the keeping of the law. Drawn from his "Notes on Justification," Cranmer quoted Galatians 3:21; 2:21; 5:4; and Ephesians 2:8-9.[67] Rejecting the argument of the King's Book that grace and human works mutually augmented each other in the pursuit of inherent righteousness,[68] Cranmer concisely stated his own black-or-white approach to justification by paraphrasing Romans 11:6 as "the sum of all Paul's disputation" on the matter: "if justice come of works, then it cometh not of grace; if it come of grace, then it cometh not of works." Cranmer then turned to Acts 10:43 to confirm that Paul's view was universally held by the biblical writers: "'Of Christ all the prophets,' saith St Peter, 'do witness, that through his name all they that believe in him shall receive the remission of sins.'"[69]

Having shown wide biblical support for solifidianism, Cranmer then proceeded to do the same with the fathers, since for Protestants *sola Scriptura* did not mean that the writings of the ancient church had no value. Indeed, Cranmer consciously patterned his biblical hermeneutic on patristic practice, quoting in the "Homily on Salvation" both Chrysostom on all things necessary for salvation being found in Scripture alone and Augustine on his commonplace method of exegesis.[70] Rather, the sound witness of the best of the early Christian writers was extremely important to Cranmer, since he realized that the Protestants were no more exempt from the human con-

---

[65]Null, *Thomas Cranmer's Doctrine of Repentance*, pp. 214-17.
[66]Long before Hooker, Cranmer specifically used Scripture, tradition and reason as his theological method: "[T]he Archbishop collectyng both his arguments, authorities of Scriptures, and Doctors together, caused hys Secretarie to write a fayre booke therof for the king, after this order. First the Scriptures were alledged, then the Doctours, thirdlye folowed the Argumentes deducted from those authorities" (John Foxe, *Actes and Monuments* [London: John Day, 1570], p. 1355).
[67]See Cox, *Miscellaneous Writings*, pp. 205, 208-9.
[68]Lacey, *King's Book*, pp. 157-63.
[69]Cox, *Miscellaneous Writings*, p. 130.
[70]Ronald B. Bond, *Certain Sermons or Homilies (1547) and A Homily Against Disobedience and Wilful Rebellion (1570)* (Toronto: University of Toronto Press, 1987), pp. 62, 66.

dition than the scholastics had been before them. He was adamant that any conclusions resulting from Protestant biblical collation could never be novel in the history of the church. Some prior stream of sound patristic witness had to confirm that their contemporary exegesis had been validly derived from *sola Scriptura*.[71] Hence Cranmer now made a patristic commonplace in support of solifidianism. After asserting that "all the old and ancient authors, both Greeks and Latins," supported justification "only by this true and lively faith in Christ," Cranmer quoted from Hilary, Basil and Ambrose. He added that he could have just as easily included supportive extracts "that we be justified by faith only, freely, and without works" from "Origen, St Chrysostom, St Cyprian, St Augustine, Prosper, Œcumenius, Photius, Bernardus, Anselm, and many other authors, Greek and Latin."[72]

Satisfied that he had shown sufficient biblical and patristic support for justification by faith, Cranmer at last turned to his chief theological argument in its favor:

> This proposition, that we be justified by faith only, freely, and without works, is . . . most plainly to express the weakness of man, and the goodness of God; the great infirmity of ourselves, and the might and power of God; the imperfectness of our own works, and the most abundant grace of our Saviour Christ.

Since "this doctrine advanceth and setteth forth the true glory of Christ, and suppresseth the vain-glory of man," Cranmer argued that to reject solifidianism was to be "an adversary of Christ and his gospel, and for a setter-forth of men's vain-glory."[73] Naturally, Gardiner cried foul, but with the support of the Edwardian regime, Cranmer simply went ahead and published the homily, making this argument standard preaching in English parish churches.[74]

Having now defended justification by faith on the basis of Scripture, tradition and reason, Cranmer concluded the homily with an exhortation to

---

[71]See Ashley Null, "Princely Marital Problems and the Reformers' Solutions," in *Sister Reformations: England and the German Empire in the Sixteenth Century*, ed. Dorothea Wendebourg (Tübingen: Mohr Siebeck, 2010), pp. 133-49.

[72]See Cox, *Miscellaneous Writings*, pp. 130-31.

[73]Ibid., p. 131.

[74]"In all this dyscussyon no man could have cause to saye, 'Alas, good poore people, what meaneth men to teache you justyficacion by workes, to the diminution of Godes glory?' Their is no cause to crye oute so" (Gardiner to Cranmer, shortly after July 1, 1547; James Arthur Muller, ed., *The Letters of Stephen Gardiner* [Cambridge: Cambridge University Press, 1933], p. 345).

lively faith made known through the practice of a godly life. For if justification was the work of God for humanity, humanity's dutiful response was to live to glory God and serve one another. Cranmer noted that both Paul and James agreed that saving faith produced good works, or else it was not true faith. However, Cranmer did not merely rely on duty as a sufficient motivation for the Christian life. Saving a massive biblical and patristic commonplace on the importance of good works for the following "Homily on Faith," Cranmer concluded the "Homily of Salvation" with his characteristic appeal for the renewal of the affections. Based on his reading of Romans 8, he clearly outlined how a true understanding of grace would move human hearts from fear to loving gratitude as expressed in the service of God and neighbor:

> Therefore . . . considering the infinite benefits of God, shewed and exhibited unto us mercifully without our deserts . . . so making us his dear beloved children, brethren unto his only Son our Saviour Christ, and inheritors for ever with him of his eternal kingdom of heaven: these great and merciful benefits of God, if they be well considered . . . they move us to render ourselves unto God wholly, with all our will, hearts, might, and power to serve him . . . [and they] do move us for his sake also to be ever ready to give ourselves to our neighours. . . . These be the fruits of the true faith, to do good, as much as lieth in us, to every man, and, above all things, and in all things, to advance the glory of God.[75]

A Confirming Conversion Narrative

Thus Cranmer's "Homily on Salvation" proved to be the opposite of his annotations to Henry's corrections. Whereas the latter concentrated on defending solifidianism, the former had focused on describing the renewal of affections in the child of God that justification by faith produced. These two themes were thoroughly integrated only a few months after the introduction of the *Book of Homilies* in a further publication from the regime's religious campaign—the remarkable autobiographical conversion narrative of Queen Katherine Parr, the widow of Henry VIII.[76] Here was a firsthand account of how the English evangelical construal of Pauline theology con-

---

[75]Cox, *Miscellaneous Writings*, p. 134.
[76]Katherine Parr, *The Lamentacion of a Sinner* (London: Edward Whitchurch, November 5, 1547).

vinced the heart and mind of a key establishment figure.

According to Katherine, the divine gift of living faith first opened her eyes to the truth that her salvation was totally dependent on "Christ crucified." "Then I beganne (and not before) to perceyue and see myne owne Ignoraunce and blindnes." Realizing how stubborn and ungrateful she had been to refuse to rely on Christ alone earlier, "all pleasures, vanities, honour, riches, welth, and aydes of the world beganne to waxe bitter unto me."[77] This alteration in her affections was the turning point for Katherine: "[T]han I knewe it was no illusion of the deuill, nor false, ne humain doctrine I had receyued: when such successe came thereof, that I had in detestacion and horrour, that which I erste so muche loued and estemed."[78]

By the light of living faith Katherine now recognized that her "synnes in the consideracion of them, to be so greuouse, and in the number so exceding" that she deserved eternal damnation.[79] Yet she saw that her prior penitential works had only been a "hynderance"—the more she had sought "meanes and wayes to wind" herself out of her sinful state, the more she had in fact become "wrapped and tangled therin."[80] Consequently, she now put all her hope in one thing only—the promise of full, free and immediate pardon in God's "own Woorde."[81] "Saynt Paule sayeth, we be iustified by the fayth in Christe, and not by the deades of the lawe." Therefore, "by this fayth I am assured: and by thys assurance, I fele the remission of my sinnes." Experiencing assurance brought the "inwarde consolacion" of having imputed right standing with God: "I feele my selfe to cum, as it were in a newe garment, before god, and nowe by his mercye, to be taken iuste, and rightwise."[82] Hence, "all feare of dampnacion" was gone for those who with justifying faith "put their whole hope of saluacion in hys handes, that will and can performe it."[83] Having before "passed therto with great feare," Christians were now "bolde through the spirite" because "the sure hope of resurrecion" brought them joy.[84] Katherine admitted that true believers

---

[77]Ibid., sigs. B5v-B6r.
[78]Ibid., sig. B6r.
[79]Ibid., sig. A8r.
[80]Ibid., sig. B1v.
[81]Ibid., sig. B2v.
[82]Ibid., sigs. F7r; B3v-B4v.
[83]Ibid., sig. F7r.
[84]Ibid., sig. C6v.

would still fall into sin because of their human "frailty." Yet such failures only served to cause them to humble themselves, acknowledge God's goodness and "cum to hym for refuge and helpe."[85] Now freed from all fear because of the love of God in bringing her to certain salvation, Katherine finally found the power to love God in return:

> Yet I neuer had this unspeakable and most high charitie, and abundant loue of god, printed and fixed in my hart dulye, tyll it pleased god of hys mere grace, mercy and pitie, to open myne eyes, makyng me to see, and beholde with the eye of liuely fayth. . . . Then began I to dwel in god by charitie, knowing by the louyng charitie of god in the remission of my sinnes, that god is charitie as Saint John sayth. So that of my faythe (wherby I came to knowe god, and wherby it pleased god euen because I trusted in hym, to iustifie me) sprang this excellent charitie in my harte.[86]

Convinced that nothing could separate them from the love of God in Christ, Christians were "not by this godly fayth presumptuously enflamed, nor by the same becum they leuse, idell or slowe in doinge of godly workes." Rather, they were "so much the more feruent they be in doing moste holy and pure workes, which god hath commaunded theym to walke in."[87] Consequently, Christians were not "hierlinges for meede, wagies, or rewarde," but "louyng children" who served him "without respect of lucre, gayne or hyer."[88] For "the loue of god printed in [their] hartes" kept them "backe from runnyng astray."[89]

"Hirelings for wages" or "children with love printed on their hearts"—Gardiner and Cranmer's two competing armorial badges on the battlefield of Tudor court religious politics were clearly well known to Katherine, herself a veteran partisan and near victim. As a doctor of both civil and canon law, Gardiner could not but see salvation as a matter of due divine process. Cranmer's eventual affective construal of Pauline soteriology led him to a different conclusion, forcing him in his forties to switch sides.

Of course, that was the story that the Flicke portrait set out to tell for the

---

[85] Ibid., sig. C5v.
[86] Ibid., sigs. B5-B6. Note the printed marginal comment: "Charitie immediately foloweth liuely fayth."
[87] Ibid., sig. F6v.
[88] Ibid., sig. F7r.
[89] Ibid., sig. G1r.

ages, how Cranmer came to be the first Protestant archbishop of Canterbury. The intricate, multilayered curtain of church tradition had to be pulled back so light could shine on Scripture alone once again, in particular on the soteriology of Paul. For only the free and certain promise of salvation made possible through justification by faith had the power to allure human hearts back to God, and only as "children with love printed on their hearts" would the English people have the perseverance to repair the broken panes in their church and society. In that light, were we able to ask his Grace what passage he is reading, surely Cranmer would say, "Romans 8."

10

The Texts of Paul and the Theology of Cranmer

Jonathan A. Linebaugh

[A] notable qualitie or virtue he hadd: to be benficiall unto his enemyes. ... For whosoever he hadd byn that hadd reportid evil of hym, or otherwaies wrought or done to hym displeasure, were the reconciliation never so meane or simple on the behalf of his adversarye ... the matter was both pardoned and clerelie forgotten, and so voluntarily caste into the sachell of oblivioin behind the backe parte, that it was more clere nowe out of memorie, than it was in mynde before it was either commensid or committed.[1]

This reminiscence from Ralph Morice, Thomas Cranmer's secretary, offers more than a description of Cranmer's character; it captures the core of his evangelical theology.[2] In his 1538 annotations to King Henry VIII's corrections to the Bishops' Book, Cranmer asks, "What were we, when [Jesus] gave his most precious life and blood for us?" And he answers: "horrible sinners and his enemies."[3] Like the apostle Paul in Romans 5:6-10, Cranmer em-

---

[1]John Gough Nicholas, ed., *Narratives of the Days of the Reformation* (London: Camden Society, First Series, 77, 1859), p. 245.
[2]For "evangelical" and the related label "gospellers" as the original designation for reformers like Cranmer in England, see Ashley Null, "Thomas Cranmer and Tudor Evangelicalism," in *The Advent of Evangelicalism: Exploring Historical Continuities*, ed. Michael A. G. Haykin and Kenneth J. Stewart (Nashville: B&H Academic, 2008), pp. 221-51, esp. pp. 226-30.
[3]John Edmund Cox, *Miscellaneous Writings and Letters of Thomas Cranmer* (Cambridge: Parker Society, 1846; reproduced by Regent College Publishing), p. 110.

phasizes the simultaneity of human unworthiness and the definitive embodiment of divine love. "God demonstrates his love for us in this way," writes Paul, "that while we were still sinners Christ died for us," and "while we were enemies we were reconciled to God by the death of his son" (Rom 5:8, 10).[4] "Sinners" and "enemies": Paul's words flow from Cranmer's pen as he characterizes the recipients of the love that is the cross of Christ. God, as Cranmer sees in the act of the one "who did not spare his own son but gave him up for us all" (Rom 8:32), is "always ready to forgive us."[5]

God, in Christ, forgives his enemies. This is both a summary of Cranmer's Reformational theology and, as will be suggested below, the main motif in his reading of Paul. But it is also what might be called the heart of his "theology of the heart."[6] In Cranmer's words, "if the profession of our faith of the remission of our own sins enter within us into the deepness of our hearts, then it must needs kindle a warm fire of love in our hearts towards God, and towards all other[s]."[7] Here, then, is the ground and catalyst for Cranmer's "notable qualitie." Forgiving his enemies was not a personality quirk of Cranmer's, and neither was it, to his mind, a simple matter of obedience to Christ's command. To be sure, Cranmer considered it "a true rule of our Saviour Christe to do good for evill," but he was likewise convinced that "it is above our frail and corrupt nature to love our enemies."[8] What "kindled a warm fire of love" in his heart for his enemies was that his own belovedness as an enemy "entered within [him] into the deepness of [his] heart." Pointing to this pattern of God's merciful love producing a mimetic love, Cranmer advised, "If any peradventure will think it to be a hard thing to suffer and forgive his enemy . . . let him consider again, how many hard storms our Saviour Christ suffered and abode for us."[9] For Cranmer, the divine "I love you" spoken in the "I forgive you" of the cross creates its own echo: faith in God and forgiveness for others. Cranmer's habit of forgiveness, therefore, at least as he would tell his own story, was the fruit of having been forgiven.

---

[4]Translations from Paul's letters, unless otherwise noted, are my own.
[5]Cox, *Miscellaneous Writings*, p. 110.
[6]For this theme, see Ashley Null, "Thomas Cranmer's Theology of the Heart," *Trinity Journal for Theology and Ministry* 1 (2007): 18-34.
[7]Cox, *Miscellaneous Writings*, p. 86.
[8]Nicholas, *Narratives*, p. 247; Cox, *Miscellaneous Writings*, p. 110.
[9]Cox, *Miscellaneous Writings*, p. 110.

Understood this way, Cranmer's "notable qualitie," so memorably portrayed in a line from Shakespeare's *Henry VIII*—"Do my Lord of Canterbury / a shrewd turn, and he is your friend forever"—is an x-ray revealing the heart of Cranmer's theology: "God's gracious love," as Ashley Null puts it, "inspires a grateful love in his children."[10]

This chapter will interact with this core of Cranmer's theology as it is articulated as a reading of Paul. For Cranmer, the identification of God as the one who forgives his enemies is, at least in part, an interpretation of Paul's language of justification. Similarly, the insistence that the experience of being forgiven engenders a willingness to forgive is worked out, again in part, as exegesis of the Pauline expression "faith active in love" (Gal 5:6). These shared Cranmerian and Pauline *loci*—that is, the nature and basis of justification and the meaning, source and liveliness of faith—will function as icebreakers of sorts, conversation starters that will enable us to eavesdrop on a dialogue between the texts of Paul and the theology that Cranmer confessed as a reading of them.

THE QUEST FOR THE EXEGETICAL CRANMER

Cranmer did not write a commentary. He wrote prayer books and sermons, kept extensive notebooks organizing the discoveries unearthed in the books in his famously vast library, offered marginal comments during the formative stages of what would be public documents, penned a preface to the Bible (1540), maintained prolific correspondences with political players at court and religious reformers on the Continent, participated in the crafting of a theological confession, and engaged in (transcribed) debates related to the Lord's Supper and other topics du jour. This means that locating texts or passages that can be called readings of Paul is not as easy as pulling a commentary on Galatians or Romans off the shelf.

Further complicating this quest for the exegetical Cranmer is the reality of political constraints on his publications during the Henrician period. It was not until the death of Henry VIII and the subsequent accession of the

---

[10]Ashley Null, "Conversion to Communion: Thomas Cranmer on a Favourite Puritan Theme," *Churchman* 116 (2002) : 239-57 (p. 250). For an extended discussion of this theme, see Ashley Null, *Thomas Cranmer's Doctrine of Repentance: Renewing the Power to Love* (Oxford: Oxford University Press, 2000). The Shakespeare quotation is from *Henry VIII*, act V, scene III, lines 176-77.

nine-year-old Edward VI on January 28, 1547, that Cranmer's theological publications could match his theological positions. Edward VI reigned for just over six years, but his short rule witnessed a proliferation of public Protestant formularies. In addition to the *Book of Common Prayer* (1549 and 1552), the *Articles of Religion* appeared in 1553. Cranmer's first publication project, however, was the *Book of Homilies* (1547), which, as Null says, "was designed to be both a manifesto of the Edwardian regime's theological agenda and the means of implementation."[11] It is here in the homilies, especially the third, fourth and fifth, which address "Salvation," "Faith" and "Good Works," respectively, that we come closest to a sustained interpretation of Paul. That Cranmer is the author of these three public, serial sermons is evident from their obvious derivation from his research notebooks, known as the "Notes on Justification"[12] and "Cranmer's Great Commonplaces."[13] These three homilies, together with the research notes on which they are dependent and Cranmer's aforementioned annotations to Henry VIII's corrections to the Bishops' Book, will serve as the main textual sources for this consideration of Cranmer's reading of Paul.

The Justice of God the Father and the Justification of God's Ungodly Children

Having just cited Romans 3:20, 22, 23-24; 8:3-4; 10:4; and Galatians 2:16, Cranmer writes, "In these foresaid places the apostle toucheth specially three things, which must concur and go together in our justification."[14] His enumeration is a summary of his exegesis: (1) "upon God's part, his great mercy and grace"; (2) "upon Christ's part, justice, that is, the satisfaction of God's justice" by the "shedding of his blood"; (3) "upon our part, true and lively faith in the merits of Jesu Christ."[15] What Cranmer calls "our part" will be considered below as Cranmer's notion of a "true and lively faith"

---

[11]See the chapter by Ashley Null in this volume, p. 224.
[12]The "Notes on Justification" are included in Cox, *Miscellaneous Writings*.
[13]My access to CGC is limited to those sections that Ashley Null has either translated or transcribed in his various publications on Cranmer. Null is currently engaged in a project to produce a critical edition of "Cranmer's Great Commonplaces." As Cox notes, there is also strong and "nearly contemporary" external evidence attributing these homilies to Cranmer (*Miscellaneous Writings*, p. 128 n. 1).
[14]Cox, *Miscellaneous Writings*, pp. 128-29.
[15]Ibid., p. 129.

converses with Paul's phrase πίστις χριστοῦ ("faith in Christ") and the antithesis that defines it ("not by works of the law"). This section, however, will let Cranmer's claims about "God's part" and "Christ's part"—that is, the coming together of divine justice and grace in the sending and self-giving of the Son—talk to the texts of which they purport to be an interpretation. Put heuristically: If the Cranmerian references to the justice and grace of God in Christ are readings of the Pauline announcement of "the righteousness of God" and the justification it effects, what might the Pauline texts that make this announcement say to the theology derived from them?

That Cranmer understands himself to be interpreting Paul's phrase "the righteousness of God" (δικαιοσύνη θεοῦ) when he says that "in our justification" there is a convergence of "God's mercy and grace, but also his justice" is evident in the way he ends the sentence: "which the apostle calleth the justice of God."[16] For Cranmer, what Paul calls "the righteousness of God" is revealed in "the mystery of our redemption" (cf. Rom 3:24)—that is, the cross of Christ on which God "tempered his justice and mercy together," leaving sinners neither in the "prison of hell, remediless for ever," nor "delivered . . . without justice."[17]

It is worth recalling that in Cranmer's carefully ordered collection of homilies, the "Homily of Salvation" followed the homily on the "Misery of Mankind." This reflects Cranmer's Reformational understanding of the order and function of the law and the gospel:

> The commandments of God lay our faults before our eyes, putteth us in fear and dread, and maketh us see the wrath of God against our sins, as St Paul saith [referring to Rom 3:20]. . . . The gracious and benign promises of God by the mediation of Christ sheweth us, (and that to our great relief and comfort,) . . . that we have the forgiveness of our sins, be reconciled to God, and accepted, and reputed just and righteous in his sight.[18]

This sequencing of the homilies also allows Cranmer to open the "Homily of Salvation" with an assumption: "Because all men be sinners and offenders against God . . ."[19] The result of this hamartiological starting point is that

---

[16] Ibid.
[17] Ibid.
[18] Ibid., p. 113.
[19] Ibid., p. 128.

"no man can be justified by his own good works because that no man fulfilleth the law," a conclusion Cranmer offers as a reading of Galatians 2:21; 3:21.[20] This "excludeth the justice of man"[21] and means that the only hope for justification—that is, the forensic pronouncement that one is judged righteous by God[22]—is the miracle of "another righteousness," a *iustitia aliena* "received from God's own hands" in the form of the "forgiveness of sins."[23]

It is this miracle, this promise of the "impossible," that Cranmer hears in Paul's proclamation that "the righteousness of God has been revealed" (Rom 3:21). With Paul's Abraham, he is "hoping against hope" (Rom 4:18), crying out from the conclusion that "all, both Jews and Greeks, are under sin" (Rom 3:9), that "no one is righteous" (Rom 3:10), that "all sinned" (Rom 3:23), and that therefore "by works of the law no human being will be justified" (Rom 3:20).[24] To Cranmer's exegetical ears, Paul's "word of the cross" (1 Cor 1:18) is at once a confirmation and a contradiction of this conclusion—the announcement of an event that goes through "the wrath of God revealed from heaven against all ungodliness" and to a new and antithetical conclusion: "there is now no condemnation" (Rom 8:1). For Cranmer, the name of this new conclusion effected by the cross is justification. The death of Jesus weaves a heretofore unimagined tapestry as the "justice and mercy of God [are] knit together": the curse of the law is carried out (Gal 3:13) and yet those who "have offended, and have need of the glory of God" are "justified freely by his grace."[25] Cranmer's quotation of Romans 3:23-24 indicates that this underlining of the disjunction between the divine verdict—"righteous"—and the inherent status of the justified—"unrighteous"—is offered as an interpretation of Paul.

In emphasizing this contradiction, Cranmer captures the core of Paul's announcement in Romans 3:21-24. As Paul pivots from the impossibility of justification (Rom 3:20) to the promise of justification (Rom 3:21-26), he dramatizes the disjunction between the universality of human sin and

---

[20]Ibid., p. 130.
[21]Ibid., p. 129.
[22]*Iustificare subinde significat, iustum pronuntiarie, declarare, aut ostendere* (CGC II, fol. 84r).
[23]Cox, *Miscellaneous Writings*, p. 128.
[24]On the "impossible," see ibid., p. 129.
[25]Ibid.; Cranmer speaks of Jesus "fulfilling the law perfectly and thoroughly" (ibid.).

the somehow stronger word of justification: "All sinned... and are justified" (πάντες ἥμαρτον... δικαιούμενοι; Rom 3:23-24). Grammatically, the objects of the divine saving action implied in the passive participle δικαιούμενοι ("being justified"; Rom 3:24) are the sinners of 3:23, and thus, as James Dunn construes this Pauline paradox, "it is precisely those who have sinned and fallen short of God's glory who are justified."[26] In Cranmer's words, "God justified us when we were sinners."[27]

The "scandal and folly" here (1 Cor 1:23) is not lost on Cranmer. "Here," he says, "may man's reason be astonished" because what Paul calls "the justice of God" appears to be an instance of injustice in which, with seeming forensic schizophrenia, God locates and labels unrighteousness (Rom 3:23) only to create its opposite with the word of justification (Rom 3:24).[28] For Cranmer, then, justification, as a forensic word, is a creative word—a *verbum efficax*, to use Luther's phrase.[29] Searching for an analogous action to the "infinite benefits of God, shewed and exhibited unto us mercifully and without deserts," Cranmer sees a consistent pattern of grace in the economy of the one "who not only created us from nothing... but also, whereas we were condemned to hell and death eternal, hath given his eternal Son... to the intent to justify us and restore us to life everlasting."[30] This echoes Paul's language in Romans 4: God is "the one who justifies the ungodly" (Rom 4:5), "gives life to the dead" and "calls non-being into being" (Rom 4:17). The linking of liturgical predications suggests an analogous form of divine activity in the acts of creation, resurrection and justification.[31] Nothingness, death and sin are the site at which God utters a creative counterstatement: creation, life, salvation. Following this Pauline pattern, Cranmer hears God's

---

[26]James D. G. Dunn, *Romans 1-8*, Word Biblical Commentary 38A (Waco: Word, 1988), 1:168. Following C. E. B. Cranfield (*A Critical and Exegetical Commentary on the Epistle to the Romans*, International Critical Commentary [Edinburgh: T&T Clark, 1975], 1:205), I take as the subject of Rom 3:24 the "all" of Rom 3:23 while recognizing that Rom 3:24 continues the main theme from Rom 3:21-22.

[27]*Iustificavit nos deus cum peccatores essemus* (CGC II, fol. 104v). Cf. Rom 5:6-10.

[28]Cox, *Miscellaneous Writings*, p. 129.

[29]Cf. LW 5:140.

[30]Cox, *Miscellaneous Writings*, p. 134; cf. the quotation from Augustine in CGC II, fol. 255r: *Gratis creati, gratis et iustificati sumus*.

[31]Jonathan A. Linebaugh, *God, Grace, and Righteousness in Wisdom of Solomon and Paul's Letter to the Romans: Texts in Conversation*, NovTSup 152 (Leiden: Brill, 2013), pp. 152-54; cf. Ernst Käsemann, *Commentary on Romans*, trans. G. W. Bromiley (Grand Rapids: Eerdmans, 1980), p. 123.

justifying verdict as a reality-determining declaration: justification is a word spoken to us "while we were [God's] enemies" (Rom 5:10) that "mak[es] us [God's] dear beloved children."[32]

For both Paul and Cranmer, however, justification is not a groundless divine fiat. Rather, justification, understood as God's creative counter-statement to sin, is a word of new creation anchored in the cross. "All the world being wrapped in sin," writes Cranmer, "God sent his only Son our Saviour Christ into this world . . . and by the shedding of his most precious blood, to make a sacrifice and satisfaction . . . to his Father for our sins."[33] Jesus' "'for us' fulfilling [of] the law perfectly and thoroughly" to which Cranmer refers climaxes as the curse of the law is carried out in the "condemning of sin in the flesh of [God's] son."[34] This reading runs with the grain of a passage like Galatians 3:10-13 in which the law's conditional promise of life (Gal 3:12, quoting Lev 18:5) is contravened by the universality of the deuteronomic curse: "Cursed be everyone who does not abide by all things written in the Book of the Law" (Gal 3:10, quoting Deut 27:26).[35] In this context, redemption from the curse is a consequence of Christ "becoming a curse for us" (Gal 3:13). On the cross, the deuteronomic curse is not cast aside; it is carried out—"cursed is everyone who is hanged on a tree" (Gal 3:13, quoting Deut 21:23). When addressing the *locus* of atonement, however, the Pauline texts Cranmer gathers are predominately from Romans, especially Romans 3 (though references to Romans 8 and 10 appear as well).[36] This suggests that his description of the movement from condemnation to

---

[32]Cox, *Miscellaneous Writings*, p. 134. For Cranmer's filial understanding of justification, especially in his reading of Rom 8 in the annotations, see the section titled "Paul for Cranmer the Solafidian," in the previous chapter, pp. 216-24.
[33]Ibid. Cranmer here quotes Rom 8:3-4.
[34]Cox, *Miscellaneous Writings*, p. 128.
[35]For this reading of Lev 18:5 in early Judaism and Paul, see Preston M. Sprinkle, *Law and Life: The Interpretation of Leviticus 18.5 in Early Judaism and in Paul*, WUNT II.241 (Tübingen: Mohr Siebeck, 2008).
[36]Cranmer organized his research notes and homilies by *loci communes* ("commonplaces"—i.e., recurring and significant topics), thus participating in the humanist practice of Erasmus and Melanchthon. In Cranmer, this means that a discussion of a particular locus is often followed by quotations from or references to numerous texts that address the given topic. The preceding explanation, therefore, functions as a synthetic reading of multiple texts rather than a detailed exegesis of a particular passage. For Cranmer's use of the *loci* method, see Ashley Null, "Official Tudor Homilies," in *The Oxford Handbook of the Early Modern Sermon*, ed. Peter McCullough, Hugh Adlington and Emma Rhatigan (Oxford: Oxford University Press, 2011), pp. 348-65 (esp. pp. 353-54).

no condemnation via Jesus' substitutionary suffering of the law's curse on the cross is offered, in part, as a reading of Romans 3:21-26. And this Pauline passage, I think, has something to say to Cranmer's reading of it.

As noted above, Cranmer is singing in a Pauline key when he characterizes justification as a creative contradiction effected by the cross: the unrighteous are called righteous through the redemption that is in Christ Jesus (Rom 3:23-24). There is, however, what might be called a Pauline harmony that Cranmer does not seem to hear: the disjunctive and reality-determining word of justification is, for Paul, a forensic word from the future. Reading Romans 3:25-26 in conversation with Romans 2:4-5 will explain what I mean.

The oft-noted lexical link between Romans 2:4 and Romans 3:26 (ἀνοχή, "patience") occurs within parallel plot lines. In both Romans 2:4-10 and Romans 3:24-26, ἀνοχή is used to characterize an era in contrast to a time defined by the disclosure of divine righteousness (δικαιοκρισία τοῦ θεοῦ, Rom 2:5; δικαιοσύνη αὐτοῦ, Rom 3:26). As Günther Bornkamm observes, in Romans "the periods of salvation history" are "placed in contrast to each other as the time of patience and the time of the showing of righteousness."[37] This observation is offered by Bornkamm as an exegesis of Romans 3:25-26, but, as it stands, it functions as an equally apt description of the implicit plot line of Romans 2:4-5. The present is the time of God's kindness and patience and concludes with the coming apocalypse of God's righteous judgment (Rom 2:5). Within this narrative sequence, the end of the era of divine patience is the arrival of the eschaton in the form of a future judgment (Rom 2:5-10).

Romans 3:24-26 tells a sequentially similar yet drastically different story. Whereas Romans 2:4-6 contrasts the *present* era of patience with the *future* enactment of justice in the form of a judgment "according to works," Romans 3:25-26 presents the *past* as the time of the ἀνοχή τοῦ θεοῦ ("the patience of God"), the time in which God delayed the revelation of his righteous judgment "by passing over former sins," and juxtaposes this era not with the *future* "day of wrath" but with the *present* demonstration of divine righteousness that is the cross. Thus, in narrative terms, God's act of putting Jesus forward as an ἱλαστήριον ("place of atonement" and/or "propitiation") is

---

[37]Günther Bornkamm, "The Revelation of God's Wrath," in *Early Christian Experience* (New York: Harper & Row, 1966), p. 49.

functionally parallel to "the revelation of God's righteous judgment." In other words—and here we arrive at the Pauline harmony Cranmer seems not to have heard—the "now-time" (νῦν καιρῷ) of Jesus' death is the eschatological enactment of the future judgment; it is, to borrow Hans Urs von Balthasar's words, "the full achievement of the divine judgment."[38] Expressed in terms of the parallel between Romans 2:5 and Romans 3:25-26, the present "demonstration of divine righteousness" (ἔνδειξιν τῆς δικαιοσύνης αὐτοῦ, Rom 3:25, 26) is the occurrence of the promised "revelation of God's righteous judgment" (ἀποκαλύψεως δικαιοκρισίας τοῦ θεοῦ, Rom 2:5). The "now" of the cross is the "day of wrath" (Rom 2:5), the day God shows himself "to be just" (εἰς τὸ εἶναι αὐτὸν δίκαιον, Rom 3:26; cf. Rom 3:5).

The cross, however, is not the justification of God alone. As the καί ("and") that links the predicates "just" and "justifier" (Rom 3:26) indicates, the death of Jesus is simultaneously the event of divine judgment *and* human justification; it is, to borrow Justyn Terry's phrase, "the justifying judgment of God."[39] According to the righteous decree of the righteous God (Rom 2:5; 3:5-6), sinners "are worthy of death" (Rom 1:32; cf. Rom 6:23a). The death of Jesus, in the first instance, is the demonstration of divine righteousness because it is the enactment of this decree: the cross is the condemnation of sin and as such the fulfillment of "the righteous decree of the law" (Rom 8:3-4; cf. Gal 3:10-13). In other words, the gracious sending and self-giving of Jesus (Rom 3:24-25; 8:32; Gal 2:20) is not the circumvention of God's contention with sinful humanity (Rom 1:18; 3:9-20); it is the completion of that contention in the eschatological judgment that is God's condemnation of sin in the flesh of his Son. But—and here we return to the linking of "just" and "justifier"—the condemnation of sin (Rom 8:3) grounds the noncondemnation of the sinner (Rom 8:1). The cross, then, is the "correspondingly" that connects human unrighteousness and God's wrath (Rom 1:18; 3:5), but the "correspondingly" of divine judgment contains and effects the "nevertheless" of justification (Rom 3:24, 26). The arrival of God's eschatological

---

[38]Hans Urs von Balthasar, *Mysterium Paschale*, trans. A. Nichols (Edinburgh: T&T Clark, 1990), p. 119.

[39]Justyn Terry, *The Justifying Judgement of God: A Reassessment of the Place of Judgement in the Saving Work of Christ*, Paternoster Theological Monographs (Milton Keynes, UK: Paternoster, 2007).

judgment in the "now" of Jesus' death rewrites God's future word of justification (Rom 2:13; 3:20) in the present tense (Rom 3:24, 28; cf. the aorist in Rom 5:1). Justification, then, is not a separate verdict from the one that God will speak at final judgment, nor is it "an anticipation of the future verdict."[40] Justification *is* the final verdict—a forensic word from the future spoken in the arrival of God's eschatological judgment that is the "now" of Jesus' death (and resurrection; cf. Rom 4:25).

A forensic word from the future: Cranmer does not indicate that he hears this harmony. But he never tires of singing the melody: The God who judges ungodliness on the cross is, in that way, the God "who justifies the ungodly" (Rom 4:5).

FAITH AS THE FINGER OF JOHN THE BAPTIST

"What," asked Karl Barth, "is the *sola fide* other than a faint echo of the *solus Christus*?"[41] For Cranmer, the answer is obvious: nothing. What was obvious to Cranmer and Barth, however, has become obscure to an increasing number of Pauline scholars. Referring to an essay by Gerhard Ebeling, Richard Hays suggests that the great weakness of the Reformational "understanding of 'faith' and 'justification' in Paul is that it offers no coherent account of the relation between the doctrine of justification and Christology."[42] Within this rhetorical context, the translation of Paul's phrase πίστις Χριστοῦ ("Christ-faith") is a line in the sand: translate the genitive phrase as "faith in Christ" and your reading of Paul is anthropological, anthropocentric, contractual and now even Arian; but interpret πίστις Χριστοῦ as "the faith/faithfulness of Christ," and thus as a compressed reference to the narrative of Jesus' life and death, and your exegesis is christological, theocentric, covenantal and Athanasian.[43]

---

[40]N. T. Wright, "New Perspectives on Paul," in *Justification in Perspective: Historical Developments and Contemporary Challenges*, ed. B. L. McCormack (Grand Rapids: Baker Academic, 2006), pp. 243-64 (on p. 260).

[41]*CD* IV/1, p. 632.

[42]Richard Hays, *The Faith of Jesus Christ: The Narrative Substructure of Galatians 3.1-4.11*, 2nd ed. (Grand Rapids: Eerdmans, 2002), p. xxix; quoting Gerhard Ebeling, "Jesus and Faith," in *Word and Faith* (London: SCM Press, 1963), p. 203.

[43]Hays introduced the "anthropological-christological" contrast (*Faith of Jesus Christ*, pp. xxv-xxvi). The expansion of the contrast to include "anthrocentric-theocentric" is most notable in the work of Douglas Campbell, as are the "contractual-covenantal" and "Arian-Athanasian" distinctions that he borrows from James Torrance's critique of federal theology. For Campbell, see especially *The*

The question is whether this contrast resonates with Cranmer's reading of Paul. Does Cranmer's rendering of πίστις Χριστοῦ as "faith in Christ" untie the Pauline knot that links justification and Jesus? Is the notion of "righteousness by faith" that Cranmer articulates as a reading of Paul anthropocentric? Cranmer does say that "faith," the third of the "three things" the "apostle toucheth . . . which must concur and go together in our justification," is "our part."[44] To place these words within an anthropocentric context, I will suggest, would be to commandeer a Cranmerian phrase against Cranmer, for whom "justification is not the office of man, but of God."[45] To the point: for Cranmer, "faith in Christ" is christocentric.[46] The *sola fide*, which for Cranmer is an interpretation of a Pauline antithesis—"not by works of the law, but through faith in Jesus Christ"—is an anthropological negation and a christological confession: "Faith alone" excludes the human as the subject of salvation and confesses Christ, "who is now the righteousness of all them that truly do believe," as the *one* by, in and on the basis of whom God justifies the ungodly.[47]

Paul does not present faith as an abstraction; he presents it in an antithesis: "a person is not [οὐκ] justified by works of law [ἐξ ἔργων νόμου] but [ἐὰν μή] through faith in Jesus Christ" (διὰ πίστεως Ἰησοῦ Χριστοῦ, Gal 2:16; cf. Rom 3:28). For Cranmer, this formulation indicates what faith is not: "faith in Jesus Christ" is not a "work of the law." According to his "Notes on Justification," Cranmer concludes that "when St Paul said, 'We be justified freely by faith without works,' he meant of all manner of works of the law, as well of the Ten Commandments, as of ceremonials and judicials."[48] For Cranmer, then, whatever faith is (see below), it is em-

---

Deliverance of God: An Apocalyptic Rereading of Justification in Paul (Grand Rapids: Eerdmans, 2009). For Torrance, see "Covenant and Contract: A Study of the Theological Background of Worship in Seventeenth-Century Scotland," *SJT* 23 (1970): 51-76; "The Covenant Concept in Scottish Theology and Politics and Its Legacy," *SJT* 34 (1981): 225-43. Interestingly, in the essay Hays quotes, Ebeling anticipated this rhetorical situation and warned that we must "not let ourselves be impressed by the labels . . . like 'anthropological approach'" ("Jesus and Faith," p. 202 n. 1).

[44]Cox, *Miscellaneous Writings*, p. 129.
[45]Ibid., p. 131; cf. CGC II, fol. 226v.
[46]For a parallel argument in relation to Luther's understanding of "faith in Christ," see Jonathan A. Linebaugh, "The Christo-Centrism of Faith in Christ: Martin Luther's Reading of Galatians 2:16, 19-20," *New Testament Studies* 59, no. 4 (2013): 535-44.
[47]Cox, *Miscellaneous Writings*, p. 130.
[48]Ibid., pp. 207-8. Cranmer cites passages from Rom 2; 3; 4; 5; 7; 8; 9; 2 Cor 3; Gal 2; 3; Eph 2; Phil 3; Tit 3.

phatically not a work—not even, to quote Hays, a "bizarre sort of work in which Christians jump through the entranceway of salvation."[49]

Romans 4:3-5 can clarify Cranmer's point. As Paul's citation of Genesis 15:6 indicates, Abraham is the unambiguous subject of the verb πιστεύω ("believe"; Rom 4:3), and yet the antithesis of Romans 4:4-5 makes it impossible to interpret this human act as a "work." Precisely as the subject of πιστεύω, Abraham is ὁ μὴ ἐργαζόμενος ("the one who does not work"; Rom 4:5)—he is χωρὶς ἔργων ("without works"; Rom 4:6)—and his justification is therefore the act of "the one who justifies the ungodly" (Rom 4:5). Faith, it seems, as an anthropological action, is an anthropological negation. It is the act of the ungodly in the absence of "works" (Rom 4:5, 6); it is what is present and possible when works are not. In this sense, and to borrow from Barth again, faith is "the great negation"—the site of nothingness, death and sin at which God operates out of the opposite, speaking creation (Rom 4:17), life (Rom 4:17) and salvation (Rom 4:5).[50] Faith, in other words, is a human "yes" to the divine "no" that is God's judgment against sin in the death of Jesus. Cranmer joins voices with Paul to say that "boasting is excluded" (see Rom 3:27) because the one who has faith "doth not boast himself . . . but knoweth himself certainly to be unworthy" and therefore "advanceth not himself for his own righteousness, but knowledgeth himself to lack true justice and righteousness."[51] Faith says "no" to the human; that is what the excluded option ("not by works of law") in the Pauline antithesis teaches Cranmer.

But, to recapitulate the argument above, the object of faith is the God who acts in Jesus to judge *and* justify the ungodly. Faith lives in this contradiction: it is an anthropological "no" because it says "yes" to the eschatological judgment of the cross. But, to anticipate Cranmer's positive definition of faith, it is also a theological "yes" because it hears in God's "no" of judgment the merciful surprise that is the "yes" of justification. This "no" and "yes" that Cranmer hears in the Pauline formula "justified by faith

---

[49]Richard B. Hays, "ΠΙΣΤΙΣ and Pauline Christology: What Is at Stake?," in *Pauline Theology, Volume IV: Looking Back, Pressing On*, ed. David M. Hay and E. Elizabeth Johnson (Atlanta: Scholars Press, 1997), p. 56. For further engagement with Hays and contemporary Pauline research on this point, see my *God, Grace, and Righteousness*, pp. 155-60.
[50]*CD* IV/1, p. 621.
[51]Cox, *Miscellaneous Writings*, p. 130. Cranmer cites Phil 3.

without works of the law" (Rom 3:28; Gal 2:16) is expressed in the "Homily of Salvation" as exegesis of Paul's words:

> This proposition, that we be justified by faith only, freely, and without works, is spoken for to take away clearly all merit of our works, as being insufficient to deserve our justification at God's hands, and thereby most plainly to express the weakness of man, and the goodness of God; the great infirmity of ourselves, and the might and power of God; the imperfectness of our own works, and the most abundant grace of our Saviour Christ; and thereby to ascribe the merit and deserving of our justification unto Christ only . . . this doctrine advanceth and setteth forth the true glory of Christ, and suppresseth the vain-glory of man.[52]

Faith acknowledges one's "weakness," "infirmity" and "imperfectness"—that's the anthropological "no." But this same faith confesses God's "goodness," "might and power" and the "grace our Saviour Christ"—that's the christological "yes." And this, for Cranmer, is "the very true sense of [Paul's] proposition." It "excludeth the justice of man" as it sings the song *solus Christus*: "We put our faith in Christ, that we be justified *by him* only."[53] Justification by faith, for Cranmer, is a way of saying and safeguarding the soteriological cornerstone: justification by Jesus.

The only alternative Cranmer can see to this exclusively christological confession is a soteriology that is in fact an expression of original sin. To make "justification . . . the office of man," either "in part, or in the whole," is the "greatest arrogancy and presumption of man," and makes the sons of Adam and daughters of Eve who have been seduced by the serpent's whisper, "you will be like God" (Gen 3:5), "adversar[ies] of Christ and his gospel."[54] Faith, however, is the opposite of idolatry; it affirms the dependence of the creature in both creation and redemption and therefore says, "justification is the office of God only, and it is not a thing which we render unto him but which we receive of him; not which we give to him, but which we take of him."[55] Faith, then, is not what justifies; it is the confession that nothing and no one but Christ can. In Cranmer's words:

---

[52]Ibid., p. 131.
[53]Ibid., pp. 129, 132 (italics added).
[54]Ibid., p. 131.
[55]Ibid.

> The true understanding of this doctrine, that we be justified freely by faith . . . is not, that this our own act to believe in Christ, or this our faith in Christ, which is within us, doth justify us, and merit our justification unto us (for that were to count ourselves to be justified by some act or virtue that is within ourselves): but the true understanding and meaning thereof is, that although we hear God's word, and believe it; although we have faith . . . we must renounce the merit of all our said virtues, of faith, hope, charity, and all our other virtues and good deeds . . . as things far too weak and insufficient and unperfect to deserve remission of our sins, and our justification.[56]

Faith, in other words, does not trust in faith; it "trust[s] only in God's mercy"[57] because, as Cranmer records in his "Notes on Justification," "neither faith nor charity be the worthiness and merits of our justification, but that is to be ascribed only to our Saviour Christ, which," and here Cranmer quotes Romans 4:25, "was offered upon the cross for our sins, and rose again for our justification."[58]

This reading of the Pauline antitheses catches their christological confession. In Romans 4:4-5, for example, as Halvor Moxnes observes, the antithesis between "works" and "faith" is unbalanced by the addition of the predication "the one who justifies the ungodly," which directs the reader "not to faith *per se*, but to God, in whom one believes."[59] The salvific subject here is not believing Abraham—he is "the one who does not work"—but the justifying God. This pattern reverberates throughout the chapter. Abraham's faith lives at the disjunction between the content of God's promise ("so shall your offspring be"; Rom 4:18) and empirical reality ("his body was as good as dead" and "Sarah's womb was dead"; Rom 4:19). The ground for this "hope against hope" (Rom 4:18), however, is not Abraham's faith but the one in whom Abraham believes: "the God who makes alive the dead and calls non-being into being" (Rom 4:17) and "raised from the dead Jesus our Lord" (Rom 4:24).[60] Similarly, the contrast between "law" and "faith"

---

[56]Ibid., pp. 131-32.
[57]Ibid., p. 132.
[58]Ibid., p. 209. Cranmer also cites Tit 3:5 at this point in this "Notes."
[59]H. Moxnes, *Theology in Conflict: Studies in Paul's Understanding of God in Romans*, NovTSup 53 (Leiden: Brill, 1980), p. 42.
[60]The passive forms of ἐνδυναμόω and πληροφορέω in Rom 4:20, 21 suggest that even Abraham's believing is generated by God through the promise (cf. Rom 10:17). Cranmer can make a parallel point, saying "a true and lively faith . . . is the gift of God" and is therefore "not ours, but God's

in Romans 3:21-22 is made asymmetrical by the identification of faith's object: Jesus Christ. Faith, because it is "apart from law," is a pointing away from self and, because it is "faith in Jesus Christ," is a pointing to the singular saving subject that Cranmer calls God's "most dearly-beloved Son."[61] In Cranmer's most precise (and I think deeply Pauline) formulation, it is not that faith justifies but that "Christ is now the righteousness of all them that truly do believe in him."[62]

For Paul, to say that "the righteousness of God" is "the righteousness of God through faith in Jesus Christ" is to say that God's eschatological act of judgment and justification is irreducibly and exclusively singular—it is Jesus Christ. Cranmer, as a reader of Paul, puts it this way: "We put our faith in Christ, that we be justified by him only."[63] Rather than qualifying Paul's christological singularity (*solus Christus*) and his underlining of God's gracious unconditionality (*sola gratia*), Cranmer says *sola fide* as their echo and affirmation (cf. Rom 4:16; 11:6).[64] Expressed with Paul's pen, faith's motto is "not I, but Christ" (Gal 2:20). Cranmer's image is of faith as the finger of "St John Baptist," which "put the people from him, and appointed them," not merely with assent but with "sure trust and confidence" "unto Christ."[65]

It's Alive: Faith Active in Love

The homilies on faith and good works, officially entitled "A Short Declaration of the True, Lively, and Christian Faith" and "An Homily or Sermon of Good Works Annexed unto Faith," center on two characteristics of faith: "First, that this faith doth not lie dead in the heart, but is lively and fruitful in bringing forth good works. Second, that without it no good works be done, that shall be acceptable and pleasant to God."[66] For Cranmer, this is a mutual necessity: good works inevitably flow from faith; in the absence of faith there is an absence of good works. In this sense, Cranmer's phrase "lively faith" is a double entendre: faith is both alive and life giving—it

---

working in us." Cf. CGC II, fols. 251v, 252r.
[61]Cox, *Miscellaneous Writings*, p. 131.
[62]Ibid., p. 130.
[63]Ibid., p. 132.
[64]In the "Homily of Salvation," Cranmer cites Rom 11:6 as "the sum of all Paul's disputation in this" (ibid., p. 130).
[65]Ibid., pp. 132-33.
[66]Ibid., p. 136.

"worketh by charity" and it "doth give life to works."[67]

Galatians 5:6 provides Cranmer with an antithesis to the "idle, unfruitful, and dead" "persuasion . . . whereby [a person merely] knoweth that there is a God, and assenteth unto all truth of God's most holy word."[68] Whereas this *fides historica* (i.e., faith in the facts of history) is a "dead faith," "a sure trust and confidence of the mercy of God through our Lord Jesus Christ, and a steadfast hope of all good things to be received at God's hand" is a "lively faith."[69] Cranmer can therefore identify the "faith which is wholesome and clearly evangelical" by quoting Paul: it is "the faith which he says works by love" (Gal 5:6).[70] In its Pauline context, faith is both freedom from the curse of the law (Gal 3:13, 22-26) and freedom for the love of others (Gal 5:13). The law "locked up everything under sin" (Gal 3:22), but the coming of faith (Gal 3:23, 25), which is the coming of Christ (Gal 3:24), establishes a filial freedom ("you are children of God"; Gal 3:26) and unlocks love for others (Gal 5:6, 13).

In his "Great Commonplaces," Cranmer, with help from Augustine, traces this Pauline transition from slavery to sonship, insisting that while fear is a sign of slavery, faith lives in the space of filial freedom.[71] Cranmer can both join Paul in saying "Whatsover work is done without faith, it is sin" (Rom 14:23) and follow the Pauline move from faith to love: faith is "the ground of all good works."[72] Reading Romans 14:23 and Galatians 5:6, it seems, compels a double confession: "nothing is good without faith" (an interpretation of Rom 14:23); "faith of itself is full of good works" (an interpretation of Gal 5:6).[73] Following Augustine, Cranmer understands "good deeds to be measured . . . by the ends and intents for which they be done." Because faith is the antithesis of the "antichrist" ambition to justify one's self, "faith it is that doth commend work to God."[74] Faith, in other words, extracts

---

[67]Ibid., p. 135.
[68]Ibid.
[69]Ibid. For Cranmer's understanding of faith as *fiducia* (sure, personal trust), see Null, *Thomas Cranmer's Doctrine of Repentance*, pp. 165-66.
[70]CGC II, fol. 261v.
[71]CGC, fol. 247r; cf. Null, *Thomas Cranmer's Doctrine of Repentance*, p. 167.
[72]Cox, *Miscellaneous Writings*, pp. 141, 142.
[73]Ibid., p. 143.
[74]Ibid., p. 131: "for man cannot justify himself by his own works . . . that were the greatest arrogancy and presumption of man that the antichrist could erect against God, to affirm that a man might by his own works take away and purge his own sins, and so justify himself."

works from the satanic scheme of self-salvation and locates them within the responsive gratitude that is the echo created by God's prior and unconditioned grace.

The logic here is related to what might be called Cranmer's affective anthropology. Echoing Philipp Melanchthon's first edition of the *Loci communes* (1521), Cranmer understands the decisions of the will to be determined by the desires of the affections—we choose what we love. This means that any reorienting of the human will results from a replacing of the human heart. No wonder Cranmer confesses "we have no power of ourselves to help ourselves" (collect for the second Sunday in Lent). If death and resurrection are required for the will's redirection, then as Cranmer's collect for the fourth Sunday after Easter prays, it is "Almighty God who alone canst order the unruly wills and affections of sinful men." For Paul, as the parallel between Galatians 5:6 and Galatians 6:14-15 suggests, the reality of a faith that is active in love results from the cosmos-crucifying-and-recreating event that is the cross of Christ (Gal 5:14-15). "Lively faith," to combine Cranmerian and Pauline language, is a "new creation" (Gal 6:15). In Cranmer's words, "a loving heart" is what "doth follow" from "true Christ faith."[75] It is the "great and merciful benefits of God" that "move us to render ourselves to God" and "for his sake also to be ever ready to give ourselves to our neighbours."[76] As Null summarizes: "When the good news of justification by faith was proclaimed, the Spirit, working through God's Word, assured believers of their salvation. This new confidence in God's gracious goodwill towards them reoriented their affections, calming their turbulent hearts and inflaming in them a grateful love in return."[77]

Faith, for Cramner, is the opposite of fear; it is "sure trust and confidence in God's merciful promises."[78] It is, in other words, the presence of "the profession of our faith of the remission of our own sins" in "the deepness of our hearts."[79] Faith is being loved. And such belovedness, for Cranmer, "must kindle a warm fire of love in our hearts towards God, and towards all

---

[75]Ibid., p. 133.
[76]Ibid., p. 134.
[77]Null, "Thomas Cranmer and Tudor Evangelicalism," p. 241.
[78]CGC II, fol. 247; Cox, *Miscellaneous Writings*, p. 133.
[79]Ibid., p. 86.

other[s]."⁸⁰ Cranmer's "notable qualitie" is a parable of this, a biographic reading of Romans 5:10 and Galatians 5:6, you might say. His "sure trust" in God's reconciliation of him "while [he] was an enemy" (Rom 5:10) was active in love (Gal 5:6)—or, in this case, leniency. The fruit of having been forgiven as an enemy was a habit of being "benficiall unto his enemyes." This, as Cranmer understands himself within the Pauline grammar of "faith," is "freedom"; and "freedom" is faith active in love—it is the affective certainty of being loved by God (faith) leading ineluctably to love for others.

LET US PRAY

Thomas Cranmer's 1552 *Book of Common Prayer* is "the only effective attempt ever made to give liturgical expression to the doctrine of 'justification by faith alone.'"⁸¹ This is the opinion of Gregory Dix, and to the extent it is correct it can also be said that Cranmer's second prayer book is, in part, a liturgical expression of his reading of Paul, the apostle of justification by faith. Paul, in other words, is among those who taught Cranmer to pray. The words of absolution, for example, are littered with Pauline language; the inclusion of the reading of the Decalogue with the refrain "Lord, have mercy on us" reflects Romans 3:20 ("through the law comes the knowledge of sin"); the Pauline pattern of the word creating the faith that communes with it (see Rom 10:17; 1 Cor 10:16) is followed in the elimination of the *epiclesis*, a change that makes the reception of the bread and wine—the "feeding on him in your hearts by faith"—the immediate response to the words of institution; one of the four "comfortable words" comes from the Pauline corpus (1 Tim 1:15); all self-offering is reserved for the postcommunion prayer, making the presentation of one's self as a "living sacrifice" a response to having received "God's mercies" in the "full, perfect and sufficient sacrifice, oblation, and satisfaction" of Christ "once offered" (cf. Rom 12:1).⁸²

The thesis is confirmed: Cranmer, in part, learned to pray from Paul. It seems fitting, therefore, to conclude this conversation by inviting Paul to join Cranmer in a prayer that employs his theological grammar. Pauline

---

⁸⁰Ibid.
⁸¹Gregory Dix, *The Shape of the Liturgy* (Westminster: Dacre, 1945), p. 672.
⁸²For a full consideration of these changes to the liturgy and several others in addition, see Null, *Thomas Cranmer's Doctrine of Repentance*, pp. 236-47, who concludes by describing "the solafidian shape of the liturgy as a whole" (p. 244).

texts regularly turn on an adversative: "I am unworthy . . . but [δέ] by the grace of God I am what I am" (1 Cor 15:9-10); "by works of the law no human being will be justified . . . but [δέ] now the righteousness of God has been disclosed" (Rom 3:20-21; cf. Gal 1:13-16; Eph 2:1-6). This Pauline pattern shapes the "Prayer of Humble Access." I can hear Cranmer saying, "Let us pray," and (I think) I can hear Paul saying: "We doe not presume to come to this thy table (O mercyfull Lorde) trusting in our owne righteousnesse, *but* in thy manifolde and great mercies: we bee not worthye, so much as to gather up the crommes under thy table: *but* thou are the same Lorde whose propertie is always to haue mercye . . ."

In Conclusion

The Story *of* Reformation Readings

Gerald Bray

The Making of the Reformers

It is a common theme of the essays in this book that each generation is shaped by the work of its predecessors and cannot be understood without them. Neither we today nor the Protestant reformers of the sixteenth century were exceptions to this rule. The reformers had inherited a tradition of piety and learning that was well over a thousand years old and that had shaped the entire culture of Western Europe. They read the Bible from childhood in the Latin translation of Jerome, known to us as the Vulgate and first published in AD 410, and studied it through the eyes of the great fathers of the church, especially Augustine, whose personal experience of conversion drew him close to the apostle Paul. Augustine wrestled with Paul's epistle to the Romans in particular and developed the Pauline themes of predestination and of salvation by grace to a degree that was unequaled in ancient times and that would continue to haunt the Latin church for centuries. Men like Jerome and Augustine thought for themselves and did not feel particularly indebted to a canonical tradition of biblical interpretation, but that was not true of their successors. For the best part of a millennium, biblical and theological study in the Western church was rooted in their writings, along with those of men like Ambrose of Milan, Gregory the Great and Bede, the great commentator of Jarrow. Original thought did not disappear, but it was contained within the framework of a traditional authority that was attributed to these "fathers of the church" and eventually codified in works like the famous *Sentences* of Peter Lombard (d. 1160), which became the premier theological textbook of the later Middle Ages.

Until about 1200, serious reading of the Bible took place mainly in the monasteries, where it was set in the context of liturgical prayer and devotion. But with the emergence of universities in the late twelfth and early thirteenth centuries, biblical study moved out of the cloister and into the classroom, where the text was analyzed and expounded in a way that is recognizably the ancestor of modern practice. The classification of knowledge into distinct disciplines, the systematic study of texts and the lecture style we are familiar with today all derive from patterns developed in that academic world. The change of venue and technique also led to the development of new hermeneutical principles. Where monastic reading of Scripture had tended toward allegorical interpretation, the academic study of the Bible went in the opposite direction. Preference was given to the literal sense of the Latin text, though there were men like Andrew of St. Victor who understood the importance of learning Hebrew and Greek. The practical difficulties of finding teachers and procuring texts was such, though, that it was impossible for most people to venture beyond Latin, which was the official language of the church. The liturgy contained fixed words and phrases from both Hebrew (*alleluia, amen*) and Greek (*Kyrie eleison*), but that was as far as it went.

Medieval university lecturers drew on an ancient tradition of commentary writing, but they reshaped it to suit the needs of students trained in the art of theological disputation. Commentaries became extended analyses of portions of the biblical text, which was now subdivided into chapters to make this easier. The main purpose of these exercises was to demonstrate how each of these chapters should be read in the light of the whole Bible. One of the most popular exponents of this method was Nicholas of Lyra (c. 1270-1340), whose *Postills* (as his notes were called) were so widely circulated that they became the first biblical commentary to be printed. The reformers cannot be understood apart from this background. Most of them were either university lecturers or theologically educated preachers whose aim was to teach their congregations as if they were all divinity students. The style and the content of academic discourse is everywhere present in their writings, some of which (like Luther's commentaries on Galatians and Bucer's on Ephesians) were lecture notes taken down by students and then edited for publication. Most of the commentaries we possess were not written for the average churchgoer but for the pastors who watched over them, because they needed to learn what their task was and how they ought to go about it. This explains why, at a time when the reformers were translating the Bible into vernacular languages and producing a vast amount of instructional material for their congregations in their mother tongues, the commentaries were almost all in Latin, which remained the academic language until the eighteenth century.

THE IMPACT OF THE RENAISSANCE

Yet however traditional they were in some ways, the reformers were very conscious that they were "new men," operating in a world that had not been known to their ancestors. Seldom has any generation been more aware of breaking with its past than they were, and the Reformation would not have occurred otherwise. There had been reform movements throughout the Middle Ages, some of which left enduring traces in monastic orders, friars and different kinds of piety (like devotion to the reserved sacrament) that can still be found in the Roman Catholic Church today. At first, some people believed that Protestantism would turn out to be another of these renewal movements that would eventually be integrated within the church. That this did not happen is largely due to a general consciousness, shared by both the reformers and their opponents, that a fundamental change had occurred and that the traditional patterns of medieval church life could not contain the new spirit that was abroad.

There were two developments in particular that facilitated this awareness. The first was the invention of printing. Johann Gutenberg published his Latin Bible in 1456, and by the end of the fifteenth century printed books were becoming the new means of communication. They guaranteed that the educated elite of Western Europe could read the same thing at the same time, an information revolution comparable to the recent invention of the Internet. The second was the rediscovery of a vast store of ancient learning that had previously been ignored or unknown. This is what we now call the Renaissance, which was characterized by an increasingly secular (though not irreligious) tendency generally referred to as "humanism." After Erasmus published his critical edition and Latin translation of the New Testament in 1516, it was no longer possible to be a serious biblical scholar without a thorough mastery of both Greek and Hebrew. Latin remained the scholarly language for everyday purposes, but anyone who confined himself to the Vulgate (as John Wycliffe had done in the 1370s) would not have been taken seriously as a scholar. Much of what Erasmus did had already been proposed by Lorenzo Valla (1404–1447), but as Valla died before the invention of printing, it was Erasmus who became the torchbearer of the new humanism, whose slogan was *ad fontes*—to the sources.

From the modern perspective, the efforts of the Erasmian humanists often seem crude and mistaken, but this is because the source material available to them was much less extensive than what we possess today and a lot of it circulated under false names. Works were regularly attributed to Augustine or Jerome in order to buttress their authority, when in fact they were written by very different people, many of them medieval monks. Citations from lesser-known church fathers have to be treated with great caution, since many of them are falsely attributed. In particular, works defending transubstantiation often bore the names of men like Cyprian or Eusebius of Emesa, even though they were composed centuries later. If they found their way into Peter Lombard's *Sentences*, as many of them did, they acquired a spurious canonical authority that was almost impossible to challenge until modern methods of literary detection were developed.

The humanists were able to ransack the monastic libraries of Western Europe for manuscripts, but archaeology and its subdisciplines (like epigraphy, numismatics, comparative philology and so on) remained inaccessible to them. Erasmus did not even realize that the Greek text of the New Testament that he prized so highly had evolved over centuries of constant use in the Byzantine Empire and in many places was not as good as the one Jerome had used for his translation of the Vulgate. Because of this, he was inclined to criticize Jerome for mistaking the original text when the Vulgate represents an earlier and better form of it, an error that he passed on to his many disciples. A classic example of this is the longer ending of the Lord's

Prayer, which Erasmus thought was authentic because it was found in his Greek manuscript, but which we now know was a later addition. As for Hebrew, the humanists knew nothing beyond the Masoretic Text and were mostly ignorant of other Semitic languages, which have subsequently thrown light on our understanding of many Old Testament words and expressions.

Given these limitations, it is remarkable that sixteenth-century commentators were as sophisticated as they were. They appreciated that Hebrew had its own literary styles and conventions, and that these frequently underlay the Greek text of the New Testament. For example, they knew that the Hebrew word *shalom* meant "prosperity" as well as "peace" and interpreted Paul's epistolary greetings and farewells accordingly. Their literary training in the classics made them sensitive to rhetorical devices to a degree that equals (and often surpasses) the awareness of many modern scholars. They were perfectly capable of interpreting the literal sense of the texts they had and were not afraid to castigate even the most eminent of their predecessors for lapsing into allegory in order to explain difficulties. Where divergent interpretations were possible, they usually mentioned each of them in turn and then argued for their own position, much in the way that a modern critic would. But whereas earlier generations (and many of their Catholic contemporaries) would have felt bound to submit to the authority of someone like Jerome, the reformers felt free to agree or disagree with the patristic tradition if they felt that it rested on weak premises. To that extent they had moved beyond the mindset of their predecessors, and in this sense we can still recognize them as genuinely modern in their approach.

THE PATRISTIC TRADITION AND PAUL

That the Reformation was in large measure a movement of Pauline theology can scarcely be doubted, and this was affirmed by the reformers themselves. Where the early church had often read the New Testament through the eyes of John, using the prologue to his Gospel and the great farewell discourses as sources for their trinitarian theology, the reformers concentrated on the Pauline epistles, which to their minds expressed the heart of the gospel message. They never denied their ancient theological inheritance and were happy to affirm it whenever the biblical text pointed them in that direction, but instead of concentrating on the person and natures of Christ as the church fathers had done, they focused their attention on his person and work instead. They were further attracted to Paul because he was an unusual kind of apostle. Living as they did in a church whose titular head claimed to be a direct successor of Peter, they were impressed by a man who had received his preaching commission directly from Christ and who was prepared to confront Peter on his weakness in defending the principles of the gospel against the Judaizers of the early church. Paul's boldness in this respect appealed to the reformers, who believed they were doing much the same thing in their own day. They did not want to reject "Peter" (the pope and the Roman church) any more than Paul did, but they were determined to correct his errors in the same spirit of loving forthrightness.

They were also determined to imitate Paul in showing concern for the spiritual welfare of the churches under their care. To them Paul was a pastor as much as an evangelist, and his epistles reveal his pastoral role more than anything else. They knew from their own experience how easily a church could fall away from preaching the gospel if it lacked good teaching and sustained discipline, and much of their interest in Paul focused on this. They also knew from experience that a faithful minister of the gospel will suffer persecution for his efforts, and here again Paul provided an obvious model, not least because he did not let his chains stop him from proclaiming the message. Most important of all, though, Paul was a model of what God can do with the least promising material. Here was a man who had persecuted the church of God but who had been rescued from his folly and turned around to become the great evangelist of the early church. He was living proof, not only that a person is saved by faith and not by works, but that this salvation is God's choice and not ours. No one had been less eager to become a Christian than Saul of Tarsus, and yet God intervened to save him in spite of himself. Furthermore, when Paul looked back on that in later life, he realized that what happened to him on that day was no freak occurrence but the age-old plan of God, which he had been working out in the young Saul even in the days of his unbelief. Paul became what he was, not by his own free will, but by the election and predestination of God, and with this the reformers closely identified themselves.

When it came to the corpus of Paul's epistles, the reformers accepted the tradition that had been handed down to them, including the Pauline authorship of Hebrews. For example, because Galatians was very similar in content to Romans, it was generally believed that Paul had abridged what he had said to the Romans in his letter to the churches of Galatia. The reformers thought that Paul had written Romans first, and not (as most modern scholars would claim) the other way around. In fact, this makes little practical difference to their exposition, except that occasionally they refer back to Romans in their commentaries on Galatians and ask their readers to consult their commentaries on the "earlier" epistle for further details. As a result, their exposition of Galatians is sometimes shorter than it would otherwise be, but that is all. The reformers also followed ancient tradition in linking Galatians with Ephesians, Philippians and Colossians. Not all of them went as far as Calvin, who wrote a single commentary on all four as a group, but they generally agreed that they belonged together. Today we would agree that Ephesians and Colossians are both prison epistles, although modern scholars often doubt their authenticity (especially that of Colossians), but the others do not fit into the overall scheme. Furthermore, the reformers were convinced that Ephesians is just as clear an exposition of the gospel as Romans and Galatians are—perhaps even more so! To their minds, the fact that Ephesians concentrates so heavily on predestination was proof of this, because predestination was the ultimate assertion of divine sovereignty (and therefore of the irrelevance of human works) in salvation. The idea that this emphasis on predestination might suggest that Paul was not the author of Ephesians never crossed their minds.

As far as Paul's life and career were concerned, the reformers had nothing to go on beyond the New Testament and the assertions of the fathers of the early church. Their critical sense was sharp enough to see that it was difficult to connect what Paul says in Galatians 2 about his confrontation with Peter with what Luke writes about Paul's visit to Jerusalem in Acts 15, but this did not worry them unduly. They tended to think of them as two separate events and felt free to use Acts 15 as the key to understanding Galatians 2, because even if the occasions were different, the theological message was the same—Paul was right and the leaders of the Jerusalem church were wrong about circumcision and the place of the Mosaic law in the church. The reformers were content to leave the historical details unharmonized and were prepared to allow for a variety of possible solutions to the problem. As they saw it,

Paul's main concern was not with the Jerusalem church but with the false apostles who claimed to be its representatives and who were leading the Galatians astray. Such false apostles were less in evidence at Ephesus or Colossae, but the reformers still believed that Paul wrote to the Ephesians and the Colossians because he was conscious of the ever-present threat which they posed. In terms of dating, they knew that Paul wrote the prison epistles toward the end of his life, but they did not speculate on whether or not he was later released from prison. They saw Ephesians as a follow-up to the speech that he had given to the elders of the church at Miletus (Acts 20) and measured the success of its teaching by the report on the church found in Revelation 2:1-7, which they (correctly) assumed to be later in date. Beyond that they could not (and did not) go.

In regard to the witness of the fathers of the church, the reformers had a high opinion of Jerome, though this was tempered by the fact that the Jerome they knew included the Pauline commentary of Pelagius, which had been recycled under his name. The error was not discovered until the nineteenth century, so the reformers mistakenly accused Jerome of being weaker on justification and predestination than he really was. The reformers also had a good knowledge of Augustine and quoted him frequently, though they made surprisingly little use of his unfinished commentaries on Romans or his commentary on Galatians. The other Latin father they often quoted was Ambrose, though here again there was a confusion of identity. The Pauline commentary preserved under his name was in fact the work of an unknown presbyter who was writing at Rome sometime around AD 380. Erasmus realized that it was not the work of Ambrose, and seventeenth-century editors dubbed the unknown author "Ambrosiaster," the name that has stuck to this day; but although the reformers knew what Erasmus thought, they disregarded his judgment. As a result, they went on referring to the commentary as the work of Ambrose, thus giving him higher marks as a commentator than he deserved.

Of the Greek fathers, the reformers had some knowledge of Origen, much of whose work was preserved in a Latin translation by Rufinus, but they made little use of him because of his reputation as the father of allegorical interpretation. More to their liking was John Chrysostom, who enjoyed a number of important advantages in their eyes. First of all, he was a

Greek who spoke the language of the New Testament as his mother tongue and could therefore be trusted to have understood it correctly. Second, Chrysostom had been largely unknown in the Latin West during the middle ages, so he benefited from the notoriety of novelty. Third, no one could accuse him of being under the thumb of either the pope or the emperor. On the contrary, he had stood up to the secular authorities of his day and had suffered for it—just like many of the reformers themselves. Fourth, Chrysostom avoided allegorical interpretations as much as possible and plumbed for the literal sense of the biblical text, as the reformers also did. Finally, and most important of all, Chrysostom was a preacher whose "commentaries" were really homilies and whose main concern was to educate and edify the Christian public. This was what the reformers thought their own exegetical work was all about, and Chrysostom gave them a role model who was without parallel in the patristic period. Not surprisingly, he was their favorite church father and the one whom they were least likely to criticize, although, as always, they were prepared to do so if they had to.

The fathers of the church were important to the reformers because they represented a witness that predated the rise of the papacy and the medieval scholasticism that the reformers so disliked. By showing that Augustine (in particular) agreed with them on certain controversial points, they were pointing out the antiquity of their beliefs and justifying their claim to be recovering the ancient gospel, not inventing something new and heretofore unheard of. They were far from being patristic fundamentalists, but they respected the great exegetes of the past for the faithfulness with which they had studied the Scriptures and let the texts speak for themselves. Unlike the medieval scholastics, the reformers did not try to force the Bible into a particular philosophical paradigm, but let it determine what their agenda should be. The picture they presented was idealized and not altogether accurate, but it enabled them to appropriate the legacy of the past without being subservient to it, and that was what they wanted.

THE THEOLOGICAL CRISIS OF THE REFORMATION

The reformers were fully engaged in the Renaissance humanism of their time, but if that were all there was to say about them, they would be known today as followers of Erasmus, and Martin Luther would now be as obscure to nonspecialists as his contemporary Johannes Reuchlin is. Some of the greatest humanists were never attracted to the Reformation, and Erasmus himself broke with Luther when he realized that Luther was not just a moral reformer with a broadly humanist agenda. At the heart of the Reformation lay a theological crisis that led to the formulation of the doctrine of justification by faith alone as the essential touchstone of the gospel. Volumes have been written about this, and it is difficult to speak of an agreed scholarly consensus. On the one hand, it can be shown that the ancient and medieval church had a doctrine of justification by faith, because it had always believed that only by faith in Jesus Christ can a person be forgiven and stand in the presence of the holy and righteous God. The reformers recognized this and never claimed to have discovered anything fundamentally new. Their argument was that they had recovered the ancient teaching of the church in its pristine purity by going to the sources and reading them for themselves. On the other hand, they also believed that something had gone seriously wrong with the theology of the late medieval church. Scholars differ as to whether the church was teaching false doctrine (as the reformers claimed) or merely obscuring the truth, but everyone agrees that many sixteenth-century Christians were confused about the true nature of grace and salvation. This was most obvious at the level of popular devotion, but not only was the church doing little to correct the problem, in some cases (like the sale of indulgences) it appeared to be manipulating the credulity of the masses for its own benefit.

To understand how this situation had arisen, we must go back to the writings of Anselm of Canterbury (1033–1109), one of the greatest of medieval theologians. As he understood it, by sinning against God the human race had piled up an enormous debt to him, which no amount of effort or goodwill on our part can ever repay. Knowing this, God sent his Son into the world to pay the price for our sins. By suffering and dying on the cross, Jesus of Nazareth satisfied the wrath of God against human sin, and by his resurrection from the dead and ascension into heaven, he took that payment back to God the Father. There he pleads for us by offering his sacrifice on our behalf, and in the sacraments of the church, direct access to that sacrifice is made available to those who believe. In principle, there is enough "merit" in Christ's sacrifice to pay for the sins of the whole world, but only those who draw on it through the ministry of the church actually benefit from it.

The church provided various "means of grace," or channels of communication, by which Christ's sacrifice could be applied to our lives. The first and most important of these was baptism, which cleansed the person who received it from original (or birth) sin. After that, the other sacraments were established in order to provide supplementary doses of grace that were needed to take away postbaptismal sins. The snag was that the church could refuse this grace to those whom it deemed unworthy of it. To be "excommunicated," as this refusal was called, was the medieval equivalent of having a bank card swallowed by an ATM—it cut people off from the source of the grace they needed in order to live. This gave the church and its priests enormous power over the lives of individuals, but it raised as many problems as it solved. For one thing, many priests were corrupt and unworthy of their office, which made some people question whether God had really entrusted his saving grace to them. For another, it seemed unfair to treat all sins as being equally serious, and it was unclear how much grace was needed to pay for particular ones and how the right quantity could be obtained.

Late medieval theology was preoccupied with this problem. Sins were categorized into "mortal" and "venial" types, and lists were drawn up of the penances that a Christian would have to do in order to gain enough grace to pay for them. Those who were still in debt when they died went to purgatory, where they could continue to pay it off after their deaths. Eventually they would clear their account and be admitted into heaven, a process that could be shortened by doing good works on earth that would then be counted as a kind of voucher that would be redeemable in purgatory. These vouchers were called "indulgences," and they came in many different values. As time went on, the church hit on the idea that these debts could be repaid in cash as well as in penitential acts, and it was this that led to the infamous sale of indulgences that so scandalized Luther. If indulgences could be sold, it followed that the grace of God could be purchased, and by 1500 the forgiveness of sins had become big business.

Money has a powerful hold on people, and by the late fifteenth century the church had become a bottomless pit of corruption. Popes and bishops lived in ostentatious luxury, paid for by the sweat and fears of ordinary believers, though relatively few people were aware of that. It was mainly the humanist elite that was scandalized by the combination of ignorance and greed that it saw in the clergy, and Erasmus was one of their greatest critics. Then came Martin Luther. Unlike Erasmus and his colleagues, Luther had a deep sense of his own sinfulness, and as a young monk he used all the means of grace he could find to purge himself of his unrighteousness. There is no doubt that he went to an extreme in this, and his superiors in the monastery advised him to desist from his constant fasting and self-flagellation. But Luther wanted to get rid of the sin in his life and could not rest until he had done so, which effectively meant that he would never be at peace with God because he could not achieve sinless perfection. It was a terrible dilemma for him and led to long periods of intense soul-searching akin to a form of spiritual depression.

Luther's breakthrough came when he read in Romans 1:17 that "the just will live by faith." We know that the meaning of this verse did not become clear to him immediately, and that during the years 1515 through 1519 he continued to wrestle with its implications. The theological issue he had to resolve can be put like this: Did Jesus die for sins (things), or did he die for sinners (people)? Is God's grace a substance that can be obtained from the church and applied to sins for their healing, or is it a relationship with him that he makes available to those who believe in Christ? The Reformation was born when Luther understood that Jesus came to save sinners by uniting them to himself in a personal relationship that Luther described as "justification by faith alone." Once that was accomplished, the blood Christ shed on the cross was sufficient to atone for all their sins—past, present and future. There was no need to supplement this sacrifice with works of penance or devotion, which could add nothing to what God has already done. Furthermore, it was impossible to curry favor with God, because he had already declared whom he had chosen for salvation. Salvation was a free gift from God that believers appropriated by trusting that Christ has done what is needed on our behalf.

For Luther this was a message of enormous liberating power. In his own words, a believer is *simul iustus et peccator*, a justified sinner who can stand in the presence of God because he is confident that Christ has paid the debt of his sins. To him this was the only way salvation could ever be possible, but it is typical of the spiritual darkness of his age that two powerful misunderstandings of his teaching almost immediately surfaced to haunt him.

The first was the belief that he was teaching a doctrine of sinless perfection. To the medieval mind, it was obvious that if the means of grace are no longer necessary, it must be because the person concerned has become perfect. In this way of thinking, justification (being declared righteous before God) was the direct corollary of sanctification (being made holy in oneself), which Luther vehemently denied. In response to this confusion, the reformers uncoupled justification from sanctification and made them two distinct things. Justification is a once-for-all declaration of our innocence in the sight of God, something that is possible only in and by the action of Christ. Sanctification, or growth in grace, is the fruit of justification, which exists in individual believers to different degrees but does not determine their standing before God.

It was this aspect of Luther's message that produced the second great misunderstanding, when some of his hearers concluded that if we are justified by faith alone, then sanctification was completely unnecessary. If a person was saved by faith and not by works, what was the point of good works? If the law of Moses had given way to the gospel of Christ, did this not include the moral precepts of the Ten Commandments along with all the temple rituals and circumcision? Critics of Luther (and a few of his more radical followers) said that his teaching destroyed all morality and undermined the social order. To this, Luther declared that good works have an essential role to play in the Christian life, but they must be understood in an entirely new way. In the medieval understanding, they were born of the fear that without them salvation would be unobtainable. By declaring that forgiveness of sins comes by grace through faith, Luther removed the fear generated by the knowledge that our works are never good enough to satisfy God, but at the same time faith provided a new context in which good works could be performed for their own sake. Believers have been set free to do them because we have been born again into a new life with Christ. In other words, works are the result of our salvation, not the cause of it. If there are no good works in a person's life, there is no salvation either, but this is not because good works are the cause of salvation; it is because good works are the inevitable consequence of saving faith.

As this doctrine took hold, the power of the medieval church over Luther and his followers crumbled away. Purgatory and indulgences were the first things to be rejected, followed not long afterward by sacramental penance. With no grace to be mediated, there was no more need of the medieval priesthood, which was transformed into a company of pastors whose main qualification was their ability to preach the Word faithfully to their people. Sermons replaced the sacraments as the focal point of Christian worship, and trust in God became more important than trust in the counsels of the church. The net effect of all this was to bring the Bible and its exposition back to the center of Christian worship. That meant that the Scriptures had to be taught clearly and comprehensively, so that ordinary church members would understand what their faith was all about. The Bible had to be widely circulated in the vernacular tongue, so that everyone in the church would have the opportunity to read it, but the unskilled would have to learn how to understand its message, and this is where the writing of biblical commentaries became so important.

The reformers believed that the Bible was God's gift to the church and that for the most part its message was clear enough. Needless to say, they also believed that what they taught was its theology and that they shared the apostles' priorities and understanding of what churches were and how they should be organized. The reformers recognized that there were textual difficulties in the Bible that needed to be resolved, including problems of translation that only specialists could explain, but their main concern was to exhort people to submit to the truth that it proclaims without being unduly distracted by secondary details. Knowing what the Bible says was one thing, but obeying it was quite another, and it was to call believers to obedience that God had sent his pastors to the church. As good shepherds they did not have to give their lives for the sheep in the way that Christ had done, but they still had to protect them from losing their salvation to prowling wolves who might take advantage of textual difficulties or accidental mishaps that had occurred in the process of the Bible's transmission. Those who wrote commentaries were preachers and teachers who were not merely informing God's people of his will and intentions for them but protecting them in the enjoyment of the salvation they had in Christ.

This spiritual dimension of the reformers' task has to be understood and appreciated if we are to have any hope of understanding them. What gave special force to the reformers' biblical interpretation was their belief in the centrality of the work of the Holy Spirit in the formation of the church. They were convinced that the outward forms of religious observance were of no value without the indwelling presence of the Spirit in the lives of believers. That presence could not be artificially induced by the sacraments, as the medieval church had tried to do. Baptism was not a kind of spiritual vaccination that took effect whether the recipient believed it or not. Nor was holy communion "the food of immortality" in the sense that the church had come to understand this. Merely consuming consecrated bread would not put Christ into a person's life, though obviously that was what a doctrine of transubstantiation implied. Even faith, understood as intellectual assent to a creed, was not enough. Only a spiritual transformation would suffice, and that was a work of the Holy Spirit that no human agency could either dispense or withhold.

How could one know whether this spiritual transformation had taken place? Here the answer of the reformers was that the Spirit had given the Bible to the church as God's Word. The truly spiritual person would therefore be someone who was passionately attached to the Scriptures and who would submit to them as his guide to the Christian life. Whatever was taught in them he would believe, and whatever was not in them he would ignore or reject. There was some leeway on this second point, to the extent that practices not found in the Bible might be adopted for practical purposes (like meeting for worship on Sunday morning), but these things were matters of indifference (*adiaphora*) that could not be imposed on anyone as a requirement for salvation. In other words, spiritual authority was transferred from the church as the body of Christ headed by the pope to the Bible, which was God's Word inspired by the Holy Spirit and equally accessible to all in whom that Spirit dwelt.

Reading the Reformation Paul

The Pauline epistles had a central importance in the reformers' overall scheme of biblical interpretation, or hermeneutics, because Paul, more than anyone else, explained how the Bible should be read. It was Paul who laid out the meaning of the creation and fall of Adam and who expounded the true significance of the covenant that God had made with Abraham. The Jewish view that Moses the lawgiver was the founder of Israel was overturned by saying that he had done no more than codify covenant principles that the people had been unable to keep on their own. The resulting law was a good thing in itself, but in spiritual terms it was second best and could do no more than identify the nature of the spiritual decay that affected the human race after the fall of Adam.

Keeping the law was an impossible ideal, and those who promoted such observance were cutting people off from the grace of God, which alone could save them. By sending his Son into the world to pay the price of sin, God had fulfilled the law and made it redundant as far as obtaining salvation was concerned, though it continued to restrain and reveal sin in the old age, even as it showed the children of God what love for their Father expected of them. Christians who were filled with the Holy Spirit could understand what the law was getting at, and although they were not expected to fulfill it and thereby gain life (which would have been impossible), they could nevertheless look to it as a yardstick against which to measure their own behavior, which would, of course, both diagnose ongoing sin and identify the form of freedom.

This message resonated with the reformers because they believed that the church of their day had fallen into a spiritual trap not unlike that of the ancient Jews. This belief was not a product of their imagination, because it had considerable evidence to back it up. After Christianity was legalized in the Roman Empire, there were attempts to create a Christian society based on ancient Israel. This went to such an extreme that there were even churches built according to the dimensions of Solomon's temple. The clergy was turned into the Christian equivalent of Levites, forming a distinct class within the body politic and living off tithe revenue rather than owning land themselves. The Eucharist was interpreted as a sacrifice in which the Lamb of God was symbolically slain by a priest who was specially consecrated for that purpose. In the twelfth century theologians developed the doctrine of transubstantiation, which was canonized at the Fourth Lateran Council in 1215. According to this doctrine, the bread and wine presented at the Eucharist were transformed into the "real" body and blood of Christ, so that the sacrifice was not just a memorial but a reenactment (or "re-presentation") of Christ's death on the cross. It would be hard to get any closer to the pattern of Old Testament temple sacrifices than that.

There were differences between the Old and New Testaments, of course, notably the fact that Christian priests were supposed to be celibate and did not constitute a hereditary caste as they did in Israel. But this was explained by saying that the Jewish system was "carnal," being rooted in physical generation, whereas the Christian equivalent was "spiritual," since priests were (supposedly) chosen by God and given the grace to live the life of the celibate angels as evidence that their true home was in heaven.

In the developed medieval system, the priesthood, along with monks and nuns, constituted a distinct society of "spiritual persons" (the title actually used to describe them) on whom the laity were dependent for access to God. Spiritual persons were expected to live according to a rule that involved numerous devotional exercises that were intended to bring them closer to God. At the heart of this system was the sacrament of penance, which was administered by the priests. The penitent was expected to confess his sins to a priest and receive a punishment of sorts (which was his "penance"), from which he would be absolved on completing it and admitted to the fellowship of the Eucharist. Just as in ancient Israel there was a rite of purification that was required before access to the atoning sacrifice could be granted, it was the priesthood that determined whether the rite had been performed adequately or not.

This point has to be understood, because modern critics of the reformers claim that Luther and his followers knew nothing about Second Temple Judaism and therefore misunderstood what Paul was saying about the so-called works of the law. It is true, of course, that no Christians in premodern times knew much about Judaism, but it is remarkable how close the medieval church came to replicating it. The church did not teach that people earned their admission to the covenant of grace by works. All baptized persons were in the covenant of grace and members of the new Israel already, so their spiritual status was exactly the same as that of the ancient Jews—and what is more, they also understood that they had been saved by grace. As in Second Temple Judaism, the works enjoined on those within the covenant were designed to prevent the loss of salvation that would inevitably occur if they sinned after baptism, and there was no atonement for it. Saul of Tarsus did not persecute the church because he was trying to earn favor with God, but because he was trying to protect the boundaries of the covenant, and the medieval church was doing exactly the same thing. Its members were already baptized and "born again" in Christ, but they had to be protected against the wiles of the devil, and the works enjoined on them served that purpose. Advocates of the "new perspective" on Paul who criticize Luther for failing to understand the spiritual nature of Second Temple Judaism do not show that they realize this, and so they fail to grasp just how much Luther's background resembled that of Saul the Pharisee.

Of course it is true that in many ways the reformers had little idea of what the early Christian communities were like and tended to read them in nonhistorical ways. For example, Luther naively imagined that Paul's epistle to the Galatians was of special relevance to his own people because both the Germans and the Galatians were of Celtic stock and therefore subject to the same ethnic defects. We smile at this today, but it would be quite wrong to dismiss what Luther says about the epistle merely because of that. The comparison he made was really irrelevant to his argument, because at bottom, every human being—Galatian, German or whatever—is a sinner in the sight of God. Luther's lectures on Galatians were addressed to Germans in the first instance, but they spoke to the whole world because he touched on something fundamental about human nature and our separation from God. One might add that it was for precisely the same reason that Paul's epistle to the Galatians transcended its original context and became a message for the entire church.

Modern scholars are widely read in the literature of early and rabbinic Judaism and have discovered that it teaches a covenant of grace. But so what? It is possible to read the scholastic theologians of the late Middle Ages and find a doctrine of justification by faith in them just as much as in Luther. Modern ecumenical dialogues have pointed this out in joint statements on justification that both Protestants and Catholics have signed in good conscience. Does this mean that Paul was saying nothing particularly new and that belief in Christ was just a more efficient and universal form of the covenant faithfulness advocated by the Jews? Was Luther merely stating the obvious? If so, how do we account for the seismic impact that both Paul and Luther had? There must be something more to what they said than this.

The problem with the reformers' modern critics is that they downplay the spiritual dimension that makes sense of the teaching of both Paul and Luther. However much the two men lived in completely different worlds, and however little Luther and his contemporaries understood Paul's historical situation, they were united at the spiritual level, which transcends the limits of time and space. The great questions of sin, death and redemption do not change from one age to another, and neither are they bound by context or culture. We know this because in the modern world we see how culturally naive evangelists can preach the gospel to pagan tribes who are converted when they hear its message, even though they have never read the Old Testament, let alone the writings of Second Temple Judaism. How is that possible? What is it that makes headhunters in New Guinea turn to Christ when sophisticated professors at Oxford or Harvard turn up their noses at him? The latter have infinitely more access to the facts and have inherited a cultural tradition that has been shaped by them, but it is the illiterate tribesmen who hear the Word of the Lord and are converted. Why?

The answer is given by Paul himself in his first letter to the Corinthians. He tells them that the message he preached was a scandal to the Jews and folly to the Greeks (Gentiles), but to those who were saved it was the power and wisdom of God. This power and wisdom was not the result of clever arguments. The men to whom Paul preached on the Areopagus in Athens were probably the most sophisticated group of people he ever spoke to, but they were also the ones most resistant to his message. The reason for this is that the people who had all the clever arguments and relied on them for their justification lacked the Spirit of God dwelling in their hearts. This is what Paul had, and what Luther and his fellow reformers also had. And it is this connection between Paul and reformers that so often seems to be missed, both by the Catholic apologists of the early sixteenth century and the modern critics of the reformers.

Modern scholars who immerse themselves in cultural contextualization theories and try to explain everything through that prism do not consider that there is a transcendent spiritual dimension that links people across such divides. This dimension is not necessarily Christian—the pagan classics can also move us in ways that go beyond our immediate context. If that were not the case, those classics would have died a long time ago because they would not speak to anyone. Homer and Plato understood the pains of the human heart, but they had no answer to them. Paul came along with a message that touched the same deep wounds but provided a way of healing them. Luther discovered the same thing when he read Paul, not because he related to Paul's original context (of which he knew little or nothing), but because he was on the same spiritual wavelength as the apostle. That in turn was a work of the Holy Spirit, who bears witness with our spirits that we are children of God, as Paul said to the Romans.

It was at that level that the reformers connected with Paul and understood what he was getting at. When the message sank in, it changed their lives, and in changing their lives, it changed the church. Their modern critics are primarily interested in intellectual enlightenment, which they believe they have found and need to communicate to whoever will listen. The Reformation followers of Paul and Luther, by contrast, were seeking spiritual transformation, which comes to those to whom God chooses to reveal himself. Those today who have had that experience understand both Luther and Paul and have no difficulty reconciling the two, even if they would not think of Luther's Germans as distant cousins to the Galatians. They are one with both men in the Spirit, just as they are one with the saints of every age. They do not need a new perspective on Paul or on the reformers in order to get their message, but a new life in Christ, which Paul and the reformers both had. With the right hermeneutical key in place, they can make sense of both and reconcile them in the all-embracing power of the Spirit of God.

Contributors

Michael Allen is associate professor of systematic and historical theology at Reformed Theological Seminary in Orlando. He is the author of several books, including *Justification and the Gospel: Understanding the Contexts and Controversies*, *Karl Barth's Church Dogmatics: An Introduction and Reader* and most recently (with Scott Swain) *Reformed Catholicity*.

John Barclay is the Lightfoot Professor of Divinity at the University of Durham. He is the author of many books, including most recently *Paul and the Gift*.

Gerald Bray is research professor of divinity at Beeson Divinity School and distinguished professor of historical theology at Knox Theological Seminary. Among many publications in historical and systematic theology, he has recently edited the inaugural volume, *Galatians, Ephesians*, of the Reformation Commentary on Scripture series.

David Fink is assistant professor of religion at Furman University. His dissertation at Duke University was titled "Divided by Faith: The Protestant Doctrine of Justification and the Confessionalization of Biblical Exegesis."

Wesley Hill is assistant professor of biblical studies at Trinity School for Ministry. He has most recently written *Paul and the Trinity*.

Robert Kolb is the mission professor emeritus of systematic theology and director of the Institute for Mission Studies at Concordia Seminary in St. Louis. Author of numerous books, he is perhaps most widely regarded for editing (with Timothy Wengert) *The Book of Concord*.

Jonathan Linebaugh is lecturer in New Testament studies in the Faculty of Divinity at the University of Cambridge. He is the author of *God, Grace, and Righteousness in Wisdom of Solomon and Paul's Letter to the Romans*.

Brian Lugioyo is associate professor of theology and ethics at Azusa Pacific University. He is the author of *Martin Bucer's Doctrine of Justification*.

Ashley Null currently holds a research post funded by the German Research Council at Humboldt University of Berlin and is a visiting fellow at the Faculty of Divinity at the University of Cambridge and St. John's College, Durham University, while he edits a five-volume edition of Thomas Cranmer's notebooks. He has written *Thomas Cranmer's Doctrine of Repentance*.

Dane Ortlund is senior vice president for Bible publishing at Crossway Books. He is the author of numerous books on the New Testament and the Christian life, including *Zeal Without Knowledge: The Concept of Zeal in Romans 10, Galatians 1, and Philippians 3*.

Mark Seifrid is professor of exegetical theology at Concordia Theological Seminary. He has written widely on the theology of the apostle Paul, most recently publishing a commentary on 2 Corinthians.

Scripture Index

Old Testament

Genesis
1, *84*
1–5, *175*
1:2, *175*
3:5, *248*
6:5-6, *175*
6:18, *175*
15:5, *113*
15:6, *113, 247*
17:1-6, *113*

Exodus
3:14, *147*
19–20, *158*
29:37-38, *158*
33, *139*
33:19, *154*

Leviticus
14:10, *136*
18, *242*
18:5, *242*
26:10, *36*

Deuteronomy
7:6-8, *156*
21:23, *242*
27:26, *242*
29:29, *153*
30:15-20, *132*
33:11, *131*

Psalms
14:2, *158*
18:1, *33*
31:3, *37*
32:1-2, *113*
68:10, *103*
69:9, *103*
98:2, *112*
142:2, *158*

Ecclesiastes
9:1, *130*

Isaiah
20:22-23, *78*
26:3, *37*
45:8, *112*
46:12-13, *112*
49:8, *207*
51:6-8, *112*
53:12, *82*
56:1, *112*
59:20, *104*
61:10-11, *112*

Lamentations
3:4, *37*

Ezekiel
43:25, *136*

New Testament

Matthew
6:11, *148*
20:1-16, *218*
25, *215*

Luke
1:6, *137*
10:27, *45*
24:45-49, *77*

John
1, *116*
1:17, *82*
1:29, *82*

Acts
1:3, *176*
1:7, *181*
2:47, *183*
6:1, *182*
6:14, *182*
7:30, *177*
7:41, *180*
7:44, *180*
10:43, *228*
15, *261*
20, *262*

Romans
1–2, *119*
1–4, *111*
1–8, *103, 241*
1:1–3:20, *81*
1:3, *102*
1:5, *117*
1:6-7, *111*
1:13-15, *102*
1:16, *19*
1:16-17, *14, 86, 112, 113*
1:16–4:25, *110*
1:17, *266*
1:18, *244*
1:18-20, *87*
1:29, *78*
1:32, *244*
2, *246*
2:4, *243*
2:4-5, *243*
2:4-6, *243*
2:4-10, *243*
2:5, *243, 244*
2:5-10, *243*
2:13, *245*
2:16, *110*
2:17-29, *106*
3, *242, 246*
3:1-9, *98*
3:5, *244*
3:5-6, *244*
3:9, *240*
3:9-20, *244*
3:10, *240*
3:20, *54, 88, 158, 226, 238, 239, 240, 245, 253*
3:20-21, *254*
3:20-31, *88, 89*
3:21, *82, 240*
3:21-22, *241, 250*
3:21-24, *240*
3:21-26, *110, 114, 240, 243*
3:21–5:21, *81*
3:22, *110, 226, 238*
3:23, *227, 240, 241*
3:23-24, *238, 240, 241, 243*
3:23-25, *227*
3:24, *239, 241, 244, 245*
3:24-25, *244*
3:24-26, *243*
3:25, *244*
3:25-26, *88, 243, 244*
3:26, *201, 243, 244*
3:27, *247*
3:28, *245, 246, 248*
4, *81, 82, 90, 241, 246*
4:1-5, *113*
4:1-25, *98*
4:3, *247*
4:3-5, *247*
4:4-5, *247, 249*
4:5, *241, 245, 247*
4:6, *247*
4:6-8, *113*
4:9-12, *90, 99*
4:9-25, *111*
4:12, *117*
4:13-25, *117*
4:15, *54*

4:16, *250*
4:17, *111, 114, 241, 247, 249*
4:18, *240, 249*
4:18-22, *113*
4:19, *249*
4:20, *249*
4:21, *249*
4:24, *249*
4:24-25, *110*
4:25, *82, 113, 245, 249*
5, *84, 246*
5-8, *111*
5-11, *190*
5:1, *91, 110, 112, 114, 245*
5:1-11, *98*
5:1-21, *114*
5:1-8:39, *110*
5:1-11:36, *109*
5:3-4, *91*
5:6-10, *235, 241*
5:8, *236*
5:10, *236, 242, 253*
5:11, *110*
5:12-17, *84*
5:12-21, *114*
5:15, *84*
5:15-16, *114*
5:16, *115*
5:17, *115*
5:17-21, *78*
5:18, *115*
5:20, *54*
5:21, *110*
6, *81, 92*
6-8, *114*
6:1, *114*
6:1-11, *117*
6:4, *117*
6:7, *115*
6:11, *119*
6:17, *111, 117*
6:23, *110, 244*
7, *54, 92, 93, 246*
7-8, *67, 93*
7:7-25, *54*
7:14-20, *93*
7:25, *110*
8, *135, 181, 217, 218, 219, 222, 230, 233, 242, 246*

8:1, *93, 218, 240, 244*
8:3, *78, 218, 244*
8:3-4, *227, 238, 242, 244*
8:4, *115*
8:5, *222*
8:6, *223*
8:9-11, *148*
8:12-13, *223*
8:14, *222*
8:15, *222*
8:17, *219, 220*
8:25, *95*
8:26-27, *92*
8:28-30, *111*
8:29-30, *108*
8:30, *108, 115, 218*
8:32, *236, 244*
8:33, *137*
8:38-39, *218*
8:39, *110*
9, *16, 94, 108, 139, 140, 144, 145, 246*
9-10, *155*
9-11, *94, 99, 103, 104, 106, 107, 108, 111, 154, 155, 156, 157, 161*
9-16, *94*
9:1-5, *103, 144*
9:1-11:36, *114*
9:3-5, *102*
9:6-13, *156*
9:7-11, *108*
9:11, *108*
9:12, *111*
9:14-16, *108*
9:14-18, *108*
9:14-21, *103*
9:15, *154*
9:18, *103*
9:18-24, *108*
9:25-26, *111*
9:27-28, *78*
9:30-33, *103, 110*
9:30-10:21, *114*
10, *192*
10:1-4, *103*
10:1-21, *110*
10:4, *227, 238*
10:6-8, *112*
10:16, *117*
10:17, *112, 249, 253*

11, *155*
11:6, *228, 250*
11:8-10, *103*
11:8-11, *103*
11:11-16, *104*
11:15, *104*
11:16-24, *102*
11:17, *112*
11:17-24, *110*
11:20, *112*
11:20-21, *103*
11:22, *103*
11:25-27, *103, 112*
11:25-32, *104*
11:26, *104, 156*
11:26-27, *104*
11:27, *104*
11:29, *103*
11:32, *103*
12, *95*
12-16, *81, 94*
12:1, *253*
13:14, *95*
14, *96*
14:1-23, *102*
14:23, *251*
15:1-3, *103*
15:5-13, *103*
15:14-22, *102*
15:19, *101*
15:23, *101*
15:25, *101*
15:25-29, *102*
15:26, *102*
15:27, *102*
16:26, *117*

1 Corinthians
1, *170, 179, 192*
1-2, *86*
1:2, *182*
1:9, *181*
1:17, *184*
1:18, *179, 240*
1:20, *178*
1:23, *191, 241*
1:26-31, *60*
1:29, *192*
1:30, *195, 198*
1:31, *192*
2, *170*
2:2, *177*

2:5, *177*
2:6, *185*
2:14, *135, 177*
2:14-15, *178*
2:15, *178, 179*
2:16, *177*
3, *170*
3:1, *170, 184*
3:6-7, *183*
3:10-15, *184*
3:11, *214*
3:12, *184*
3:18, *178*
4, *170*
4:3, *215*
4:4, *198*
4:13, *216*
4:15, *184*
5, *170*
6, *170*
6:8, *192*
6:11, *195, 197, 199*
7, *170*
7:8, *185*
7:35, *178, 185*
8, *171*
8:1, *204*
9, *171*
9:5-7, *173*
9:13, *186*
9:26-27, *173*
10, *171, 174*
10:8, *174*
10:11, *202*
10:16, *253*
10:26, *178*
11, *171, 174*
11:1-2, *185*
11:2, *174*
11:3, *174*
12, *171*
12:12, *173*
13, *171*
13:1-3, *204*
14, *171*
14:18-20, *185*
15, *171, 207*
15:1-5, *207*
15:3, *208*
15:3-4, *207*
15:9-10, *254*
15:11, *203*

Scripture Index   279

15:12-19, *208*
15:17, *207*
15:20, *207*
15:23, *207*
15:45, *207, 208*
16, *171*
16:9, *173*

2 Corinthians
1, *171*
1:3-4, *147*
1:6, *173*
1:8, *173*
1:9, *182*
1:12, *174*
1:15, *173*
1:20, *200, 206*
1:22, *206*
2–3, *171, 173*
2:6, *185*
2:10, *173*
3, *246*
4, *171*
4:4, *173, 189*
4:5, *173, 185*
4:6, *173, 177*
4:10, *173*
4:17, *173*
5, *171, 198*
5:1, *173*
5:3-4, *177*
5:4, *173*
5:5, *206*
5:10, *202*
5:14, *185, 201*
5:16, *198*
5:17, *204, 207*
5:18, *185, 193, 198*
5:19, *202*
5:21, *198*
6, *172*
6:2, *207*
6:5, *173*
6:7, *198*
7, *172*
7:11, *173*
7:12, *173*
8–9, *172*
8:2, *173*
8:9, *192*
9:4, *189*
9:11, *173*

10, *172*
10:7, *173*
10:8, *185*
10:10, *188*
10:17, *174, 192*
11, *172*
11:3, *176*
11:20, *173*
11:30, *182*
12, *172, 180*
12:4, *180*
12:11, *173*
12:19, *182*
13:7, *182*
13:9, *173*

Galatians
1, *192*
1–2, *40*
1–4, *178*
1:1-5, *37*
1:3, *61*
1:4, *41, 58*
1:6, *61*
1:6-9, *58*
1:6–2:21, *37*
1:9, *33*
1:10, *42*
1:10-17, *65*
1:11, *60, 66*
1:11-17, *55*
1:13-16, *254*
1:15, *61*
1:16-17, *63*
2, *59, 246, 261*
2:1-10, *56*
2:1-14, *59*
2:5, *58*
2:6, *60*
2:6-9, *60, 61*
2:11, *30*
2:11-13, *30*
2:11-14, *56, 61, 62*
2:14, *57, 58, 61, 62*
2:15-16, *52, 62*
2:15-21, *52, 62*
2:16, *41, 42, 57, 59, 62, 226, 238, 246, 248*
2:16-21, *52*
2:17, *197*
2:17-18, *63*
2:19, *60, 63*

2:19-20, *63, 66, 246*
2:20, *54, 63, 244, 250*
2:21, *42, 52, 62, 228, 240*
3, *174, 245, 246*
3–4, *64*
3:1, *42*
3:1-5, *65*
3:1-9, *40*
3:1–4:31, *37*
3:2-5, *52*
3:3, *54*
3:6, *57*
3:6-29, *57*
3:8, *57*
3:9, *57*
3:10, *242*
3:10-12, *52, 57, 62*
3:10-13, *242, 244*
3:10-22, *40*
3:12, *242*
3:13, *30, 65, 94, 240, 242, 251*
3:15-21, *59*
3:19, *54*
3:19-25, *52*
3:21, *62, 228, 240*
3:22, *65, 251*
3:22-26, *251*
3:23, *49, 54, 251*
3:23-25, *54*
3:23–4:7, *40*
3:24, *251*
3:24-25, *49*
3:25, *54, 251*
3:26, *251*
3:26-28, *57*
3:28, *60, 64, 174*
4, *40*
4:1-7, *65*
4:3, *65*
4:4-6, *148*
4:6, *178*
4:7, *40*
4:8-9, *40, 65*
4:8-10, *59, 61, 65*
4:9, *42*
4:10, *56*
4:12-20, *60*
4:14, *42*
4:21-31, *65*
4:24, *40*

4:29, *54*
4:1535, *178*
5–6, *60, 64*
5:1, *37*
5:1–6:18, *37*
5:2, *42*
5:2-6, *52*
5:2-12, *56, 59*
5:4, *52, 62, 228*
5:6, *37, 41, 49, 53, 59, 60, 237, 251, 252, 253*
5:7, *42*
5:13, *251*
5:13-25, *61*
5:13–6:10, *54*
5:14-15, *252*
5:15, *60*
5:17, *30, 54, 61*
5:22-23, *53, 60*
5:23, *59*
5:24, *60*
5:26, *60*
6:1-5, *60*
6:2, *59, 64*
6:8, *61*
6:8-10, *60*
6:12-13, *60*
6:12-14, *57*
6:12-15, *56, 59*
6:14, *42, 60, 63, 66*
6:14-15, *68, 252*
6:15, *58, 59, 60, 252*
6:18, *61*

Ephesians
1, *132, 155, 156*
1–4, *151*
1:1, *159*
1:1-2, *146*
1:3, *131, 146, 148, 149, 160*
1:3-6, *126, 129, 144, 153, 154, 155, 156, 157, 160, 161*
1:4, *133, 136, 149, 150, 151, 152, 157, 158, 160*
1:4-6, *151*
1:5, *138*
1:6, *140, 160*
1:8, *160*
1:14, *206*
1:15, *157*

1:20, *149*
2, *246*
2:1-6, *254*
2:5, *160*
2:6, *149, 160, 207*
2:8, *155, 160*
2:8-9, *160, 228*
2:8-10, *66*
2:9, *66*
2:10, *160*
2:11-22, *156*
4:2, *157*
4:15, *157*
4:16, *157*

5:2, *157*
5:19, *148*
5:27, *159*
6, *181*
6:12, *132*

Philippians
3, *192, 246, 247*

Colossians
1, *147*
1:22, *159*
3:1, *148*

2 Thessalonians
2:13, *86*

1 Timothy
1:15, *15, 253*

2 Timothy
1:9, *66*
2:18, *207*

Titus
3, *246*
3:5, *66, 249*

Hebrews
8:8, *37*

2 Peter
1:10, *158*

1 John
2:3, *137*
3:21, *137*
5:2, *137*

Revelation
2:1-7, *262*

www.ingramcontent.com/pod-product-compliance
Lightning Source LLC
Chambersburg PA
CBHW022002220426
43663CB00007B/930